D0206724

OTHER BOOKS BY FREDERICK FRANCK:

Days With Albert Schweitzer   1959
My Friend in Africa   1960
African Sketchbook   1961
My Eye Is In Love   1963
Outsider in the Vatican   1965
I Love Life   1967
Exploding Church   1968
Simenons' Paris   1969
The Zen of Seeing   1973
Pilgrimage to Now/Here   1973
An Encounter With Oomoto   1975
The Book of Angelus Silesius   1976
Zen and Zen Classics, Selections from R.H. Blyth   1978
The Awakened Eye   1979
Art As a Way   1981
The Buddha Eye, Editor   1982
The Supreme Koan   1982
Echoes From the Bottomless Well   1985
Life Drawing Life   1989
A Little Compendium on That Which Matters   1989
On Being Human Against All Odds   1991

Readers:

Au Pays du Soleil
Au Fil de l'Eau
Croquis Parisiens
Tutte le Strade Portano a Roma

ZEN
AND
ZEN
CLASSICS

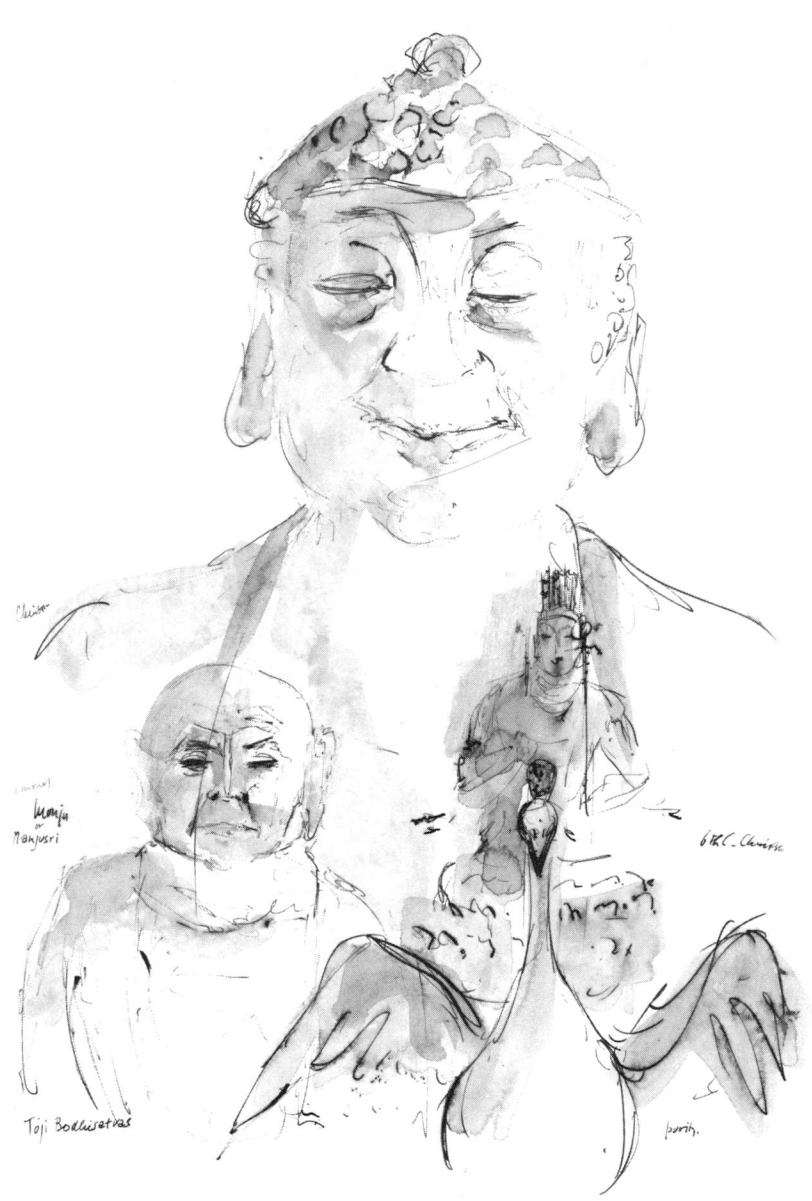

Chinese

Manju
Manjusri

6th C. Chinese

Toji Bodhisattvas

purity.

Toji temple Bodhisattvas.

Selections from R. H. Blyth

ZEN
AND
ZEN
CLASSICS

Compiled and with drawings by Frederick Franck

Heian International, Inc.

The selections in this book appeared in *Zen and Zen Classics* by R.H. Blyth; Volume One © 1960 by R.H. Blyth; Volume Two © 1964 by R.H. Blyth; Volume Three © 1970 by R.H. Blyth; Volume Four © 1966 by Tomiko Blyth; Volume Five © 1962 by R.H. Blyth; with permission of their publishers, The Hokuseido Press, Tokyo, Japan.

HEIAN INTERNATIONAL, INC.
P.O. BOX 1013
UNION CITY, CA 94587

First Heian Edition 1991

1 2 3 4 5 6 7 8 9 99 98 97 96 95 94 93 92 91
Printed in the United States of America

ISBN: 0-89346-353-1

For Claske, Lukas
and my revered Friends
Abbot Kobori Nanrei
and Kondo Akihisha

INTRODUCTION

When you meet a master swordsman,
show him your sword.
When you meet a man who is not a poet,
do not show him your poem.

—RINZAI
(ninth century)

Zen is no longer an exotic import. If there ever was a Zen fad, it wore off long ago in the fifties and sixties and has been succeeded by newer fashions. It has survived, however, as an ever-deepening influence. In some form or other—often completely unrecognized—Zen ideas and Zen values have percolated and deeply affected Western consciousness. They are exerting a powerful, pervasive influence on the world view, the spiritual attitudes and the quality of religious experience of innumerable people of different religious affiliations or none. Often these people are not even aware of this influence or of its origin in Zen. Nor are they even remotely connected with the many Zen centers that have sprung up in America and to a lesser extent in Europe. These centers, often founded and led by Japanese Zen masters, are apt to display a kind of Zen fundamentalism and taste for *Japonaiserie* that makes one suspect that the essential implications of the Zen attitude to human existence are still in the process of being fully assimilated and appropriated.

To my mind, R. H. Blyth is destined to become the indispensable interpreter of, and initiator into, Zen for the Western mind. His writings, until now far too inaccessible to the Western reader, seem to me the catalyst needed for a profound integration of Eastern and Western spirituality.

Reginald Horace Blyth was born in London in 1898. His earliest contact with the Orient came when as a young man he taught in India. In 1924 he moved from India to Korea (it was then under Japanese rule), where he taught English and became deeply interested in Buddhism. Under Kayama Taizi Roshi he started the study of Zen that would remain his central concern for the rest of his life. It was his commitment to Zen that made him move to Japan in 1940. He soon found a job as a teacher of English, but when the war broke out in 1941, he was interned as an enemy alien. In the internment camp near Kobe he finished his first book, *Zen in English Literature and Oriental Classics,* published by Hokuseido Press in 1942. This was followed by part of his authoritative four volumes on haiku. When the war ended he moved to Tokyo, taught at several colleges and universities, and finally became English tutor to the Imperial Crown Prince. He wrote assiduously: more than a dozen titles were published in the course of one decade. Among these were: *Senryu* (1950), *Japanese Humour* (1957), *Oriental Humour* (1959), *Zen and Zen Classics,* Vols. I, II, VII (1960–64), *Japanese Life and Character in Senryu* (1961), *Edo Satirical Verse Anthologies* (1961), *A History of Haiku,* Vols. I, II (1963–64).

Jumpei Nakatsuchi, president of Hokuseido Press, told me that he often advised Blyth to look for a publisher in England or America so that his books might reach a wider public. Blyth refused: "You are my friend, and you just go on publishing me." Manuscripts kept coming incessantly, often dropped off by Blyth as he bicycled through the Tokyo traffic on his way to lectures in the Imperial Palace. Domestic conflicts darkened his last years but did not seem to interfere with his productivity. They may, however, according to his doctor, have undermined his health. Blyth died in 1964 at the age of sixty-six.

After forty years in the East, steeped in Oriental philosophy, religion and literature, he remained a Westerner—and a proverbially eccentric Englishman at that—too deeply rooted in European culture to become a mock Oriental. His long residence in Japan gave him a deep familiarity with Japanese culture, and his position as tutor to the Crown Prince brought him in intimate contact with that culture at its most unadulterated formal and traditional level. He admired Japanese culture without ever becoming obsequious to it. He was a free spirit, and the rich humor that pervades all of his writings made him poke gentle fun at Japanese idiosyncrasies, and direct rather less gentle ridicule at those esthetic and folkloristic *Japonaiseries* to which Westerners who have only recently discovered Zen all too easily become addicted. His awareness and sensitivity kept him from mistaking such froth for the substance of Zen. He was exceptionally endowed with poetic sensibility, and he saw all artistic and spiritual humbug and cant as being antithetical to both the poetic spirit and the radical authenticity that Zen demands.

He became a close friend of D. T. Suzuki, who introduced Zen to the West, a feat whose importance has been compared to the discovery of nuclear energy. Suzuki wrote of Blyth: "To those of us who knew him, he was first and foremost a poet with a wonderfully keen and sensitive perception." Blyth on his part dedicated his books to Suzuki as "the only man who can write about Zen without making me loathe it," or "the greatest Japanese of this century," and spoke of Suzuki as the person "who taught me all I don't know."

Faithful to his Western heritage, he never disowned his Christian roots. On the contrary, his practice of Zen deepened, distilled and refined his insights into Christianity's profoundest meanings. His lifelong contemplative testing of Gospel texts led him to a totally liberated "new" Christian consciousness, utterly different from the synthetic "Christian Zen" appropriated by some clerics for the benefit of their moribund institutions. Blyth speaks with his characteristic irreverent reverence of both Christianity and Zen. Where he discovers evasion, hypocrisy or unveracity in either, he exposes and derides it mercilessly.

I discovered Blyth's *Zen in Oriental Literature and English Classics* more than twenty-five years ago. It was the first present I gave to Claske, who became my wife. The five volumes of *Zen and Zen Classics* I have reread countless times. They never lost their freshness. Each time I found treasures I had overlooked. Each time I was delighted anew. While in Japan I was told that Hokuseido intended to let them go out of print, and it was suggested that I select what seemed to me most precious of the more than eleven hundred pages and make this into one manageable volume. I could not think of a more honorable and useful assignment. Volume IV, the *Mumonkan*, which by itself is 340 pages, I felt could not be excerpted without mutilating it. I hope it will be published separately.

My task proved to be both a delightful and a desperate one, for Blyth is not a systematic, much less an academic writer. He is perhaps the first Western "Zen fool," a successor to the poets Hanshan, Ryōkan and Sengai, of whom there have been many in the East. He says somewhere: "To write about Zen is not difficult. What is difficult, is to write *by* Zen. And if we don't write *by* Zen, we shouldn't write at all. If we don't live by Zen, there is no point in living." He certainly wrote "by Zen"—that is, in direct and total response to each day's life-experience—and what he wrote apparently went to press as it came to Nakatsuchi's desk without any editing to speak of. Hence *Zen and Zen Classics*, this inexhaustible treasure trove, is also a disheveled one, lacking organization and containing many redundancies that editing could have avoided. I have attempted to bring a semblance of order to it by organizing the material under fourteen chapter headings. Sayings, mondo and koan—insofar as they are not quoted in preceding chapters—have been gathered in Chapter XIV. To add commentary of my own seemed quite superfluous. To use a Zen idiom: it would merely be adding legs to the snake.

It has been hair-raising having to pick and choose from what is so obviously both lived and written "by Zen." I have had to discard much that I found painful to discard, and I was constantly reminded of the Zen story of the butcher who was carving a pig. When a customer said, "Now, cut me a particularly fine piece of meat!," he threw down his chopper and exclaimed, "Now, think for a moment, is this not all particularly fine meat?"

It hurts me deeply, for instance, not to be able to include all Blyth's commentaries on the *Hsinhsinming*, that compendium of that profound good sense called wisdom, by Sengtsang, the Third Patriarch of Zen, who died in 606. Certain mondo and koan now so well known that I saw "One hand clapping" glibly used in a *New Yorker* advertisement I eliminated for that reason, in order to accommodate others, with the comments by Blyth. The saints, sages and poets he quotes are of imperishable validity. But to me his own comments are not a whit less momentous. Each time I have opened *Zen and Zen Classics* I have rediscovered a joy, a jewel, whether in the form of a guffaw or a tender embrace. Blyth never fails to jerk me out of the busy doldrums. He is indeed a Master.

Blyth has the eye that never sleeps. Neither does his ear, his intellect, his memory, his rare sensitivity. He is always ready to catch the uncatchable, able to see into the unseeable. And so he helps us see into that Self-Nature, that unattainable Buddha Nature, that True Self, which is the very core of our being/non-being. If one must speak of his "faith," it is that without the full realization of this core, our journey from birth to death misses both point and destination. Like those earlier Zen fools, he is a paradigm of sanity. If sometimes he rambles on, amuses himself with free association, I enjoy this poet's rambling and the freedom of his associations enough not to interfere. Where he contradicts himself he is not unaware of it: he prefers life to deadly consistency.

He remains the lifelong, wakeful questioner, but a questioner who knows that the right question contains the answer within itself, and that the wrong question can receive only a nonsensical answer. He is the persistent analyzer of That Which Matters, which resists all attempts at intellectual analysis, yet has to be grasped if life is not to slip through our fingers. Zen, he realizes perfectly, is undefinable. Still, he makes such heroic efforts to give us glimpses of its nature—again and again, and from every conceivable angle—that he succeeds betters than anyone else in presenting a clear and reliable vision of what Zen might be and what it definitely is not.

Being a visionary and a poet, he shies away from all dry exegesis. He seems to sing his Zen in every possible key and in all the modes. To his perceptions, whether of Zen—which, he holds, can be grasped only by the poetic faculty—music, painting or poetry itself, he brings an instantly available erudition, a phenomenal memory of the whole of Western and Eastern literature, much of it in his own translations from Japanese, Chinese, French, German, Italian.

"It is," he wrote, "the nature of man (that is to say his biological nature) to harden into something or other. Eternal life means having it without hardening, having it abundantly and overflowingly," and he quotes his beloved poet Ikkyu:

> To harden into a Buddha is wrong
> all the more I think so
> when I look at a stone Buddha . . .

and

> Deeply thinking of it
> I and other people
> there is no difference
> as there is no mind
> beyond this Mind.

Blyth himself is like "other people" . . . only more so. He will never make you feel, as Zen Masters, certified or self-appointed, are apt to do, that he is Zennier than Thou.

It is this man's unhardened mind I rejoice being able to share with you, a mind so alive, vital and unsolemn that it remained free from all traces of Zen-upmanship. It is a mind that never lost its capacity for wonder: a delightfully sane mind. Long after his death, Blyth, like the best of Bodhisattvas, goes on bestowing his blessings on us searching mortals, refreshing our eyes and ears and spirits, laughing away our conceits and evasions. He pulls us by the ears, twists our noses, and if nevertheless we threaten to doze off, he uses his hossu-stick with the virtuosity of an Ummon or Rinzai.

He never preaches in the usual sense of the word, although he says: "Whether there is an audience or not, before ten thousand people or alone, in the middle of the Sahara, in the prime of life or at the point of death, you must preach, you must let your light shine before men . . . Preaching means giving Something to Somebody. It is in a way the opposite of prayer, which is receiving Something from Somebody."

He never moralizes, and here and there he might strike the puritan as amoral. But here we touch an aspect of Zen that has misled many into believing that Zen promotes libertinism or at any rate an absence of ethical norms. Only raw, unripened and pseudo-Zen, non-Zen, would fit this. The Awakened mind, for whom the other's reality is fully as real as his own, is incapable of harming the other, for there is no "other": "I am neither I nor other." "All beings have (or "are," to speak with Dogen) the Buddha Nature." To be an enlightened man is to respect this Buddha Nature fully, is to be harmless and compassionate to man or beast, is to live "according to God's Will."

No one who is seriously concerned with Zen can fail to be immensely enriched by the constant self-confrontation Blyth's writings impose, by the innumerable witty pinpricks and infuriatingly sharp little stabs, all too *à propos*, by which he deflates his own as well as our self-importance and illusions of attainment, "those petty and infantile personal stories people tell to exemplify moments of 'enlightenment.'" He reminds us that "an enlightenment which requires authentication, certification and congratulation" is a fake, or at least an incomplete one, and that "enlightenment is not a state but an activity." Far from the usual boasting about the rigorous disciplines he had to subject himself to, he observes: "The Way may be attained by a shout of astonishment."

"You can't learn Zen from a book." True, true! Still, you can learn more from the right book than from the wrong guru or rōshi. You cannot get it from a book if you rush through it to get to your next "spiritual" paperback or weekend "experience." If you race through this particular book in a few evenings, all I can promise you is a worthwhile entertainment. If on the other hand you find enough in it to keep you going back to it for, let's say, twenty years, you may—looking around you and within—make some remarkable discoveries. If after adding another ten years such discoveries still elude you, the book has failed. It was not for you, and your money will, weather permitting, be cheerfully refunded.

As far as I am concerned, Blyth's openness, sanity, faith and fearlessness, his inimitable style, remain a constant delight even if it sometimes becomes appropriately uncomfortable. I can always count on him to give me those fresh inklings of Zen, the Zen of Buddhism and that of Christianity, which—officially—you cannot learn from a book, not even from what is "written by Zen," unless you read it by Zen, as a Zen breviary.

I owe him unbounded gratitude, this most lovable person I failed to meet in the flesh, although I had been reading and rereading him for so many years. I hope you will find with me that Ikkyu's poem

> The figure of the Real Man
> standing there . . .
> just a glimpse of him
> and we are in love

written six hundred years ago, refers to R. H. Blyth.

If I add a few of my drawings, especially of the Nō play, for which I share Blyth's reverence and devotion, it is as a small nosegay offered to his undying spirit, and also perhaps because a book of mine without any drawings looks too much like someone else's.

FREDERICK FRANCK

ZEN
AND
ZEN
CLASSICS

1 | WHAT IS ZEN?

The reader of this book will be confused by it, but this is the destiny of man, since many are the roads, but all lead to the same conclusion, confusion. If I am asked, "Are you for, or against Zen?" the answer is, both, not neither. The great fault of Christians is that they never criticise (fundamentally) Christianity. No one, or almost no one, criticises democracy or communism (fundamentally) in the countries where they are the "national treasure." No Buddhist ever calls the Buddha a bit of a fool; blasphemy laws still exist in England.

Zen is the essence of Christianity, of Buddhism, of culture, of all that is good in the daily life of ordinary people. But that does not mean that we are not to smash it flat if we get the slightest opportunity. And we are not going to attack foxy (false) Zen, or the hypocrites and time-servers who support it, but Zen itself in its highest and sublimest forms. Nothing is sacred but one's own foolish and contradictory intuitions. By "intuition" is meant here that which I myself find in common with all so-called "great men" without exception, and with a good many "little" men. It is thus purely subjective, dangerous, and indeed variable, but the great thing is to have courage, and say again and again, "All that can be shaken shall be shaken!" and if nothing remains, let it be so.

*

There is nothing harder to write about than Zen. No, this is not so. There is nothing harder than really to write, because really to write means to write by Zen. To write, or eat, or sing, or die by Zen is difficult. Really to write about Zen means writing by Zen about writing or eating or singing or dying by Zen. So to write about Zen is not difficult; what is difficult is to write by Zen. And if we don't write by Zen we shouldn't write at all. If we don't live by Zen, there's no point in living.

*

What is Zen? Zen means doing anything perfectly, making mistakes perfectly, being defeated perfectly, hesitating perfectly, having stomach-ache perfectly, doing anything, perfectly or imperfectly, PERFECTLY. What is the meaning of this PERFECTLY? How does it differ from perfectly? PERFECTLY is in the will; perfectly is in the activity. Perfectly means that the activity is harmonious in all its parts, and fully achieves its proposed end. PERFECTLY means that at each moment of the activity there is no egoism in it, or rather, that our ego works together with the attraction and repulsion of the Egoism of the nature within and without us. Our pain is not only our own pain; it is the pain of the universe. The "joy" of the universe is also our joy. Our failure or misjudgement is that of nature, which never hopes or despairs, but keeps on trying.

Zen is at once irresistibly attractive and unutterably repulsive. Zen draws us to it for many reasons. First, because at last we have a belief which we need not believe in. No dogmas, no ritual, no mythology, no church, no priest, no holy book,—what a relief!

Second, Zen, even the word itself, enables us to perceive that all our deepest experiences of life, of music, of art, music, poetry, humour and so on, however varied they may be, and deriving as they do from the most widely different circumstances, have all a similar "taste" or odour, a common element that seems fundamental. This idea is of course dangerous in its monistic, scientific, philosophical, unpoetical tendency, and we need all the more to insist upon the variety, the plurality, the disparateness of Zen. But we must have a unity as well as a

the great Buddha of Nara

diversity, and so the word Zen usually refers to this depth of oneness in our depth of life. But just as deep is our experience of difference. For a thing to exist at all it must have this separateness; at the same time it has no existence if only separate. Spengler describes the different "Zens" of the various world cultures, of which, with an instinct of genius (or it may be mere nationalism and misanthropy) he denies the inter-comprehensibility, that is, their essential identity. The same mistake is often made in regard to ego-lessness, in Japanese *muga*. Egolessness alone won't do, and to bring in the Over-Soul or something of that sort won't do either, for if we pinch the Over-Soul it won't shriek. What we want is something unpinchable and pinchable, and the ego is pinchable. So we must have *muga*, egolessness, and at the same time *yuga*, ego-fulness; then we are all right, as Shakespeare was when he was Hamlet and at the same time Shakespeare, a Danish prince and an English playwright.

Third (the third reason why Zen is so acceptable), Zen makes us realise that, as Hazlitt said, only "what interests is interesting." Zen is interest. Zen makes the mountains more mountainous, and the valleys more valeful, and yet at the same time the lower the mountain the better, and the shallower the valley. We begin to have an idea of what we have always been looking for without knowing it. Zen is the universal standard of judgement we have all been looking for. Zen is good taste.

What is odious about Zen is what people say about it (all of them with the exception of Suzuki Daisetz); the photographs of Zen monks in their fanaticism, bigotry, superstition, and standardisation; the pettifogging and infantile personal stories supposed to exemplify moments of enlightenment; the commentaries on the *Hekiganroku* and *Mumonkan* or koans, with their esotericism and superiority-complex; foreigners (no exceptions) who pretend to understand Zen, and bamboozle themselves and (some of) their readers by adding their own legs to the snake. Nobody understands Zen; nobody can explain it; writing books about it is effrontery and impertinence. In fact, Zen is itself a kind of impudence. On the other hand it is the essence of modesty, the modesty of nature. Let us combine the two.

*

Zen arises spontaneously, naturally, out of the human heart. It is not a special revelation to any person, class, or nation. Thus to say it came from India to China and from China to Japan is nonsense. One might as well say that the air we breathe in one country comes from another. Further, the claim of Zen that it is "a special transmission," and that this line runs from Sakyamuni through the intervening twenty six patriarchs to Bodhidharma, Huike, Sengtsan, Taohisin, Hungjen, Huineng, down to the rōshi of the present day, is nothing but obscurantism, exclusivism, false patriotism, pedantry, and egoism; the absence of the Zen spirit.

From the Zen—the poetical, the transcendental—point of view, "never man spake such as he," is true of anybody, and in the last resort, of everybody, and our seeing the truth or not seeing it is a question of will; we will to see or will not to see, just as a crow wills to be black, and a snake wills its legs away.

Nevertheless there is after all a history of Zen in time. Cause and effect are just as real as they are unreal. If then we find the spirit of Zen in Homer, Epictetus, Plutarch, Marcus Aurelius, The Bible, *The Inferno*, Eckhart's *Sermons, King Lear, Don Quixote*, the works of Bach and Mozart, *A Week on the Concord*, Stevenson's *Fables*, we may properly search for historical relations, for a special transmission inside as well as outside the scriptures; we may depend on books, as we trace the connections between all these direct pointings to the soul of man, seeing into their nature and attaining, even for a brief moment, Buddhahood.

*

The "Four Statements of the Zen Sect" are usually ascribed to Bodhidharma (Japanese: Daruma), who according to legend brought Zen from India to China in the 6th century, crossing the sea on a reed.

He arrived at Canton with his begging bowl, and settled at Loyang, where he sat wall-gazing for nine years, becoming known as the wall-gazing Brahmin, though actually he belonged to the ruling and military class. The cave where he sat became Shōrinji Temple. He is said to have died at the age of a hundred and forty or fifty, some say by poison, some that he returned to India. These four statements are:

1. No dependence on words and letters.

To apply this to poetry, whose medium is words and phrases, may seem absurd. It is like pictures without paint and music without sound. But words are a peculiar medium, in being the vehicle for all communication, whether poetical or otherwise. It is the darkness and silence of things, of which the ordinary poetical meaning is the light and sound.

2. A special transmission outside the Scriptures.

There is a transmission from poet to poet of the spirit of poetry deeply similar to that of Zen from monk to monk. A poet knows another poet by indubitable yet invisible signs; the same is true of the artist and the musician.

> Two came here,
> Two flew off,—
> Butterflies.
> —Chora

In this verse, the ordinary poetical meaning is discarded; what remains is that dark flame of life that burns in all things. It is seen with the belly, not with the eye; with "bowels of compassion."

3. Direct pointing to the soul of man.

How can there be such a thing as pointing without a finger? How can art subsist without a medium? What is this silence that speaks so loudly?

> A fishing village;
> Dancing under the moon,
> To the smell of raw fish.
> —Shiki

4. Seeing into one's nature and the attainment of Buddhahood.

Attaining Buddhahood means attaining manhood, being a citizen of the world, of double sex; besides this Shakespearean state, it emans attaining childhood, beast-hood, flower-hood, stone-hood, even word-hood and idea-hood, and place-hood and time-hood.

As for the skin,
What a difference
Between a man and a woman!
But as for the bones,
Both are simply human beings.

—Ikkyū

In speaking of Zen, especially in its relation to forms of culture, it is necessary always to bear in mind the difference between Zen as a "system" of paradoxes evolved in India and China during a period of three thousand years, and Zen as Zen, that is, the spontaneous, individually created timeless-activity-in-time of an undivided mind-body. This is the substratum, the *basso ostinato* of the historically developed consciousness of Zen.

Zen is not a religion; it is religion. Zen is not a value, it is value. What is often mistaken for Zen is some value. A bullfighter's Zen is wisdom, but it has no love in it. Christ's Zen is love, but it lacks wisdom. Buddha's Zen is truth, but where is the humanity? We may say, if we like, that Zen is of two kinds, partial and total. The Zen of art, the Zen of Nō is partial, and the Zen of a Zen abbot is partial. Total Zen, that penetrates and interpenetrates the whole of a man's life, that stops him reading the newspapers, and writing articles for magazines,—this is not our concern here.

*

True Zen then must make people not hate animals, not wish to kill them, not rejoice in their violent or natural death. It must make one wish to reduce as much as possible the unnecessary, that is, the meaningless, that is, the Zen-less, unpoetical suffering in the world. To put the matter in an extreme form, no man has true Zen in him, no man has real *satori*, that is, poetry, who is not, or does not become, a vegetarian. Expressing it more mildly, to the extent that he does not actively reduce the amount of useless, fruitless pain in the world, to that extent a man's Zen is a swindle, a self-swindle, a Self-swindle. I am not saying, by the way, that there is anything "wrong" with bull-fighting. In my modest way I am simply saying that there are other, "better" ways of passing one's only life on this planet. "Better" means deeper, more mean-

ingful, more poetical, more Zen-ful, with bigger and better
bulls more gloriously killed.

*

What is Zen? Zen is the unsymbolisation of the world and
all the things in it. Of course, the Zen masters use metaphors
and similes, they even use symbols, but these are not to be
taken seriously. One thing does not mean another. Above all,
we are not to look behind things for their meaning. When the
hand is raised, all things are raised with it, but the hand does
not signify all things. In this sense, animism is the sine qua
non for Zen, but we must also say that a man is a tree walking. A human being is as subject to cause and effect as the
lowliest existence. A stone is as free as a seraph. When it
rains, Christ's blood falls from the firmament. Zen means the
freedom to be bound; we are bound by all within and without
us. We cannot escape from a thing, as Plato tried to, on the
wings of an abstraction, a Form, a function. One thing contains everything within it, and nothing can be withdrawn from
it without injury to itself and to the withdrawer. What matters
therefore about any thing is its allness. Adjectives soon become abstract nouns, "allness," and the world is impoverished
to cram the human brain with non-existences, leaving meaningless matter to be examined for a meaning. God is not love.
God is not loving. God is someone loving something, or something loving someone. In the beginning was no word, neither
was there, as Faust asserts, any act. In the beginning was a
speaker, an actor. In this matter Christianity and even Mo-
hammedanism is right, and Buddhism and Zen are wrong. God
is a person, and Heaven is a place. Contrary to the Book of
Revelation, without time nothing can exist, especially the timeless, and "Eternity is in love with the productions of time."

*

To an occidental, the forms and ceremonies of a Zen temple, and the feudalistic, not to say militaristic ranking of the
priests may seem un-Zen-like, and worse still, disagreeable.
The rules and regulations, the chantings and genuflections of
a Zen temple may be, not justified, but excused to some extent, on the ground that they continue a two thousand years

tradition from India through China and Korea to Japan. But this argument would allow us to eat one another.

*

Zen, whatever Zen may be, is the result of the combined genius of the Indian and Chinese peoples. The Buddha attained enlightenment, but hardly seemed to be able to communicate it to others. He recommended a moral and self-controlled life as the means to it. In the seventh and eighth centuries A.D. Chinese monks began to "explain" what that enlightenment was, and devise a technique for gaining it, by-passing the old Indian schema. We can trace in those twelve or thirteen centuries a thread of Zen running through the *Upanishads*, the sutras and the undoubted enlightenment of many monks in China, Korea, and Japan up to the present time, nearly three thousand years of history. We can also go to the great thinkers and poets and musicians and artists of any times and places, and see and hear in them the religious enlightenment in spheres unknown to the Buddha. This we may also call Zen, a Zen which transcends history, and is not confined to the Far East. Without some depth of thought and intuition Zen can hardly make its appearance, and that is why we find it in Eckhart and Christ and Bach. But this is not the same as solemnity and over-seriousness; we find it also in Cervantes and Mozart and Lewis Carroll.

*

An objection to the radical criticism of Zen is that since Zen cannot be defined, has no dogmas, is beyond teaching, and is essentially non-dichotomous, it cannot have even any good points, let alone bad ones. To put the matter in another way, Zen is the best of everything, the perfected latent in the imperfect, the absolute itself, so we can neither praise nor blame it, only live in it with humble gratitude. Christ also says, "Be ye perfect, even as your Father in Heaven is perfect," and it may be admitted that sometimes some of our actions are perfect, are Zen-like, in the sense that they are the best possible under the given conditions for that particular person with his unavoidable limitations. But a "perfect" act by an imperfect being is still far from perfect in the real sense of the word.

The early Christian mystics used the word "deification," not altogether heretically, to express the *union mystica*, but is the God with whom they were "oned" as intolerant, uneducated, unhumorous, tone-deaf, unpoetical, inartistic, cruel, and stupid as they often were? So with Zen. My Zen kills cats with horror, but not so Nansen's. Enō laughs zazen to scorn, but what do others say? Dr. Suzuki sees Zen in a bull-fighter; I see it in the bull. "If you have not had *kensho,* what you say about Zen is not worth listening to." But how little sense and sensibility, how much pride and prejudice is shown by many who have had it! Zen is only another absolute, but this time devoid of attributes, freedom unlimited, in nature like Eckhart's nameless Godhead, so that we wound ourselves in attacking it.

> One day, when Tanka, 738–824, was staying at Yerinji Temple in Changan, it was so cold he took one of the three Buddhas of the Buddhist Trinity in the Hall, and burned it to make a fire to warm himself. The monk in charge burst out, "What do you mean by burning my Buddha?" Tanka poked about in the ashes with his stick, and said, "I am burning it to get the sarira." [Sarira is an indestructible substance always (said to be) found in the ashes of a saint after cremation.] The monk said, "How should a wooden Buddha have any sarira?" Tanka said, "Well, there's no sarira so far, let's take the other two Buddhas, and burn them too!"

A swindler of the religious type always jumps about between the absolute and the relative according to convenience. To bow before a wooden image is nonsense; to desecrate it is nothing. To offer food to the spirits of the dead or the living or the unborn is superstition, and Zen, of all sects, should have been above such things. Singing national anthems, saluting the flag, public prayer, bowing at shrines, masses, regarding some things as holy, reading the newspapers, trying to become rich,—they are all folly and vulgarity, and naturally go together.

What is Zen? Zen is looking at things with the eye of God, that is, becoming the thing's eyes so that it looks at itself with our eyes. But this is not enough. Impression must always be accompanied by expression. Impression without expression is not yet impression. Expression without impression is impossible. But impression and expression are not enough. Expression without reception is meaningless. It is not expression if it is to nobody. This is why all art, all music, all poetry requires two persons. Why only two? How can you ask for a crowd, when even two minds with the same thought is almost unheard-of? The *Taittireeya Upanishad* says:

> I am this world, and I eat this world.
> Who knows this, knows.

This expresses, or records, a state of mind in which, first, there is no division between I and not-I. The relation of myself to the universe is not a problem, intellectual or emotional, because *I am it.* There is no good and evil, true and untrue, beautiful and ugly.

> If your ears see,
> And your eyes hear,
> Not a doubt you will cherish,—
> And how naturally the rain drops
> From the eaves!

*

Asceticism, "cynicism," "stoicism," animism, mysticism, humour,—these suggest the presence of Zen, just as do unconventionality, naturalness, understatement, freedom, in Western as in Eastern life and literature and art. But at the same time, as said before, there is a double flow dimly discernible in the history of humanity, in the history of humanness, from India to China and Japan, and from India to Greece-Persia-Egypt and Europe. The rate of flow was different, not merely as a result of geography, but because Greece especially and Europe also had "to overcome the world," the world in this case being the world of the pure intellect, of which the Far East knew little. The Greeks could not for a moment give up their heads, their rational questions and rational answers. The Chinese, if it is not too rude to say so, had no heads from the beginning, and the same may be said of the Japanese, who have always hated logic and psychology, and perhaps always will. The Greeks were men, the Chinese and Japanese were women, and women are always more right than men. Chinese Zen was, and Japanese Zen also, for all its Bushidō, woman-like Zen, in its unintellectuality, practicality, conservatism, superstition, unteachability, self-satisfaction, love of ritual and fancy costumes, and, except in very special cases, no sense of humour.

Stoicism was an approach to Zen through morality. When morality generalises and becomes abstract it goes far from Zen. The danger inherent in mysticism is the same. In the end it becomes vast, vague, inane. Everything is dissolved in God or in Nature. Zen never for a moment loses touch with the particular, the concrete, the thingness of things, and for that reason we may call the cave art of the Paleolithic period Zen, though mysticism was already present, and our writing about this art and about Zen is itself an example of the intellectualising, the fossilisation, the starving of Zen, that is, of life, of material-meaning.

*

Mysticism is the state of union, of re-union of a person with the impersonal. This union is only possible, of course, if the person is impersonal, and the impersonal is personal. This is part of the meaning of the Tendai philosophy of the Three Thousand Worlds, all of which penetrate each other, so that a man keeps a stony silence, and a stone looks cold, God is angry, and we forgive him; a tree sighs its bosom over us, and Hell is in Heaven and Heaven not outside Hell.

*

Zen and Mysticism may be said to form a bridge, both historical and spiritual, between Occident and Orient. Indeed the Japanese educational system might well be aligned to it. We have India as the chief fountain of world culture; the two streams running east and west, the eastern with its Chinese and Japanese art, poetry, and religion; the western and its Italian art, German mysticism and music, English poetry.

Neoplatonism entered Christianity through St. Augustine, who lived two centuries after Plotinus. The fact that Plotinus does not mention India or Indian philosophy in his works shows nothing, for he does not say anything about the Chris-

tianity by which he was surrounded, nor does he mention his
teacher Ammonius Saccus from whom he learned for eleven
years, until he was thirty nine. This probable historical connection between Zen and mysticism, corresponding to that
between Bashō and Wordsworth, explains the similarities between them. (Thoreau is even closer to Bashō than Wordsworth, this being again partly due to the Indian writings which
he received from an English friend, and which gave him that
philosophic background needed for all poetical and religious
experiences.) The differences between Bashō and Wordsworth
are those between the Chinese-Japanese mind and the German-
English mind, the latter always moving from the particular to
the universal, the concrete to the abstract, the former never
leaving the particular and the concrete however much the universal and abstract may be implicit in them.

Eriugena, the great 9th century Irish theologian, translated
"Dionysius" from Greek into Latin. This Dionysius the Areop-
agite introduced oriental mysticism directly into Roman-
Jewish Christianity, and brought about the Christian mysticism
of such persons as Hugh of St. Victor, 1096–1141, and thus
ultimately produced Eckhart, 1260–1327, the greatest of all
mystics and mystical writers.

It will have been painfully and indignantly obvious to the
reader that the word Zen has been used in a variety of ways,
sometimes as employed by the Zen sect with a mystical meaning; sometimes as a sort of religious humbug; at times as universal culture, at times as the particular enlightenment of an
individual; at others with a prophetic meaning, a Zen which
may be attained by poetical persons who see things with an
Eastern and a Western eye, who can be both non-sexual and
sexual, atheists who can be God. In any case, Zen is not something that changes and grows; it is the changing and growing
itself, and if anybody thinks that Zen is something to be
gained by doing zazen and receiving Zen diplomas, he is mistaken. If anybody supposes that Buddha or Daruma or Rinzai
attained to Zen, he is mistaken. If anybody imagines that
Christ or any other man born after him was a Christian, he is
mistaken.

*

Japan sea with wreck

The mind, the Buddha, living creatures,—these are not three different things.

—the *Avatamsaka* (*Kegonkyō*) Sutra

*

When goodness, truth, and beauty are all present, as one, there is Zen. In many of the paintings on the walls of almost inaccessible caves, in impenetrable darkness, seen only by the doubtful light of torches in smoky air that could not be breathed long, pre-historic men who were more really human than ourselves saw once more with their hands the animals they had seen with their eyes in the bright world outside. To live, to kill, to eat, to be one with things, to see things as they are, to see them as they ought to be, to know the real and the ideal, to grasp movement in stillness, and stillness in movement,—to do all this was what they did, and to do all this is Zen.

*

The *Meditation on the Four Acts*, ascribed to Daruma, is very clear in its teaching though not yet specifically Zen, the Zen that we find in the Platform Sutra, *Rokusodangyō*. The four acts are first, The Requital of Hatred, not only the hatred of people but of all things around us, the sharp corner of the table, for example. Second, Following Circumstances, which means, "He who would be first among you,—let him be servant of all." Third, Asking for Nothing, which is, "Not my will, but Thine be done!" Last, Accordance with Reality, which means the realisation that just as things have no self-nature, neither have we (and just as each thing has existence-value, so have we).

Does the universe "love" us, and do we, as individuals, rise from bad to good, and from good to better? Or are we all sinners against the Holy Ghost, guilt of what sin we know not; is the Unattainable also the Malefic? By merely continuing to live, most men tacitly admit that they think this life better than nothing at all. Zen presumes, and proves to its devotees, that its world is Good, and enables them to live a fairly untroubled, though not necessarily good, life. The word Good implies that bad is swallowed up in it. By Bad we mean that the universe is meaningless. This is however not logically con-

ceivable, since if the universe is meaningless as a whole, it is
meaningless in its parts.

*

Is the world bad, or Bad? Thomas Hardy thought it was
Bad, and that for this very reason it gives us an opportunity
for tragic integrity. If the world is Bad, let each man do zazen,
and get his satori, play and listen to the Forty-eight Preludes
and Fugues; paint pictures and look at the best of others daily;
learn the most distant foreign language, and read its poetry in
the original; build his own house, or at least a dog-kennel;
climb hills or high trees, or join the fire-brigade; be a vegetarian and an out-and-out (impossible) pacifist. If a man cannot do these things, he may creep in a petty pace to death, or
jump out of the window. A spiritually dead or unborn man
makes the greatest art and religion look what it is anyway,
foolish.

When we reject folly, regret, shame, hesitation, sin, egoism, vanity, sentiment, hypocrisy, ambition, dichotomy, we
reject our humanity. It is too big a price to pay for the peace
that passeth understanding. Yes, freedom is best, but attachment is better. To die for love, or live without it—what a
choice we must make! But there is no other alternative. You
say, "How about living with love?" The world is not arranged
like that.

A drowning man will clutch at a Zen straw. To be satisfied
with oneself, alias the world,—is not this Paradise? And it is
what Zen offers to every man.

How is it possible that a man should be enlightened, and
yet be unpoetical, unmusical, inartistic? It will be noted that
we have omitted "immoral." This suggests that Zen, in the
customary meaning of the word, that is, as the Chinese Zen
masters would have used it, is after all moralistic, or that
human beings are so, rather than musical, poetical, and artistic.
The object of (Chinese) Zen is to transcend life and death,
and, really to live. To die, to rot, and live until we do,—how
to perform this in the best possible way is the great problem
of life. Zen solves it, not exactly moralistically, but by dying
first, and then living. To do this requires moral force and
stamina. An understanding of literature, good taste in art and

music, even humour, have little to do with it, that is to say, with dying. But living, after we are once dead, really means being artistic, delighting in natural forms, entering into the nature of things through music. Thus, theoretically speaking, Chinese Zen was a preparation for life by dying, that is, by giving up our natural greediness, selfishness, ambition, liking-or-loathing.

*

Zen is the resolution of absolute freedom and invincible law. But obedience is unlimited; liberty is not. Zen asserts that when a horse in one country eats grass, the stomach of a cow in another country is filled. This is true, because I am both the horse and the cow, and the grass too, but there is some swindling here, because the fact that I am I is a different, a stronger kind of fact than the fact that I am a cow or coconut. If I assert that there is a wall before me, that is all right, but if I say there is no wall and keep on trying to walk through it I shall find myself given three more, all padded.

We must say then that there is, besides Zen, a substratum of fact, brute fact, and not pretend that by levitation, or will-power, or thought-transference, or poetic insight, or mystic ecstasy, it can be un-facted. Zen can make us lose the fear of death (though whether it should, is another question) but "the inevitable hour" is unavoidable. We live in time; we live time-lessly, and these two are the same, but they are also different. Time is our only chance to live in eternity.

*

According to Buddhism and Berkeley, all is in the mind, but this begs the question. You cannot kick a stone out of existence, as Dr. Johnson unwittingly demonstrated, but neither can you think it out of existence. "Nothing is good or bad, but thinking makes it so." This is true, but we cannot say, "A stone does not exist, or not-exist, but thinking makes it so," as far as our own thinking is concerned. If it is said that the stone exists in the mind of God, in the Dharmakaya, it is only saying that there are thoughts in the mind of God that nobody can unthink.

Zen makes the mistake of speaking two languages, and does not distinguish between them; only occasionally does it speak a third, which it should speak always. The first is the language of science, of (un)common sense. "When tired, we rest; when hungry, we eat." "A dog has the Buddha nature." It is the language of the relative world. The second is that of paradox, nonsense, mysticism. "A dog has not the Buddha nature." This is the language of the absolute world.

The third language is the real language of Zen, of poetry; it is the relative and absolute in one.

We say, "I have a pebble in my right hand"; Zen may add, "You have (also) a no-pebble in your right hand," or, "You have also a pebble in your (empty) left hand," but this is not, strictly speaking, the language of Zen, for it is not poetry. "The essence of Zen is enlightenment." This is commonsense and scientific. But if we say (remembering that enlightenment is illusion), "The essence of Zen is illusion," this is still only half the truth, the paradoxical half. That is to say, Zen should assert, "The essence of Zen is enlightenment," only if the listener or reader is forewarned that this means "Zen is (also) illusion," or, "Zen is enlightenment and illusion when they are one," or, "Zen is enlightenment and illusion when they are both two and one." "Zen has no God-concept" must mean, "Zen has (also) a God-concept." Further, an ordinary statement may be, by the speaker or to the hearer, poetry, and conversely, poetry, if read badly, becomes an ordinary statement or worse.

*

The otherness of God, the evolution theory, the doctrine of original sin, and nihilism are more attractive than this religious megalomania, this cosmic bumptiousness. The Zen masters have no doubts about (the interpretations of) their experience. A Christian does not doubt the perfection of Christ, or the good intentions of the Deity. But when Christ on the cross doubts the love of God, and when Hakuin doubts the enlightenment of Gantō, who screamed so loud in his death-agony,—then I have no doubt of them.

Finally, the Zen answer to the above critical querulousness is exactly the same as that of the Catholic Church. All the contradictions, monstrosities, absurdities, immoralities, and trivialities of the human-divine relation are "mysteries." Every criticism we make of Zen is yet another dichotomy, which we must transcend. But this is a self-contradiction in the idea of Zen itself, for Zen is not merely the abolition of difference, but the negation of sameness. To put it in a more practical way, Zen lives life and in so doing explains it. But as human beings, not animals merely, we must explain life, and this explanation makes us live our life (and in so doing explain it) more truly and deeply. Thus, thinking about Zen, criticising Zen (Zen itself, not mere accretions or malformations), showing the defects of Zen, damning Zen, this is also Zen. Truth is a creation, not a discovery. Sometimes, when I look at my dog Guppy, a very clever dog, I think how unintelligent he looks,—for a human being! Zen is like Guppy.

*

One last thing remains to say about Zen, the most difficult. Just as Greek art, in its perfection and incapacity of being transcended, had a deathly influence upon the art of Europe, and just as the music of Bach makes all that has been composed since him superfluous and frivolous or artificial, so Chinese Zen made all later Zen, as religion, imitative and second hand. But that is not what I really wanted to say, which is this. A thing that comes into existence, by its very existence, prevents itself from coming into existence. What is good, what is really good is what is about to come into existence, the ZEN which is not yet Zen. (Zen may be said to exist, in some sense, in its being created by Huineng, Linchi and so on). Zen, as religion, is no longer possible, any more than Buddhism or Christianity, except as a kind of repetition, which may be Zen, but is not ZEN. Thus Zen is tinged with certain hopelessness and nihilism, because we do not wish to repeat the discovery of other people; we wish to be the first that ever burst into that silent sea. Arnold says,

> How fair a lot to fill
> Is left to each man still.

This is true, but we do not want "a fair lot," the leftovers of other ages. Man wants what is impossible; he wants it only because, only if it is impossible. These are the authentic "airs and echoes that convey a melancholy into all our day." We must create ZEN, and perish in the attempt.

Chōkei said to Hyakujō, "Learners want to know the Buddha; what is the Buddha?" Hyakujō answered, "It's quite like riding an ox and looking for it." Chōkei said, "After we know it, what then?" Hyakujō said, "It's like riding an ox and going home on it." Chōkei asked, "How can we get to hold and preserve and follow this always?" Hyakujō said, "It's like an ox-herd, who has a stick and watches the ox so that it does not devastate the rice-seedling fields of other people."

This is milk for babes, and can hardly be called Zen at all, but Buddhism of a benign sort.

Once the monk in charge was scattering rice. Seeing him, the crows flew away. Jōshū said, "When the crows see you, they fly away; why is that?" "They're afraid of me," said the monk. "What does that mean?" asked Jōshū. Himself answering, Jōshū said, "You have a murderous spirit."

So have the crows, so has the great globe, and all that it inherits. All fear all, and rightly. Zen does not mean not fearing; it means not fearing to fear.

Kassan had a monk who went round all the Zen temples but found nothing to suit him anywhere. The name of Kassan, however, was often mentioned to him from far and near as a great master, so he came back and interviewed Kassan, and said, "You have an especial understanding of Zen. How is it you didn't reveal this to me?" Kassan said, "When you boiled rice, didn't I light the fire? When you passed round the food (*anyaku, gyōeki*), didn't I offer my bowl to you? When did I betray your expectations?" The monk was enlightened.

*

We teach Zen, if we teach it at all, by the way we write, the way we light the fire, or hold out the bowl to be filled with rice. It is also true, however, that there may be some intellectual obstacle which prevents the (physical) eye or ear or nose from perceiving truth directly. In such a case, the meaning, the intellectual meaning of the words, may cause satori, in the sense of removing that intellectual obstacle.

*

Once Chinsō was giving a monk a meal, and serving the rice himself. The monk stretched out his hand to take it, and Chinsō drew back his own. The monk made no response. Chinsō said, "Yes, I thought as much."

When we are given something we say "Thank you!" When we are refused something, we say "Thank you!" When we are called, we reply; when we are not called, we reply. When we lift a stone, it is heavy; when we don't lift it, it is heavy. God is a God of the heavy, not the weightless, for unto him all things are heavy.

One day Rinzai was out begging and came to the house of a well-off man. He said, "Another bowl more than usual, please!" An old woman came to the door and said, "What a vulgar greedy creature!" Rinzai said, "I don't see the slightest sign of food,—where is the vulgarity and greediness?" The old woman shut the door in his face.

Rinzai asked for more food to test the person of the house. The old woman, knowing something of Zen, returned the attack. Rinzai then spiritualises the matter, like Christ with the woman at the well, but the old woman sees Rinzai is too strong for her, and finds discretion is the better part of valour. The Jewish woman at the well is a Buddhist. The old Chinese woman is not.

*

II | ZEN, BUDDHISM, CHRISTIANITY, AND HINDUISM

In some ways there is more Zen about Christianity than Buddhism; certainly there is more Zen to be found in English literature than in Japanese or Chinese literature, and in Indian literature Zen is painfully absent. But first let us consider the fundamental identity of Christianity and Buddhism and Zen, and then take some equally fundamental differences. The essence of Christianity is, Christ died for you. Buddhism teaches that we have the Buddha nature. When you are the universe, there is Zen. But "You have the Buddha nature" means that you are divine, you are one with Christ. "You are the universe" is another way of saying "You are God." Thus Zen may be called the ultimate simplification of both Christianity and Buddhism, the former being clabbered up with emotionalism and theology, the latter entangled in morality and a more or less scientific philosophy.

However, the theology of Christianity is highly symbolical, and since human beings live by metaphors and similes (taken from Nature, "The Great Stereotype"), the dogmas of Christianity may be, should be, and perhaps are (subconsciously) understood in the Zen way. The creation of the universe by God means God's giving up his all-ness, becoming imperfect in order to look at his own perfection, in order to think of himself. It is the Fall of God, of which the creation and fall of Adam is a kind of close-up. The intellect is separated from the rest of the personality and judges it, and thus Christ adjures us, "Judge not!" The state of man (= the universe, God) suffers the nature of an insurrection. The Crucifixion is the giving up of the intellect, the abnegation of reason, "Not my will" meaning, not my idea, not my judgment, not my thought, not thought. But with the Resurrection the intellect is received back from the head; it rejoins the personality, and never again acts separately from it.

*

Christianity was lucky in that the Jewish myths and amalgamated cults could be interpreted with the Greek-Alexandrian mysticism—or rather, shall we say that the Early Church and later poets were able to bring out the deeper meaning latent in the Jewish Hymn of Creation and the Eastern mystery religions and agricultural rites. In the case of Buddhism, it took over the prosaic and childish theory of reincarnation, which gave man an immortality with all its disadvantages (lack of responsibility, no recollection of past lives) and none of its advantages (recompense for the useless suffering and injustice of this world, and fulfillment of man's desire not to suffer annihilation). In addition, the hyperboles and excessive ornamentation of the accounts of the Buddhas and Bodhisattvas and their realms of bliss are repulsive to the non-Indian mind, far more so than the anthropomorphism of the Bible.

The difference between Christianity and Buddhism is to some extent a difference of the national character of the peoples who created or embraced those religions. In India, people were overwhelmed by Nature, and sought to escape from the excess of life into a sublime, other-worldly, passionless, almost lifeless condition. All the things of this earth were to them *mayoi* (illusion), in themselves empty, and the cause of fruitless desire in man, desire which is the root of all evil. In Judea, where Nature is not so kind, man was correspondingly grateful for the little he received, and attributed to God his own feelings, "And he saw it was good." Judaism is yea-saying, Buddhism nay-saying. In the life of Christ, as in early Christianity, we feel little of the asceticism that comes, as in the case of Buddha, from a surfeit of good things. In this respect Zen is far closer to Christianity, at least the Christianity of Browning, though Zen would say rather, "God's in his world, all's right with Heaven."

*

To Buddha, the world is full of pain, pain that must be escaped from into Nirvana. This Nirvana is an ego-less state in which the illusory individual soul is swallowed up in the (perhaps equally illusory) World-Soul. If "life is suffering," life-lessness can hardly be considered a great evil. Buddha seems never to have thought of the Nirvana of poetry, of art, of music, of nature, of love. For this "illusory" Nirvana of love and hope and glory, the "illusory" soul is necessary, the soul in its painful peace, its peaceful pain. Without pain there is indeed no real painlessness. This is the "peace that passeth understanding," the peace of the Cross. "Take it, for it is all God offers." Here is the one paradox which Zen has always overlooked or avoided. This is perhaps the result of Zazen, which tranquillizes by immobility. We see the same falsity in Buddhist statues, which never eat, never kill mosquitoes even, never have diarrhea, never defend the helpless.

Christ was well aware of pain, but for him more important was evil, religious rather than moral evil, since it consists of alienation from God, which is lack of love. Evil is loneliness. Zen means never being lonely. Loneliness comes when we separate what are really not separated, ourselves and things.

Is God a person? Are you a person? What is a person? Has the universe a mind? According to Wordsworth,

> The Moon doth with delight
> Look round her when the heavens are bare . . .

Has the universe no mind? Darwin wrote:

> I remember well the time when the thought of the eye made me cold all over. . . . The sight of a feather in a peacock's tail, whenever I gaze at it, makes me sick.

To explain the universe in terms of material things and mechanical forces only, without any Mind whatever, is indeed as impossible and superstitious as a belief in a kind of Father

Kyoto ningyo

Christmas deity. On the other hand, animism sees everything as a soul. But this, however poetically true it may be, obscures the distinction between animate and inanimate. No doubt a stone is a person too, but it does not have or wish to have the immortality that human beings desire. The difference between a stone and a man is that a man (a poet, that is, who is the only really human being) knows what a stone is; a stone does not. To know a stone we must do two things. We must know that it is the whole universe; the whole universe is contained in it, and nothing is excluded. It is the Way, the Truth, and the Life. It is the Land of Hope and Glory. It is the hallelujahs of the saints, and the face of God. At the same time, it is only a lifeless, soulless, almost meaningless blur, though no doubt with infinite possibilities and potentialities. It is the stone which the builders rejected.

*

Mind is not produced by a mindless universe; it is involved in it from the very beginning, which "looks" forward to its end. The immortality of the soul was denied by primitive Buddhism, since the soul itself had no existence as an indivisible entity. Even now, at this late date, the expression *muga* "non-self," is used in Japanese to designate the state of mind, no-mind, in which great deeds of any kind are performed. Here Christianity, that is, the Western world-feeling, is in strong and perhaps permanent opposition. The will-to-live, the feeling of the miraculousness of our birth into this world, and our violent antipathy to extinction—this is a universal phenomenon, and it has been asked, with some pertinence, whether the whole of humanity in its long history made the great mistake of supposing that a man is "himself alone" with responsibility for his own actions, and only Sakyamuni realized that he is an illusion, like everything else, a bundle of fleeting thoughts and impressions, that vanish like a dream and leave not a wrack behind, not only at death, but at every moment.

*

Zen is said to be non-duality, non-choosing. The (weak) mind desires one-ness, the peace of an all-inclusive unity where it cannot be surprised or attacked by anything outside or unexpected, for there is nothing but this One, no place beyond it, no time but the present moment. To attain this pearl of great price, this monistic death, mystics have sold all they have or are. Art, music, poetry, nature are given up by the color-blind, the tone-deaf, the scientific, the automation-loving, in order to attain an insensitive, unquestioning, don't-care, fish-hearted, sex-less, pain-free, ambitionless, unnatural peace of mind. The mistake of Zen is its (mystical and scientific) over-emphasis on unity, its contempt for words, its excessive love of sitting. The One, as D. H. Lawrence felt, is more dangerous than the Many. The scientists search for the One, the mystics find It, but the ordinary man sees only the Many. He is pluralistic and polytheistic, and yet at the same time he is willing to die for his small piece of land, and even for no land at all. He can bear toothache better than a philosopher, and of him Thoreau wrote, "He is the great poet, not Homer or Shakespeare." The World is One, it is Many; it is not One, not Many.

*

Religion teaches us how to "overcome the world," whether it be by submission as in Jōdo Shinshū, by energy as in the Nichiren Sect, or by re-union with the Divine as in Hinduism. Popular Buddhism, like popular Christianity, is for cowards and fools like ourselves, and consists of escaping from this world to the Western Paradise, or to a Heaven of some kind or other. Humour, however, belongs very much to this world. Life is suffering, as Sakyamuni pointed out long ago; we cannot have what we want, and we must have what we don't want, but humour is not escapist. It overcomes the world, not by ascending into heaven, but by smiling at the paradoxes of life. We overcome the world by laughing at it; we overcome it in so far as we laugh at it. Humour is thus a religion. It is religion itself. It belongs to the will, to the subconscious will, and sets its will against communism and democracy and Buddhism and Christianity, and every other will, that is, every other religion.

*

Buddhism, like Christianity, hates this world. The world, the flesh, and the devil are lumped together in the New Testament. In Buddhism the world is, as said before, suffering, something we hate. Perversely, Christianity and Buddhism both tell us to love what we hate, to love our enemies, to be compassionate to the things or creatures or human beings that annoy and destroy us. Humour, on the other hand, makes us laugh at our enemies, and at our friends still more, laugh at God and the Devil, laugh at ourselves. To laugh is really to love. This we see in Hamlet and Ophelia, Othello and Desdemona, whose humourless love causes their tragedy.

*

There is a great deal of humour in Zen; no irony, but sarcasm is used in teaching. The humour is that of pure nonsense, Lear and Carroll's transcendentalism. An example. One day Weishan (Isan) called for the chief monk to come to his room, but when he came, Weishan said, "It was the chief monk I called; why on earth did *you* come?" Mysticism is almost devoid of humour, for one reason because it transcends all contradiction, the soul of wit. For another, a maliciously smiling mysticism, which would make fun of the hypocritical seriousness of orthodoxy towards the paradoxes of the Incarnation and the Trinity, could not escape excommunication. Kierkegaard has no humour, but a deep irony, which is sometimes almost too direct to be satire: "To let oneself be trampled to death by geese is a slow way of dying!" Sartre's satire is like that of Swift. Nietzsche is as humorous as a tiger at bay. Heidegger is heavy as only a German can be. In the matter of humour Zen is first and the rest nowhere.

*

What human beings seek for is a unifying principle in this apparently chaotic universe; and nonsense is one of them. The most common of these principles is science, which discovers (or creates) cause and effect. The trouble with science is that cause and effect are only too efficient as an explanation; there is no mystery, no wonder, no interest remaining. Another such principle is religion. Buddhism joins all things by giving them all the Buddha-nature, which "escalates" them somewhat mechanically to Buddhahood. Christianity marries the soul to Christ, who is one with God, but the rest of the creation seems to be omitted. According to Keats, Beauty is what makes everything meaningful, but how about the ugly things, how about ourselves even? The hymn says love is "the tie that binds" things together, but the vast empty spaces of the universe do not look particularly loving. Poetry, in the practical sense understood by Bashō and Thoreau and Wordsworth, "seeing into the life of things," is the best so far, the "life" being the existence-meaning of things animate and inanimate. Humour also is a unifying principle, since it is possible, and even desirable, to laugh or at least smile, however grimly, at all things without exception.

> Seen by the eye of faith
> The cherry blossoms
> Are always about to fall.

Religion is too prone to look only on the gloomy side of things.

> At last,
> With his dead face
> He looks like a man.
> —Kenkabō

Perhaps Kenkabō is speaking cynically, but inadvertently at least this verse justifies the Buddhist doctrine of the Buddha nature. Underneath all the greediness and vindictiveness and vulgarity of his life-long face there always lay the humanity at last revealed by death.

*

Is beauty in the eye of the beholder, or in the picture? The Buddhist answer would be that it is in the eye, the mind. The Christian reply is that the beauty is in God, faintly reproduced in the picture, and dimly seen by us. The Zen view, and the right one, is that beauty exists when and only when I am the picture. Though the picture is a bad one, or even a blank canvas, there is still Zen, if and when I am the canvas, but beauty arises when the canvas has already suffered a sea-change, a universe-change, a Zen-change. That is to say, man is (also) a social animal, a solitary hive-bee. No man liveth to himself, (or to others) and the true half-history of the world is the history of the reunification of things (pictures) and man.

If the [third] eye in the forehead is darkened
And we mistake the star on the balance for the
    measurement,
We throw away our body and soul
And blindly lead other blind people.

                              —Mumon

The Buddha Eye is the one above the other two. Originally this was the eye in the forehead of Mahesvara, the eighth of the Twenty Devas. Later the upper of the three eyes was used to signify the *one* Buddha eye *above* the relativity of the other *two*. The use is thus opposite to that of English, in which "one-eyed" means limited, and unable to see things in perspective.

Everyone has this third eye; all living things, and even inanimate things, have it. All use it without knowing it. It is with this eye that we read poetry, and, oddly enough, listen to music. We may go so far as to say that this eye *is* things as they really are, since things see themselves (only) when we use it.

The last part of the verse is interesting. Those with eyes lead those with eyes, those who have none lead the blind. All lead, all are led. The expression "the blind man leading a crowd of other blind men" comes from the *Nirvana Sutra*, Chapter XXIX, but the whole idea of this Case must come from the Chinese acrobats who, from ancient times (seen for example in pictures incised on bows still kept in the Shōsōin in Nara) performed all kinds of "stunts" at the top of a pole, often balanced on another man. Zen masters must frequently have thought, at such street scenes, "What wonderful talent! But we in Zen must go beyond even that."

                              *

Zen is not a religion. It is not "The Highest Doctrine." There is no "World of Zen." An "Anthology of Zen" is an absurdity (the Bible of Zen, the *Mumonkan* plus the *Hekiganroku*, is the universe laughing at itself). Zen is not something absolute, that we gradually approach, of which our understanding increases with experience. It is not something "once for all delivered to the (Zen) saints." It is not Truth smuggled from one esotericist to another. Zen is all that was, wasn't, is, isn't, will be, and won't. It is the billboard we can see just as much as the tree it hides. It is equally and unequally in the village slut and the Virgin Mary, in an empty tin can and "the solid frame of earth / And ocean's liquid mass." Heidegger asks, "Why is there something, and not nothing?" Zen is the something, the nothing. Zen is Bramah, and includes the swamis and the swoonies and moonies and baboonies toonies. *The Scale of Perfection*, a 14th century religious treatise, says that when we go home to a smoky house and a scolding wife—do not run out of it, "for behind this nothingness, behind this formless shape of evil, is Jesus hid in his joy." But even this must be amended; the smoky house, the scolding wife *is* Jesus in his joy. In this mysticism we have the Zen experience that illusion, that is, reality, the smoky house, *is* enlightenment, that is, reality, Jesus—but not in the same way, as Hakuin Zenji says, that ice is water. Just as ice is ice, not water, so illusion is enlightenment. And illusion and enlightenment are different, just as water and ice are the same. We may say that there is "something" which is neither ice nor water; which is both ice and water, which is either ice or water, but not both. This "something" would be like Thoreau's God, mentioned before, like Eckhart's, which also is nameless, not in the dictionary, but it is also Kierkegaard's God, not ectoplasm, not less personal but more so than even Kierkegaard himself.

It should be noted, as far as art is concerned, that just as the ordinary, so-called Christian knows nothing of the real Christianity, so Kierkegaard, in *Either/Or*, was outside the real aestheticism, which is as profound as we like to make it. Kierkegaard had no more understanding of music than Bernard Shaw. He listened to Don Juan ethically, as the story of a seducer, but Mozart himself was seduced into composing it. Mozart's best music is full of "fear and trembling," and of an infinite resignation to infinite suffering.

Christ was a man; he was also God. Mary was a virgin, and a mother at the same time. God created the world out of nothing. God is the author of evil, but not responsible for it. He creates imperfection, but is himself perfect. Christ died for mankind, but is far from really dead. All this is no different from a beardless bearded barbarian. The great difference between Zen and Christianity, however, is this, that Zen does not ask us somehow or other to believe in the contradiction. It requires us to become the omnipotent weak Nazarene.

*

There is no love in Zen, other than the beating and cursing, and none in mysticism, except of a nauseating, perverted, unnatural, impossible kind—the "Divine Embrace" of Suso; "my cheek on Him," (St. John of the Cross); "the Divine Bridegroom" of St. Theresa—all of which go back to the eroticism of the Orphic mysteries. In *The Hound of Heaven*, love is a cosmic bestialism.

Two thousand years of the deep experience of Christian mysticism convinces us of the existence of the God with whom certain men and women attained union (which may well be reunion). Fifteen hundred years of equally strenuous search for the truth in China and Japan under the aegis of Zen has never once, even by accident, produced the slightest inkling of a personal Deity:

A god, a god their severance ruled!

There is thus no (personal) God in Zen (Buddhism); that is the defect of Zen. There is a God in (Christian) mysticism; that is the defect of Christianity. But I believe Thoreau, as I believe the Bible (when I believe it), in the following: "His work does not lack completeness, that the creature consents." "Though we must abide our destiny, will He not abide it with us?"

(Zen) Buddhism is the religion of (the escape from) suffering. Nirvana is a state beyond (pleasure and) pain. Mysticism also is the desire for "a repose that ever is the same," an escape from loneliness. Existentialism, on the contrary, is the escaping from comfort and tranquillity of mind. It is not masochism, at least in theory, for its aim is suffering, not the pleasure of suffering. Kierkegaard says in his Journal, 1853, "To love God is to suffer." The aim of existentialism is to reign, and to reign with Him we must suffer with Him, but to suffer is to reign, to reign is to suffer. (One oblique proof of the existence of God, which Kierkegaard would have sneered at, is: God is love; love is suffering; suffering exists, therefore God does.) In any case, as far as suffering is concerned, existentialism wins all hands down, leaving Zen and mysticism trailing far behind with their joy of enlightenment and ecstasy of union.

*

Mysticism has no thought. It is pure sensation applied to the Divine. Al-Ghazzali, a Persian mystic of the 11th century, wrote in his autobiography, "The transport which one attains by the method of the Sufis is like an immediate perception, as if one touched the objects with one's hand." In Zen we think and think until thought is confronted with the abyss of Unthought, and we then jump into that abyss. Existentialism is similar, but the thinking never stops. "If the Sun and Moon should doubt, They'd immediately Go Out," says Blake the mystic. In existentialism the sun and moon are always flickering, guttering. Death and resurrection are simultaneous and endless. Mysticism is an experience of allness. Zen of this-thing-ness.

(World) mysticism is the experience of an ever-present, aboriginal oneness. It is the reunion of the I and the not-I. (Chinese) Zen, in its historical origins in the Upanishads, and for Laotse and Chuangtse, is the same; only in its method, its style, is it dissimilar, and of course a difference of style is a difference of essence. (European) existentialism is the experience of the eternal separation of the I, not from the not-I, but from the Personal Absolute that stands outside both.

*

Mysticism is a re-union of the individual soul with the Over-soul. Its mark is joy; it grasps Eternity for only short times. Zen also is an identification (together with an equally "real" separation) of the self and the Self, and thus enlightenment is the same enlightenment for everybody (in spite of the alleged "separation"). Its mark is peace of mind, and the Eternal is now, or never.

Since Zen, mysticism, and existentialism are forms of experience, the claims of all three must be conceded, for real experience is infallible. All three would say that, not in spite of, but rather because of the contradictions of experience, it

" the pine tree lives a thousand years
the morningglory but one day
yet both fulfil their destiny"..

must be believed. However, the intellect should not be forgotten. It is the intellect which tells us that the moment these three step beyond experience into explanation or synthesis or analysis or proof and disproof, we should not merely refuse to accept it but declare that it is not only not true, but false. In the world of poetry (and poetry is the common element of Zen, mysticism, and existentialism) commonsense judgements are not simply invalid; the more they are right the more they are wrong.

*

It is not easy to distinguish Buddhism from Hinduism when we go deeply into both, but what seems specifically to distinguish primitive Buddhism from earlier Indian thought is the doctrine of anatmavada, no-soul. The *Upanishads* teach in their desultory way that man is a soul; the universe is a soul; the soul of man is the soul of the universe. Against this, primitive Buddhism declared that man has no soul, the universe has no soul; both are but the parts or the whole of the Chain of Causation which is broken only when desire ceases.

*

The Buddha did not deny that Brahman, the world soul, interpenetrated all things, for to do so would have made *ahimsa*, no-killing, meaningless. But he undoubtedly taught the I-lessness of I, and that the realisation of this fully was Buddhahood. On the other hand, though there is no I, the apparent I must train itself ethically. And moral teaching is almost entirely absent in the *Upanishads*. Primitive Buddhism was a system of self-purification by which we attain to the Self. Earlier Hinduism jumped over the morality, and implied what Zen was to say explicitly long afterwards, that we are, as we are, already enlightened. Dhyana (zazen), to sit in meditation, was thus the *natural* thing for all men.

The difference between Zen and the doctrine of the *Upanishads* is this, that the *Upanishads* assert that the soul and the World Soul are unborn and undying, that is to say, timeless. Nagarjuna on the other hand declared that external things also are unborn and undying, because they are unreal and insubstantial no less than the Atman and the Brahman.

*

This doctrine of non-origination is the poetical attitude, the world of no cause and effect, no science, nonsense. Nagarjuna's other doctrine, that of dependent origination, blends the poetic and the scientific. If all things are but the effects of causes, and the causes of effects, they have no real existence and are intrinsically "empty," but at the same time, as each thing is dependent upon each other thing and all things, it is representative of them. Each is only a link in the chain of being, but as such indispensable.

*

One defect of Zen is its lack of personality, and of Personality. Zennists make fun, in very poor taste, of a personal God and of an individual soul. I myself believe in neither, but there is nothing ludicrous in the idea that personality, human or divine, is the highest form of being we can conceive. Fifty million Jews can't be wrong. In actual fact, not only we, but everything else is personal. If the I is personal, so is the not-I, for it is the universe which is thus chopped into two; animism is the essence of all true poetry and religion. This of course has nothing to do with the immortality of the soul, or a divinity that shapes our ends.

What is the conclusion to all this? It is that Zen, if it is in the end to be something at all, if it is to be all, and all in all, must be not merely Indian Zen with its quietism, or Chinese Zen with its monkish practicality, or Japanese Zen with its artistic and poetical life. As D. H. Lawrence said, the dark hand and the white hand must clasp each other, not in any mawkish pretense of friendliness, but so that the Zen of Buddhism may absorb and be absorbed by the Zen of Christianity. The Eternal Buddha has always been in Nirvana in utter peace and perfection. The Eternal Christ will never be at rest until the last sinner has been somehow or other squeezed through the pearly Gates of Heaven. (But this also is in eternity.) This "Zen" is "that something evermore about to be," the Deeper Nature that Wordsworth tells us is "opposed to nature," nature which Matthew Arnold says in *Morality* knows its own incompleteness only when it "remembers" that time

> When in the heavenly house I trod,
> And lay upon the breast of God.

Say the word "Buddha," and you wallow in mud and flounder in puddles. Say the word "Zen," and your whole face is as red as a beetroot with shame and humiliation.

—Hekiganroku

This kind of thing, strangely enough, is not to be found in Christianity. There is the word "religiosity," and "sanctimonious" as applied to particular people, but Zen feels sick with too much Zen.

*

There is the famous story of *Eisen no mimi-arai*. The Emperor Gyō sent a messenger to a hermit named Kyoyū, offering to abdicate and hand over the Empire to him. Kyoyū not only flatly refused, but upon hearing such a filthy suggestion washed his ears in the river Ei. Another hermit, Sōfu, coming there to water his ox, and seeing this, led his ox away, saying he would not let it drink such dirty water.

The old proverb, "It is a foule byrd that fyleth his owne nest," expresses the human dislike of truth, for our nest is the universe. Thus, to attack religion—not *a* religion, for that only involves persecution and perhaps death—is to be a cosmic Judas, and betray humanity,—to what?

*

A monk said to Kegon, "The loyal army builds an altar to the Heavenly Kings, and seeks for victory; the rebel army also builds an altar to the Heavenly Kings and seeks for victory; which prayer do they answer?" Kegon replied, "Heaven's rain drops its dews, and does not choose the flourishing or the declining."

This is remarkably like the rain falling upon the just and upon the unjust, though the Heavenly Kings here refers to the Four Deva-kings, giant temple-guardians brought to China by Amogha, who was the head of the Yogacara School, and who died 774. It is said that he originated the festival of feeding the hungry spirits, and he was famous for making rain and stilling storms. The Zen meaning of this adecdote must be that the universe "loves" us just as we "love" ourselves, impartially, because we are the universe.

When Ryūsen was with Kyōzan he was the tenzo (the monk in charge of the food). One day a strange monk came, and asked for a meal. Ryūsen gave him part of his own. Kyōzan already knew this, and said to Ryūsen, "That enlightened monk who came just now,—did he give you any food?" "He denied himself and passed on his alms," said Ryūsen. Kyōzan said, "You made a great profit."

This is a very charming sequel to the story of the Good Samaritan. Christians always pretend that we should think of others only, but Christ urged us to love ourselves as much as we love others (the reverse will also do).

Sōmitsu (Sengmi), and Tōzan were crossing a river together. Tōzan said, "Don't make a mistake in where you tread!" Sōmitsu said, "If I don't make a mistake how can I cross the river?" Tōzan said, "Who is he that makes no mistake?" Sōmitsu said, "He who crosses the water with an enlightened man."

This reminds us of Christian and Faithful, or rather, of Christian and Mr. Greatheart. It is the justification of the Roman Catholic Church, with its banned books. But it is true enough, the function of great men is to protect us against our worst mistakes.

> Quite apart from our religion,
> There are plum blossoms,
> There are cherry blossoms.
> —Nanpoku

This is the double mistake, the mistake of religion, and the mistake of poetry.

> The priest
> Keeps his mouth shut,
> Or speaks of Zen only.

Mr. Blyth is like this; but this is not real Zen, which will talk of anything, even of Zen.

*

One aspect of humour is lacking in Japanese Zen, though not in Chinese Zen, and therefore in Japanese Buddhism, that is, pure nonsense. The *Mumonkan* is full of preposterous stories, which must have been popular in China long before "Zen" was ever heard of. It was the genius of the Chinese Zen monks of the 8th century which perceived the Zen latent in those stories, and laughed with their conscious minds as did the Chinese illiterates with their subconscious minds. But how can we laugh with our conscious minds? To do so is Zen.

Japanese Zen is the experience of Japanese people of their humanity, that is, of the sound of water, the taste of tea, the bending of branches, the look of food on a plate, the realisation that all's right with this terrible world. There is no superstition or dogma or provincialism, no wishful thinking, nothing that stinks of India or China or Japan here. The Zen which is the essence of Christianity must in the same way leave behind the Virgin Birth, the divinity of Christ, the existence or non-existence of God. These things may and should all be kept as symbols, not of ineffable mysteries, but of our own virginity, our own divinity, our own existence, and our own non-existence.

Zen is the poetry of life, and all poetry is the same, all poetry is different. The joy at the sameness, the joy at the difference, this is ZEN.

*

Where Buddhism and Christianity make their mistakes is not in experience, which is infallible, but in the analysis of it. This analysis affects the preceding experience and that is the (only) reason for its importance. Poetic and religious experience means SEEING SOMETHING (hearing, touching, smelling and so on are included in "see"). This experience is also of its own validity, and we are as certain of it as when we merely see something. But the moment we attempt, in either case to answer the question, "And WHAT did you SEE," or, "And what did you see?" all is confusion. Note that the question may, and should perhaps always be written, "Whom did what see?" The confusion arises from the fact that what or who is seen is not separable (except in words and thought) from what or who sees, and the seeing is not separable from the thing seen. When "I" and the poetry or the truth, or my father, or the flower, or the oak tree are set against each other, both are meaningless. This is why Christ says, or John says for him, "I and my Father are one," "Ye shall be in me, and I in you," and so on. The trouble with Christians is that when they read "Christ in you, the hope of glory," they understand it in all its literality and transcendentalism, but the moment they begin to explain it, it becomes a metaphor, and "in" which means "equals," is taken as "influencing."

*

III | THE WAY

Is there such a thing as The Way? Is it not rather, as the Japanese seem to believe by instinct, that there are just as many ways as there are (types of) persons? Is there such a thing as good taste and bad taste, or only my (good) taste and your (bad) taste and his? All religion is for The Way; all experience and common sense is against it. But marriage, the ordinary marriage presumes that at least these two people have one way between them, and the marriage of two minds in general, whether in sound or words or form or colour, presupposes that the writer has his readers, the musician his audience, the philosopher his disciples,—but have they, really? Who can join what God hath put asunder?

*

Again, Nature possibly, and even probably, has A Purpose, but still more probably will change this Purpose for another if circumstances demand it. Just as we human beings are subject to all kinds of accident, so is Nature herself, and does what can be done, not what can't. A man who has a way is only a kind of animal after all. A man who thinks his is The Way deceives himself no doubt. But as Nietzsche said, some kinds of errors and delusions are as necessary for life, that is, for the Way, as truth is, perhaps more so. Nature deceives us; we deceive ourselves; but Nature also deceives herself, which means that every man must deceive himself and no other person. "Let Nature be your teacher" in this also.

*

A man is not just another animal in the universal Zoo. He is, and must believe that he is, not only a movement towards something, but to a certain extent already is that Something. The "One far-off, divine event to which the whole creation moves" is occurring here and now. But the present problem is not whether humanity has its Way or not, but whether mine is that Way or only my way. A Way implies two necessary conditions; first, people walking on it, more or less consciously; second, an ultimate goal, more or less unknown and unknowable, but believed to exist. The number of people actually walking the way is not of course so important as their quality, but it is necessary that this minority should be so to speak the spear end, not the butt end. Majorities will always persecute minorities, but the majority, though never right, is not always wrong, (usually they are just nothing at all), and therefore the minority, though never wrong, is not always right.

We talk of "right" and "wrong," but what is the standard by which to decide? The answer is clear: there is none, and even this answer cannot be made dogmatically. We may however venture a little further on this uncertain ground, and assert, as a corollary of the first sentence in Laotse, that to the extent that a way declares itself to be The Way, it is not.

*

The Way of flowers is a silent one, not that flowers don't speak because they can't, but because they don't happen to want to. Of course they would, like the stones of Jerusalem when Christ entered the city, cry out if they did happen to want to. Their expressive silence is willed, not involuntary. The life, the Way of men is also silent, but the silence is a different one, and may be in words. Thoreau says, "It takes a man to make a room silent."

*

This is the Way, but how shall we walk on it, and shall it be alone, or hand in hand, and if so, with whom? What shall we do, what shall we not do, and how shall we do it, and not do it; in this wayless world, where people have resigned themselves to spinning round like teetotums of some brand or another? Let me put my cards on the table, for I think I have a good hand, not the whole pack, certainly, but. . . .

I am a pacifist, letting other people defend me from all those millions who would rob me of my worldly goods, liberty, and life itself; a vegetarian whose shoes are made of leather; a teacher who teaches that only teachers are human, business men, politicians, doctors, lawyers and so on being mere parasitic blackmailers, and who teaches also that people are unteachable. The most important thing of all, the most human thing is, as D. H. Lawrence said, to have right relations with a particular woman. By "right relations" I mean, as Lawrence did not, that she should walk the Way (which, as is quite evident by now, means my way) in the same way as I do, albeit with a woman's legs. She must then be a pacifist, a vegetarian, a (studentless) teacher, or what is much the same thing, a (teacherless) student. In addition she must have no interest in money, her own, or other people's; no ambition, no desire "to improve her soul's estate." Anybody but Bach always and Mozart sometimes is to be listened to with only half an ear . . . Every article of daily life is to be chosen with the greatest care (not the greatest money); cups and kettles must be the best that a little money will buy. Trains, buses, buildings, streets and the people in them are all seen with the sort of horror that Dante felt as he gazed around in the Inferno. The ugliness, the stupidity, the meaninglessness! She never reads the newspapers, the advertisements, Buddhist magazines; has no recreations or amusements; always busy, she does nothing "to pass the time,"—it all sounds so terribly snobbish and highbrow! But what do Christians think they are going to do in Heaven? What books are they going to read? Do they think they are going to play Johann Strauss on their golden harps? Dante was not so cheap as to suppose that people talked shop even in Limbo. People seem to want to live greedily and vulgarly now, because they think they won't be able to do so in the next world.

*

Zen monks begging

It will be seen that this "Way" does not imply that each person is to live his own life, developing his own talents, to live as his nature urges him, in a word, to be free. He has to live as my nature tells me to live, and urges me to urge him to live. Indeed, the first step is to change his own character, to love snakes and hate jazz; to despise leaders of industry and admire the industrious ant; to abhor Buddhist societies and International Culture; to dislike socialism as much as capitalism; to love people who really love something or somebody; to be unwilling above all things to talk about The Way and such nonsense.

Further, this Way does not guarantee any kind of spiritual success, peace of mind, efficiency, good health, self-confidence, concentration of one's powers, satori, "every day spent usefully and happily," so that we leave the world a better place than we found it.

*

To go back to the original question,—are there different ways for different people, or is there One Way for everybody? The answer is that each individual, purely subjectively and with absolute freedom of choice could, (but does not) arrive at this One Way by accident. In this world, each individual life is determined Calvinistically; his character at birth decides to what extent he shall walk this Way. God, that is, Nature, decides who shall go to Heaven, i.e. walk the Way, or not. A man's efforts are of little avail. However much we support the Animal Welfare Society, it makes no difference to our real love of animals (Heaven) or real indifference to them (Hell). Teaching and writing and sitting under Bo-trees and dying on crosses have nothing to do with other people's salvation. Yet though we know this, and when we know this, and because we know this, we continue to teach and write and sit and die for others. Why? This is the Way.

A Way of Life is as good as, and no better than the people who walk it. There is no Platonic, abstract, ideal Zen; even if there were, as said before, it would have no meaning for us, for we live by our own Zen, not Zen's Zen. Buddhism long ago saw all this, and the difficulty was covered, in two senses of the word, by the doctrine of temporary teaching for those who could not enter the higher realms of Buddhist transcendence.

A monk asked Kankei, "What is the Way?" Kankei answered, "If rain is plentiful in summer, in autumn the fields are yellow." "That's not the way I mean," said the monk. "What way are you talking about?" said Kankei. The monk said, "I mean the Great Way." Kankei laughed, and nodded, and said, "The Great Way is everywhere, and gives in every direction."

The monk did not wish to hear about the Way of Nature, but the Way of Man, but there's only one Way and that is every way. We must go in every direction wherever we go.

What Takuan wanted was to deny himself, Takuan, in history, so as to affirm the Way. In one of his writings, *Ketsujōshū*, he says that we will have no troubles if we think we come into this world as guests. As guests we must praise the meal, even if we do not like it. We must put up with the heat of summer, the coldness of winter. We must be on good terms with our children and brothers and sisters, who are fellow guests. In a waka Takuan says:

> Invited by our parents,
> We came here
> As temporary guests,
> And without remaining mind,
> We go back to our native place.

Takuan's will is interesting; it might have been written by Bernard Shaw:

> Bury my body in the mountain behind the temple. Just cover it with soil and go away. Do not read any sutras; do not make an altar; do not receive obituary gifts. The clothes and the meals of the priests should be as usual. Do not ask for a posthumous title. Do not erect a tomb-stone, or make a wooden mortuary tablet. Do not write my life story.

*

Once Nansen said to the assembled monks, "The Way is not outside things, outside things there is no Way."

Jōshū asked, "What is the Way which is outside things?"
Nansen immediately struck him. Jōshū caught hold of the
stick and said, "From now on don't strike someone by
mistake!" Nansen said, "It's easy to speak of a dragon,
but difficult to please me!" and throwing down his stick
he went back to his room.

Nansen was right, but Jōshū was righter. There is no Way
outside things, but there is a Way outside things. The Way
that can be called a Way (which is not outside things) is not
an eternal way. This is what Jōshū taught his master.

A monk said to Rakan, "What is the Way?" He answered,
composing or quoting a verse:
"Lovely flowers open by the mossy roadside;
The green willows dance in the spring breezes."
The monk asked, "Who is the man who walks the Way?"
Rakan answered:
"Opening the window, he steals the moonlight;
Moving his seat, he faces the clear-flowing stream."

Rakan is speaking here in the style of *Il Penseroso*, but he
does not mean simply that the Wayfarer enjoys the beauties
of Nature, but also that his mind is undisturbed by phenomena
of every kind, and that the world is seen as a kind of pageant
(Thoreau).

*

A monk said to Nantō, "The ancient road has no tracks;
how can we advance along it?" Ōren said, "The golden
crow flies round Mount Sumeru, and makes the timeless
and time the same." The monk asked, "How can we get
to the Further Shore?" Ōren said, "The Yellow River is
clear once in three thousand years."

The monk asks about time, and Ōren says it is timeless.
The monk asks about the timeless, and is told it is time.
Thoreau says, "All the past is here present. . . . Let it
approve itself, if it can." A way exists only if people (now)
walk on it. But as for salvation, it is as difficult to attain, for
internal and external reasons, as for a cat to be averse to fish.

*

A monk asked Jōshū, "What is the Way?" Jōshū said, "The one outside the hedge." "I'm not asking about that!" said the monk. "What way are you asking about?" said Jōshū. "About the Great Way," said the monk. "Oh, the Great Road leads to Chōan (Ch'ang-an)," said Jōshū.

All teaching must be more or less malicious, and the most painful part of it all is that the monk thinks Jōshū is joking both times,—and so he is, but all the more serious both times. The path outside the hedge, and the great highway, and the bird's path through the air and the fish's through the water, and the thought's through the brain,—these are all the Way.

A monk asked Jōshū, "What is the way without mistakes?" Jōshū said, "Knowing one's mind, seeing into one's nature is the way without mistakes."

The meaning is that when once we have seen into our mind, which is the Mind of the universe, there is no mistake in the will, though there must be innumerable mistakes of thought and feeling and act.

*

A monk asked Kyuhō, "What is the Way?" He replied, "See the carts and horses going along it!" The monk asked, "How about the man walking on it?" Kyuhō hit him. The monk bowed. Kyuhō said, "Katz!"

The answer to the first question is that the only way to walk is upon the earth. The Way is any way. The second answer is transcendental. Only God walks the Way, and strikes the just and the unjust with equanimity and inequality.

A monk asked Chōsa, "What is the meaning of 'Your every-day mind is the Way'?" Chōsa said, "When you want to sleep, you sleep; when you want to sit, you sit." The monk said, "This learner does not understand." Chōsa said, "When you are hot, you cool yourself; when you are cold, you warm yourself."

This half of Zen is both more difficult to grasp intellectually and to put into practice than the paradoxical, A is not A type. This is because it is more poetical, that is to say, it is the thing as it is, simply and deeply perceived by self-consciousness.

Chōsa said, "If I once expressed the meaning of Zen, rank grasses six feet deep would cover the ground in front of the Hall."

*

Zen, to make its way in the world must advertise itself, behave eccentrically, wear fancy dress, bang drums, drone sutras,—in a word must become un-Zen. So with Christianity, so with everything of the *civitas dei*.

Ascending the rostrum, Ōbaku said, "Far better than the hundred kinds of knowledge is the nonseeking spirit. This is the best thing of all. The true wayfarer has nothing. There are not several minds. Truth is not something to be explained. That is all. Depart in peace!"

This is a good sermon, especially as to length. "Know thyself!" is converted into "Believe that there is nothing to know!" The Way is simply the pleasure of putting one foot down and then the other. There is no illuminated mind or darkened mind. Light and darkness make up one Day. Nothing can be explained. When it is brought out, it is different from when it was inside, and also, the explanation must be explained. When this happens, and it happens all over the world all the time, in churches and halls and in conversations:

The hungry sheep look up and are not fed.

Yakusan was asked by Governor Ri (Li) "What are Sila, Dhyana, and Prajna?" Yakusan answered, "This poor monk has not such useless furniture." Ri said, "Don't be so mysterious!" Yakusan said, "If you want to have what I have, you must sit on the highest mountain, go down to the bottom of the deepest sea. You don't throw off your burdens even when you go to bed; you are busy with illusions."

Sila is the precepts, Dhyana meditation, Prajna wisdom. The Governor of a State must be answered rudely, especially when he asks about Zen (which he won't). His great fault is

lack of true ambition, and he needs encouragement and stimu-
lation, though unavailing.

Yakusan's manner of death was of a piece with his life.
When he was about to die, he yelled out, "The Hall's falling down! The Hall's falling down!" The monks brought
various things and began to prop it up. Yakusan threw up
his hands and said, "None of you understood what I
meant!" and died.

What did Yakusan mean? Everything is falling down;
everything is rising up. To prop what must fall is foolish;
rather, give it a push. When some famous work of art or
monument of culture is destroyed, when a moth is burnt in a
flame, when five million Jews are slaughtered, let us do what
Yakusan did,—yell, and die.

> Perfect like great space,
> The way has nothing lacking, nothing in excess.
>   —Sengtsan

*

A monk asked Nan-yin, "What is the Way?" Nan-yin
answered, "A kite flies across the great sky; nothing remains there."

With the Way, as with God, all things are possible. But
it is the empty sky because there was a hawk flying across it.
No hawk, no sky; no sky, no hawk. Don't forget the hawk
when you look at the sky.

*

IV | BUDDHA-NATURE AND KARMA

Have all men the Buddha-Nature? What is the Buddha nature? The Buddha nature is to know (potentially, subconsciously, in practice) that we have the Buddha nature, to know too when we ask questions, that they are foolish, and the answers to them more so. This "knowing" is not that something is known; something is always about to be known. We are eternally just going to have the Buddha nature. We haven't exactly not got it, but not exactly have it. To go back to the original question: have all men the Buddha nature? We may ask a second question, a question which is more congruent with the first than most people suspect: have all men a sense of poetry, a sense of humour? If we answer yes, we look like fools; if no, ill-natured. The Christian religion says that some cannot be saved, either by the will of God (Calvinism) or by their own.

Human nature involves five elements, first, the so-called first law of Nature, self-preservation. As D. H. Lawrence said, "Art for my sake." Second, there is the equally or perhaps more fundamental (if Tolstoy was not mistaken) instinct of the preservation of others. There is marriage and procreation; there is self-sacrifice. Third, man desires the impossible, the infinite, the eternal; he wishes to be omniscient, omnipotent. The fourth is an odd one: man desires to suffer, to suffer for its own sake; this is commonly called masochism, but the pleasure in pain is to some extent a desire for a depth of experience which mere pleasure hardly gives. Last, and strongest of all, there is the desire for death, for nothingness. These five things together make up our human nature.

*

The Buddha-nature is not only ours, but that of all creatures, and even of insentient, apparently soul-less things. Every thing in the universe shall ultimately become Buddha, that is, every animate and inanimate being is of such a nature that it will become the All. This sounds very fine, and I myself feel strongly inclined to believe it. To go to Heaven together with drowned rats and sticks and stones and pimps and drunkards, even successful business men and politicians,—this suits me down to the ground. But has the dog the Buddha-nature? In spite of what Jōshū said, the answer is Yes. Must I then die like a dog? The answer again is Yes. I am not going to Heaven at all then, nor the dog nor the drowned rats and so on? No, you are not. If this is what having the Buddha-nature means, one would be just as well off without it. After all, we must ask Zen to help us out of our despair, and out of our hope as well. The truth is that we have not any specific thing that can be called the Buddha-nature, or shall we not rather say that we both have it and do not have it, at the same time. It is true that we have no immortality, but we have something far better, we have time, and we have timelessness.

> Ah, sunflower, weary of time
> That countest the steps of the sun . . .

We want to escape from time:

> Seeking after that sweet golden clime
> Where the traveller's journey is done.

*

But it is the seeking, the aspiring, the movement which is the thing. Our Buddha nature is our becoming Buddha. This "becoming" has two aspects: we are already there; our journey is already done; we have fought the good fight. But we shall never arrive there; we shall lose every battle with the stupidity and dullness of ourselves and others. We must teach the unteachable, do the impossible, make time eternal.

*

What is the poetic nature? Things mean; they mean deeply; they mean infinitely. This is their poetic nature. However, though they simply mean, and do not mean something, they mean to us, and we are meant by them. The poetry of a thing and a person arises from their conjunction. A flower by itself is everything, no doubt, but on the other hand it is nothing. A human being is the same, but when these two everythings or nothings come together, we get something; the poetic nature is activated. A poet is the true man. An unpoetical man is a monkey. But the poetical nature belongs to Nature as well as to human nature. Purpose, which is unconscious purpose, is always known by the result. It was Nature that produced the poet, and this was "that one far-off divine event to which the whole creation moves."

Nature, human nature, the Buddha-nature, the poetic nature,—these are all one thing, (though they are also different things). Humanity is implicit in the vastest, emptiest space. We speak rightly of a stony silence, or a wooden expression. The Buddha-nature is simply our own deepest nature. Moments of vision, our poetic hours, are those of Buddhahood; there is no other. Wherever we look, we see Nature, we see our human nature, we see the Buddha-nature, we see the poetic nature. All that we touch and smell and taste and hear also is so. This is the real Christian life, though we do not believe in Christianity. It is the real Buddhist life, though Buddhism is far from us. It is the life of Zen, though we have not the slightest idea what Zen is.

A monk once asked Jōshū, "Has a dog the Buddha-Nature?" Jōshū answered, "No!" Jōshū's answer can be considered in two ways, first, in its relation to the monk and his particular state of mind and circumstances; second, as a transcendent expression of reality.

(a) What made the monk ask the question? I think we may say, because he half-anticipated the answer he got. When Pilate asked Christ, "What is truth?" he really meant, "I don't want to know what truth is; it is no doubt something very tiresome and disagreeable, so please don't tell me." This is why Christ was silent. In other words, a question contains, and must contain, more than half the answer. The monk's question should perhaps have the form, "Hasn't this dog the Buddha-Nature?" He half suspected it hadn't—that is to say, that there was something suspicious about the ordinary understanding of the dog and its Buddha-Nature. As far as the words are concerned, the monk was right in suggesting that the dog had the Buddha-Nature, and the answer was "Yes!" but the monk was putting the wrong meaning into the right words, so Jōshū put the right meaning into the wrong words, to upset him, to shake him up. So, if a man says to me, "Aren't those lambs pretty little creatures?" I answer, "No!" because his meaning, with his mouth full of lamb cutlets, is not my meaning.

*

In the Kegon Sect (Hua-yen) Avatamsaka, the most important doctrine was that of the Dharma-Nature, by which name the sect was also called. The Dharmata, or Bhutatathata is conveniently defined by its synonyms, abiding dharma-nature; realm of dharma; inherent dharma or Buddha-Nature; embodiment of dharma; region of reality; reality; nature of the void, immaterial nature; appearance of nothingness, or immateriality; Bhutatathata; Tathagatagarbha; universal nature; immortal nature; impersonal nature; realm of abstraction; nature of no illusion; immutable nature; realm beyond thought; and last, the Buddha-Nature. Not all the above definitions of the Dharma-Nature, however, coincide with what is meant by "Buddha-Nature," which implies a kind of inevitable potentiality of Self-realisation, that is, of the Dharma-Nature. In other words, the Buddha-Nature is the Dharma-Nature in its self-conscious aspect.

*

The Tendai (Tien-tai) Sect taught the identity of the absolute and phenomena. Universal Buddhahood was the special teaching of this Sect, being founded upon the *Nehangyō, Nirvana Sutra.*

All sentient things without exception have the Buddha-Nature.

Even the most abandoned character who seeks to destroy his own Buddha-Nature, cannot do so.

"There are three aspects of the meaning (of Buddha-Nature or Thusness) and if you ask what they are, I answer, first, the greatness of quintessence, that is to say, all things, all existences are of Thusness, the same in their nature, neither increasing nor decreasing."

The above quotation from Yōka Daishi shows the attitude we are to adopt to the whole question of karma. The fact is, that we are bound by karma as an ordinary man is bound by a rock, or by a motor-car that won't go. The sculptor is master of the rock, the mechanic is master of the machine, in so far as they are willingly in accord with the laws of the material in which they work. And inasmuch as this obedience to law is conscious, we may say that the spiritual state of the illuminated man is that of karma becoming as it were conscious, with the psychological result that not a particle of freedom, not a particle of constraint, remains. If we can reach the "Greatness of Quintessence," the ground of our being, which is co-terminous with the ground of all being, the problem of karma is solved,—but not by transcending it. This is where Zen differs from Christian Mysticism, but agrees with Christ's "That the Glory of God may be manifested." And in fact, the problem, insoluble intellectually is solved every day, by life itself. If we say we are above karma, we are wrong (at the moment of assertion); if we say we are subject to karma, we are robots and deny our deepest experiences. If we assert that we are both above karma and subject to it, we are lying. And all our assertions are merely the leaves and branches of knowledge; they are not the Root.

There is the world of cause and effect, from which we can never for a moment escape. There is the world of no-cause, no-effect, timeless, spaceless, devoid of beauty and ugliness, right and wrong, good and bad, from which we can escape whenever we will.

*

This first Case of the *Mumonkan,* treated as a kōan, is simply Mu and nothing else, with no reference to the monk or Jōshū or the dog or its Buddha-Nature. For this reason Inoue charges Zen monks with having perverted the original meaning. Based as this Case is upon the *Nirvana Sutra,* the question should be, "What is the Buddha-Nature?" Mumon put in only half the anecdote in order to concentrate upon the "Mu," but actually Jōshū says at another time, "U," that is, "Yes." The two problems, that of Mu and of the Buddha-Nature, are two only in name.

Mu is used to reach the ground of one's nature, that is, the Buddha-Nature. Distinction is therefore intellectually valid, but experientially meaningless. If we know the kōan *Mu,* we know what the Buddha-Nature is; if we know what the Buddha-Nature is, we are in the state of Mu, the blessed state of the poor in spirit. It is a condition of the soul which we see unmistakably in Buddha and Christ, where we want nothing and yet want everything as it is, or rather, as it is becoming. We must have No *and* no, or Yes *and* yes, for Yes = No, but yes and no are opposite. Jōshū says at one time (Yes and) yes, at another time (No and) no. His Mu is No and no; his U is Yes.

*

For the practical study of Zen, you must pass the barriers set up by the masters of Zen. The attainment of this mysterious illumination means cutting off the workings of the ordinary mind completely. If you have not done this and passed the barrier, you are a phantom among the undergrowth and weeds of emotionality and intellection. Now what is this barrier? It is simply "Mu," the Barrier of the Gate of Zen and this is why the entrance to Zen is called "The Gateless Barrier of the Zen Sect."

Those who have passed the barrier are able not only to have an intimate understanding of Jōshū, but also of the whole historic line of Zen Masters, to walk hand in hand with them, and to enter into the closest relation with them. You see everything with the same eye that they saw with. . . .

The whole of this relatively long commentary may be summarised thus:

1. The Master's Barrier must be passed by cutting off emotionality and sophistication.
2. In so doing, you see and hear what the greatest men of the past saw and heard.
3. This means the unification of the microcosm and the macrocosm through Mu.
4. The result is the childlike happiness of perfect freedom.
5. To attain this state, unremitting effort is needed, but persistence will end in the birth of yet another living witness to the truth.

*

The problem here is not that of whether a dog has the Buddha-Nature or not, but whether we have it or not. The truth is that if you try to understand whether the dog has the Buddha-Nature, neglecting mankind, or try to understand whether man has the Buddha-Nature, neglecting the dog, you fail, and to that extent. When we come to consider the question of the Buddha-Nature of the dog from the point of view of Christianity, we see the deep gulf fixed between it and Buddhism. The fundamental problem, or rather, dogma of Christianity is the Divinity of Christ, that he was of a different nature from us. Modern Christian thought, however, tends towards the belief that we have, potentially, at least, the Divine Nature, and could, if pressed, admit this Divine Nature to other sentient creatures. In *Jesus, Man of Genius*, which may be taken as indicative of the direction in which Christian experience is slowly moving, Middleton Murray says:

> "The Holy Ghost . . . was simply that part or power of God which abided with Jesus, or any man after his union with God. It was not God, for God was other than himself; it was not himself for it was other than he had been. It was the God who was henceforward in himself.
>
> "Jesus believed he was the son of God, in precisely the same sense as he believed all men to be sons of God. The difference between him and other men, in his eyes, was simply this: that he knew he was the son of God, while they did not."

*

Nō: Buddhist priest and Shite in Old Man mask

One day Chōkei went to the Hall where all the monks were assembled. He called out one monk and told the congregation to bow to him. He then said, "What's so fine about this monk that I should have you bow to him?" The monks were silent.

*

It is said that the Empress Kōmyō washed a leper, in order to demonstrate the spirit of the Mahayana. We might think of this kind of thing as the solution of the problem of war and all the rest of them down to matrimonial squabbles, but it is not so. People are quite capable of bowing down to each other, and then mowing down each other.

*

A monk asked Hyakujō, "What is the Buddha?" Hyakujō asked the monk, "Who are you?" The monk said, "I am I." Hyakujō said, "Do you know this 'I,' or not?" The monk replied, "Clearly." Hyakujō held up his mosquito flapper, and said, "Do you see this?" "I do," said the monk. Hyakujō said, "I have no word."

A learner who doesn't know that he doesn't know is un-teachable.

*

An ascetic asked Kakusan, "What is the Great Meaning of Buddhism?" Kakusan bowed to him. The ascetic said to him, "Do you bow to a man of the world?" Kakusan said, "Don't you see what I am saying, that I am your famous disciple?"

Buddhism means learning, not teaching, receiving, not giving.

*

Ascending the rostrum, Baso said, "All you people, if you are enlightened, you will come out of your mother's womb and roar like a lion. You know what this roaring means?"

It is interesting how the same thing has quite an opposite effect on different people. Baso wanted to roar; that was his object of life. Why does a lion roar? Why does a bird sing? Why does a man write books? It is their nature, their Buddha nature.

*

At the bottom of Mount I, a monk had built a hermitage, and Kyōzan went there and told him what Isan had said, namely: "Most people have the great potentiality, but not the great function." The monk told Kyōzan to ask him concerning the matter, but when Kyōzan was about to do so, the monk kicked him in the chest and knocked him down. Kyōzan went back to Isan and told him, whereupon Isan gave a great laugh.

The great potentiality is the passive aspect of enlightenment, of the Buddha nature; the function is the active side of it. When Kyōzan was going to ask the monk, who was evidently a master, about the function, the monk displayed it by kicking him over. Isan also showed the function, by laughing, somewhat sadistically, at Kyōzan's discomfiture.

One day Jōshū fell down in the snow, and called out, "Help me up! Help me up!" A monk came and lay down beside him. Jōshū got up and went away.

We cannot help other people, in things that really matter. We can only look or act our fellow-feeling. Christ cannot take us to heaven. We have to go with our own wings. This is not mere *jiriki*, self-power, but a condition where *tariki*, other-power, and jiriki are one and the same thing, so strictly speaking we cannot say that Christ does not "lift us up" or that we lift ourselves up by our own faith. We can only go up, or not. But,—and this is the point of the anecdote—we must show our awareness of the rising or not rising of others. That is our humanity.

*

Once, when Jōshū was still with Nansen, Nansen took an ox into the Monk's Hall, and led him around. The head monk whacked the ox on the back three times, and Nansen took a sheaf of grass and put it in front of the head monk, who said nothing.

Has an ox the Buddha nature? Had the head monk the ox-nature?

*

Ryūge was asked by a monk, "What was it the ancients finally got, so that all their labours were over?" Ryūge answered, "It was like a robber breaking into an untenanted house."

This is a splendid reply, not merely rebuking the monk for his ambition, but also stating a fact, that we must be as empty as the room the robber breaks into, so that we can lose nothing and gain the whole (thieving) world.

*

A monk asked Ryūge, "How should we use our powers during the twelve hours (we are awake)?" Ryūge replied, "Just like a handless man clenching his fist."

As Eckhart says,

Therefore, if God is to make anything in you or with you, you must beforehand have become nothing . . . If you want to live and want your works to live, you must be dead to all things, and you must have become nothing.

*

Sozan asked a monk where he had come from. He replied, "From Seppō." Sozan said, "When you were here before, you were not satisfied; how about now?" "Now I am satisfied," said the monk. Sozan asked, "Satisfied with the gruel, satisfied with the rice?" The monk made no reply.

Sozan's last question is not merely sarcastic. The question is not whether we are spiritually satisfied or not, but materially. If we are satisfied materially we are really satisfied. If we like the gruel, and don't mind if it is a bit burnt, or has too much salt in it,—this is Paradise, this is Nirvana, this is Zen. If, however, we are satisfied about our hopes of heaven, but grumble about the food, this is Hell, this is illusion, this is un-Zen. When the monk was asked the question about the gruel and the rice, he should have answered, "I am satisfied with it, and with no gruel, and to be drowned in gruel!"

*

A monk asked Jōshū, "What is this eye of the One who never sleeps?" Jōshū said, "The physical eye of the ordinary man." He added, "Though he may be said not yet to have got the spiritual eye, the physical eye may be considered to be the same thing."

Another monk asked, "What is the eye of the one who sleeps?" Jōshū said, "The Buddha Eye; the Eye of the Law is the eye of him who sleeps."

Jōshū is trying to get the monk to give up his Oxford-Cambridge boat-race-way of looking at things. The Buddha Eye is the ordinary eye, enlightenment is illusion, the same is different; this the other half of truth so hard to jump into.

*

When a sincere man expounds a mistaken doctrine, the doctrine becomes true. When an insincere man expounds a true doctrine it becomes error (Jōshū).

*

When Hōun (Pangyun) met Sekitō for the first time, he asked "Who is he who does not accompany all things?" Sekitō put his hand over Hōun's mouth. Hōun suddenly came to a realisation.

This reminds us of Stevenson's "I will not question more." Jōshū, in his *goroku,* says that when he was with Sekitō, and anyone asked him a question (about Zen), Sekitō would say, "Shut your mouth! No barking like a dog, please!"

A nun asked Jōshū, "What is the secret of secrets?" Jōshū tapped her on the elbow. She said, "You are still holding onto something." "No," said Jōshū, "it is you who are holding onto it."

The secret of life in the tapping of an elbow,—this is what the nun would not or could not apprehend, the secret of life in the movement or stillness of every thing in all ages past or to come.

*

Daibai (Tai-mei) became enlightened on hearing Baso say "Your mind, that is the Buddha." Afterwards when he had been living in the temple on Mount Daibai, for twenty years, Baso sent someone to tell him it should be, "No mind, no Buddha," to which Daibai replied stoutly, "Others may accept 'No mind, no Buddha,' but I stick to 'Your mind that is the Buddha.' " When Baso heard this he approved of it, and said, "He has matured." From this time disciples gradually began to collect round him.

*

One day Isan ascended the rostrum and said, "You monks, you all have the form, but not the function." Kyuhō withdrew from the monks and left the hall. Isan called to him, but he did not turn his head. Isan said, "He is fit to be a vessel of the Law!"

To reply when called is of the essence of Zen. Kyuhō's refusal to reply or turn his head was a sort of super-Zen.

*

A monk asked Gensha, "The Supreme Doctrine,—is there any explanation of it recently?" Gensha said, "We don't hear such a thing often."

This grim understatement nullifies all the books on Zen that ever were or will be written. Zen is how things are said, or heard, but also how they are not said, and "those unheard are sweeter." To talk with Zen is not uncommon, and talking about Zen is more common than it should be, but to talk with Zen about Zen,—it is the rarest thing in the world.

*

One day, a monk from India came, and Kyōzan drew a half-moon on the floor, for in T'ang times India was thought to have the shape of a half-moon. The monk approached and made a circle, and with his foot rubbed it out. Kyōzan stretched out his arms. The monk dusted his clothes and went off.

All this may be taken as a kind of spiritual esperanto, but not as symbolism. The two monks, Indian and Chinese, are play-acting—it is true, but it is a deadly serious game; they are sporting with infinity and eternity. The half-circle means, "Welcome!" The whole circle means, "We are here at this point of time, in this point of place, together." The rubbing out of the circle means that you and I are not just interested in each other. The stretching out of the arms means that you and I have each [his] own path of life. The Indian monk walks away on his, the Chinese monk sits about on his. Of course all this must be far from the esoteric meaning of circles and so on.

*

One day Hofuku (Paofu), a fellow-disciple with Kuzan, was talking together with another monk, in the Tea Hall. Seeing this, Kuzan said, "Don't weave subtleties and complications!" Hofuku said, "We're not. We are making Buddhism clearer, see?" Kuzan made as if to strike him. "Where am I wrong?" asked Hofuku. Kuzan gave him a blow.

Buddhism, that is, Zen, is not to be talked about, written about, read about. Each act, each thought, each emotion is to be "performed" with the whole and undivided mind-body. That is all. If this is done, we may talk about Zen.

*

A monk asked Kuzan, "What is the Great Principle of Buddhism?" Kuzan answered, "When the golden crow appears for a moment, there is not a cloud for ten thousand leagues."

The golden crow, which has three legs, is the sun. When the sun just peeps out, the world is changed. But the sun is not a "symbol" of Buddhism or enlightenment. When we really see the sunlight we are enlightened. When we really understand Buddhism we are ensunned.

*

Sanshō said, "If someone comes, I go out to meet him, but not for his sake." Kōke said, "If someone comes, I don't go out. If I do go out, I go out for his sake."

Zen has the right attitude here. We must do something for its own sake, *and* for the sake of others, just as each thing exists for itself alone and for all other things. "A little flower is the labour of ages."

*

An old woman asked Jōshū, "I have the Five Hindrances; how can I avoid them?" He said, "All the people in the world pray that they may be born in the Heavens. You pray that you may sink into the Sea of Pain!"

The old woman wants to become a bodhisattva, who renounces Paradise to suffer with and save others.

*

There is a famous verse by Nagarjuna:

All causally produced phenomena, I say, are unreal,
Are but a passing name, and indicate the Mean.

This is the orthodox translation, "the Mean" implying an Absolute above the absolute and relative. The essence of Zen is contained in the sentence from the *Hannya Shingyō: Shiki soku ze kū, kū soku ze shiki*, which means that phenomena are real, reality is phenomenal. Primitive Buddhism taught that all combinations of things are impermanent, and therefore unreal. This was the Indian experience, and Laotse and Chuangtse perceived the same thing. But there was also the Chinese experience of the reality of each combination, repeated again and again over the centuries. According to the pre-Buddhist Hinduistic experiences recorded in the Upanishads there was Something behind all phenomena, behind all this nothing which never changes, but is nevertheless alive and creative. And one's self is that Self, identical with it. The Chinese also had this experience. They called it Zen, but would not express it intellectually, that is, partly, but only livingly, that is, wholly.

*

Just as the Kingdom of Heaven is among us and in us, so is the Kingdom of Hell. At this very moment, though we seem to be reclining in comfortable armchairs, sipping tea and discussing Buddhism with elegance and discrimination, we are, inside, at bottom, only like crabs in boiling water thrashing about with all our arms and legs. An earthquake, a toothache, a mad dog, a telephone message,—and all our house of peace falls like a pack of cards. Heaven means a state in which every possibility has been met, every bridge crossed. It is independent of tomorrow's newspaper or typhoid germs in the water. We may go through life with not a single physical pain or loss, but the possibility of them, all the troubles that never happen, are ever-present. Their baleful eyes are fixed upon us, and when will they bite? This is our constant dread.

*

Mizukagami, The Water Mirror, is an easy discourse on Buddhism with waka and kyōka (mad poems) mixed, and with notes by Mori Daikyō. One of the verses:

> The mind,—
> But if there is really
> No such thing as the mind,
> With what enlightenment
> Shall it be enlightened?

Satori is to know that there is no such thing as *satori*.

A monk said to Fuketsu, "The Western Patriarch came bringing his message; I ask you to tell me it point-blank!" Fuketsu said, "When one dog barks at nothing, a thousand monkeys show their teeth really."

"One dog barking at nothing" is Christ & Buddha and Daruma with their doctrines (or the positive absence of them) and we are the monkeys, afraid of Heaven and Hell or afraid of there being neither, or afraid of not being enlightened before we don't go anywhere.

*

V | ENLIGHTENMENT

The two doctrines of Zen most difficult to understand are, first, that illusion is, as it is, enlightenment; damnation is salvation. The second, a kind of corollary, is that there is no sin, no suffering, no morality for the Bodhisattva, and yet he spends his life saving others. The parallel to these two in Christianity would be the mediaeval idea, simple, profound, and humorous, that without Adam's sin there would be no salvation, and Christ would be still loitering in Heaven waiting for someone to die for. If we cannot solve these problems it must be because the universe is a warm thing which the stone-cold intellect can only partly understand.

*

The history of Zen from Buddha to Huineng is a funny business, partly because Zen, which abhors dichotomy, has itself a double nature. On the one hand it is individualistic to selfishness, self-reliant to aloofness. Each man must attain his own enlightenment. On the other hand, there is a flow of spirit from mind to mind, and as Whitman almost said, my enlightenment is only valid when it is everyone's enlightenment. The same is true of poetry and art and art and music; they all have this double nature. Therefore, when the Zen Sect began to be formed after the advent of Bodhidharma, it had to establish a line of communication not only from Dharma, but up to Dharma. This was a different attitude from that of the other sects of Buddhism which simply wanted to prove their antiquity; in China especially, what was old was good. For Zen, "New every morning is the sun," but it had to be the same new sun of enlightenment.

Eastern enlightenment is the full and perfect understanding that the stupidity, vulgarity, and hypocrisy of this world is quite all right just as it is. All the poems and pictures and music and significant architecture, all the natural beauty of the world may be forever destroyed,—but if so, it doesn't matter, nay, it is the best possible thing, "a consummation devoutly to be wished." This enlightenment is found in Christianity also; it is, "Thy will be done" in infinitely meaningless inanity. In the *Khuddaka-Patha* the Buddha denounces

> dancing, song, playing, music, seeing plays,

that is to say, he rejects Aeschylus, Palestrina, Shakespeare, Mozart. *But this, together with the drama of the Crucifixion, is the Western Nirvana.* Buddha was a self-proclaimed success, Christ a self-confessed failure, but the one who is defeated is always dearer to us than the conqueror; there is something cosmically significant here. Is it possible that there may be one day a Zen which shall include both the Buddha in eternal peace, and the Christ in eternal agony?

*

Any enlightenment which requires to be authenticated, certified, recognised, congratulated, is (as yet) a false, or at least an incomplete one. We are social animals it is true, but we must often resist the temptation to share our experiences. Even Kierkegaard wrote like mad in order to have at least one reader agree with him.

*

Kankei said, "When I was with Rinzai I got a ladleful, and when I was with Massan a ladleful." He added, "It is all open and unhidden in the ten directions, not a gate on the four sides, completely clear, without any attachment to anything at all, no place to take hold of it."

This is one of the best definitions of Zen. We get a ladleful of it here and there according to our (accidental) innate abilities, and our (accidental) opportunities. But what the ladle is full of we cannot put into *other* words. It is just a ladleful of Zen.

*

One day Isan went into the mountains and found Kyōzan doing zazen. He gave him a whack on the back with his staff, but Kyōzan did not turn round. Isan said, "Can you say something, or not?" Kyōzan said, "Even if I can't, I won't borrow anyone else's words." Isan said, "You have learnt something."

*

A disciple of Chōkei was Reiun (Ling-yün), dates unknown. He was enlightened upon seeing peach blossoms, that is, upon considering the lilies of the field. His *ju* upon this occasion was:

> For thirty years I visited a swordsman;
> How many times the leaves fall, the buds come out!
> But after I really saw the peach blossoms,
> Not another doubt did I have!

The first line seems to mean "studied Zen under a Master."

*

A monk bowed to (the statue of) Fugen. Daizui lifted up his mosquito-flapper, and said, "The Bodhisattvas (Monju and Fugen) are both contained in this." The monk drew a circle and threw it behind him, then stretched out his arms. Daizui told the attendant to give the monk a cup of tea.

Daizui seems to have approved of this play-acting. The drawing of a circle, in the air, means perfection, no relativity, infinity, Godhead. Throwing it behind him means getting rid of every trace of transcendentalism, absoluteness, Godhead. Stretching out the arms means going on from there to the relative. "Means" is the wrong word. The monk, if he is enlightened and enlightening, *is* the absolute, *is* the rejection of it, *is* the relative.

*

Hakuin, the founder of the Rinzai sect of Zen in Japan, was born in 1685 (Bashō died in 1684).

Once Hakuin did zazen for seven days and nights without sleeping. He records his satori on this occasion by a very good waka. (It should be noted that the "sounds" of the snow is the muffled thud of the snow falling from the trees or the roofs.)

> How I would like people to hear
> In the old temple
> Of the forests of Shinoda
> These sounds of snow falling
> Through the deepening night!

What is striking and characteristic about Hakuin is the way in which he insists upon satori as the aim of life. Satori is the pearl of great price, and a man must sell all that he has to get it. In this, in his extreme asceticism, and in what he says about the joy of enlightenment, he reminds us of the sixteenth-century Spanish mystic St. John of the Cross, who "gave his body no rest," but who says in *The Ascent of Mount Carmel*,

> Such is the sweetness of deep delight of these touches of God, that one of them is more than a recompense for all the sufferings of this life, however great their number.

Hakuin, in *Orategama*, speaks of satori as

> an event accompanied with a feeling of immense joy such as never before experienced in one's life.

This joy is not at the fact that enlightenment has been gained, nor is it the satisfaction that "a crown is laid up for me in Heaven," but joy, as Hakuin says at the beginning of his *Song of Meditation*, that

> All sentient beings are from the beginning Buddhas,

and once more at the end, that

> This very earth is the Lotus Land of Purity,
> And this body the body of the Buddha.

Hakuin does not touch our hearts as Ryōkan does; he touches something deeper, the soul with its ever-springing desire for

the Original Face revealed

truth, that living truth without which we feel we shall have
lived and loved and laughed and wept in vain.

*

When Kōkō went to see Hōgen, he was asked where he
had been recently. "With Jōshū," he answered. Hōgen
said, "I have heard about Jōshū and the oak tree; isn't this
so?" Kōkō said, "It is not so!" Hōgen said, "But everyone
says that when a monk asked about the meaning of
Daruma's coming from the West, Jōshū answered, 'The
oak tree in the front garden.' How can you say it was not
so?" Kōkō said, "My master said nothing of the kind!
Please do not insult the late master." Hōgen said, 'Truly
you are a lion's cub!"

What Kōkō was denying was that Jōshū had said something that should be repeated and interpreted and annotated
and garbled. He said it, yes, but when it was said it was finished for ever, to be forgotten like everything else.

Means are ends, and ends are means. A real religious
teacher never uses parables. A really religious man thinks
nothing of symbols or vestments of crucifixes or Buddhist
images. Or shall we say, more sweetly and therefore more
truly, when an enlightened man sees a crucifix or the tooth of
Buddha, he looks at the man kneeling before it. He really sees
not Christ or Buddha, but the Christ-nature, the Buddha-
nature.

*

Kankei visited the nun Massan Ryōnen. He said (to himself), "If what she says hits the spot, I will remain there.
If it doesn't I'll overturn the Zen seat!" He entered the
Hall, and she sent a messenger to ask, "Have you come
on a mountain-viewing journey, or for the sake of Buddhism?" He replied, "For the sake of Buddhism," so she
sat upon her seat, and Kankei approached her. She said,
"Where did you come from today, may I ask?" He replied,
"From Rokō." She said to him, "Why don't you remove
your *kasa*?" Kankei had no reply, and, making his bows,
asked, "What is Massan?" She answered, "It does not
show its peak." He asked, "Who is Massan's master?"

She answered, "There is not real form of men and women." He said, "Kwatz!" and asked, "Why then don't you change and disappear?" She said, "I am not a god; I am not a demon; what could I change?" At this Kankei knelt down, and became the gardener (of her temple) for three years.

This is a very pleasant story. The Zen nun teacher is womanly, and Kankei is defeated by her gentleness.

*

In order to be enlightened, we must first be enlightened. To understand anything at all, we must know it already. All knowledge, as Plato and Wordsworth said, is recollection. The stone turtle must first speak, then we can speak.

One day Kyōzan (Yangshan) was looking at the moon together with Sekishitsu, and asked him, "Where does the roundness of the moon go when it becomes sharp, crescent? Where does the sharpness go when it becomes round?" Sekishitsu said, "When it is sharp the roundness is still there. When it is round it is still sharp."

This is a rather good example for the difficult teaching that enlightenment is illusion, illusion enlightenment; difference is sameness, sameness difference.

Ungan raised his mosquito duster, and said, "You hear it?" "I don't," replied Tōzan. Ungan said, "You don't hear even my teaching, let alone that of inanimate things." Tōzan asked in what sutra the teaching of Buddhism by soul-less things was taught. Ungan asked him if he had not read in the Amida Kyō, "Waters, birds, trees and forests all repeat the Buddha's name, and proclaim the Law." At this Tōzan was enlightened, and made a verse:

> Marvellous! Marvellous!
> How mysterious the Inanimate-Teaching!
> It is difficult to hear with the ears;
> When we hear with the eyes, then we know it!

*

A monk said to Jōshū, "If there is a man who has left the world and he suddenly asks you what Truth is, what answer would you make?" Jōshū said, "Salt is noble, rice is common-place."

Jōshū knows that the great weakness of the higher class of human beings, those who ask such questions, is for monism, for unity and oneness. He therefore asserts the essential and unresolvable difference of things, of things we cannot live without, but which must never be confused.

*

Tokusan's enlightenment was one of the oddest, for the immediate cause was "endarkenment," the blowing out of a candle by his master Ryūtan as he was about to take it. Later, Tokusan was asked by a monk "What is bodhi (salvation)?" He answered, "Be off with you! Don't bring your dung here!" Again he was asked, "What is the Buddha?" "Just an old monk of the Western World!"

Perhaps no question, especially asked to another, is anything but disgusting in its insincerity. We all know what is what, what to do, what not to do, but pretend we don't by means of asking questions, questions about the meaning of life, the existence of God, and the immortality of the soul. With regard to the second point, to understand that Jesus is the Way, the Light of the World and so on, is not difficult. What is difficult is to understand that Christ was a carpenter, a man of sorrows, and acquainted with grief.

*

A monk said to Seppō, "The seeing into his nature of a Sravaka is like gazing at the moon at night; a bodhisattvas seeing into his nature is like the sun in the day-time. "May I ask what *your* seeing into your nature was like?" Seppō struck him three times with his stick. Afterwards the monk went to Gantō and asked him the same question. Gantō cuffed him three times.

To ask another person about his satori is like asking how much money he has in the bank, or whether he loves his wife.

Good manners applies to all things without distinction. Indeed, Zen is good taste, or rather, good taste is Zen. Perhaps, after all, beating and slapping is the only way of improving a person's taste, religious and artistic. The more we suffer, intelligently, the deeper our life. Buddha said that life is suffering, and taught us how to avoid both. This was wrong. Deep suffering is deep life. Shall we then be shallow, and dry up altogether?

*

A monk asked Kegon, "How about when an enlightened man returns to illusion?" Kegon said, "A broken mirror does not reflect; fallen flowers do not go back to the branch."

This does not mean that an enlightened man is infallible, and cannot make mistakes or do bad or foolish things. It means that he partakes of the inevitability of things. Just as the flowers make no effort to return to the branch or the broken mirror to be whole again, so the enlightened man does what he does without regret or self-pity.

*

The scholar Ryō of Sozan had a meeting with Baso, who asked him, "What sutra are you lecturing on?" "The Mind Sutra," he replied. Baso said, "By what do you lecture?" Ryō answered "With mind." Baso said, "The mind is like an actor, the meaning like a jester, the six senses like an acquaintance; how can the mind be able to lecture on a sutra?" Ryō retorted, "If mind cannot lecture, can't no-mind?" Baso replied, "Yes, no-mind can lecture all right." Ryō dusted his sleeves and began to take his departure. Baso called him, saying "Professor!" Ryō turned his head. Baso said, "What are you up to?" and Ryō had a great awakening, and made an obeisance to him. Baso said, "What on earth are you bowing for, nit-wit?" Ryō's whole body was now running with sweat. Going back to his temple, Ryō said to the monks, "I thought it could be said that all my life no one could lecture better than I on the sutras. Today, a question by Baso dissolved the ice of a lifetime." He gave up his lectures and retired far into the Western Mountains and was heard of no more.

There is something delightful about this kind of enlightenment, such a huge effect with so small a cause. A little sun and air and water, and all the flowers of spring are blooming.

*

Goei went to Sekitō, and said, "If you can say a word, I will remain here, otherwise I will go away." Sekitō simply sat there. Goei went off. From the back Sekitō called him, "Jari! Jari!" Goei turned his head. Sekitō said, "From birth to death, it is just like this. Turning the head, turning the brain, how about it?" Goei was suddenly enlightened, so he broke his staff.

Conversion, etymologically, is connected with the turning of the body-mind. What is difficult is to turn both together. When mind and body are married, we get the condition described by Donne:

"God made the first marriage, and man made the first Divorce; God married the Body and Soule in the Creation, and man divorced the Body and Soule by death through sinne, in his fall."

*

A monk said to Nansen, "There is a jewel in the sky; how can we get hold of it?" Nansen said, "Cut down bamboos and make a ladder, put it up in the sky, and get hold of it!" The monk said, "How can the ladder be put up in the sky?" Nansen said, "How can you doubt your getting hold of the jewel?"

Hōju said to Tankū, "When a man comes to you who has put away the Second and Third Roots (desire, hate, stupidity), how do you receive him?" Tankū said, "You have, in bringing up this question, already made a mistake."

One day Chinsō was up in a tower with other officials, and one of them seeing a number of monks passing, said, "Those people coming are monks on pilgrimage." Chinsō said, "It is not so." The other expostulated, "How can you say (know) that it is not so?" Chinsō said, "Wait till they get near, and I will examine them." The monks came before the tower. Chinsō called out to them, "Reverend gentlemen!" They all raised their heads and looked in his direction, "What did I tell you?" said Chinsō.

I take the story like this: Chinsō looks out of the window at the official's remark, and sees a group of monks approaching, and from their manner of walking, even in the distance, realises that they are very far from enlightened. He examines them by calling out to them in a polite way. Real monks would take no notice, but they all look up with foolish faces that bespeak the vacant mind. Even the official can see that they are without inner power and self-reliance. Enlightenment is invariably accompanied by the power to know who is enlightened and who is not, just as a love of animals (which is a form of enlightenment) enables us to distinguish the real and the sham love of animals in others.

*

One day a nun gave Reiju an earthenware bowl. He lifted it up and said, "Where did it come from?" "From Jōshū," she replied. Reiju smashed it. The nun made no remark.

The reason for this ungentlemanly behaviour was the nun's replying in the relative instead of the absolute-relative. What should she have said? She could have said "From the giver of every good and—gift," or, "From yourself," or, "All from" is "to."

*

A monk said to Bashō, "How about before the ancient Buddhas appeared on earth?" Bashō said, "A thousand years of egg-plant roots." The monk asked, "How about after they appeared?" Bashō said, "The Deva Kings roll their eyes violently."

Before Buddhism, we are animals, one almost might say vegetables, with no value or use. After Buddhism we are afraid to sin, afraid of not being enlightened.

*

Kyōgen (Hsiangyen), eleventh in the line of Zen after Daruma, was a disciple of Isan, though he was for some time under Hyakujō. Isan recognised his innate capability

of grasping the truth, and one day said to him, "I do not
ask you concerning the learning and book-knowledge you
have accumulated during your life. Before you came out
of your mother's womb, before you knew this from that,
your real self—speak, tell me what it is!" Kyōgen stood
there stupidly, unable to answer. Then, after remaining
silent for some time, he began to explain, in many words,
his view of the matter, but Isan would not listen. At last
Kyōgen said, "I beg you to explain it to me!" Isan replied,
"My explanation would express my own realization; what
would be the use of it to you?" Kyōgen went back to his
room, and searched among his books and lecture-notes
for some sentence, some passage to use as an answer, but
not one could he find. Sighing to himself (in Chinese)
Kyōgen said, "You can't fill an empty stomach with a
picture of food," and burned up all books and note-books,
and decided, "In this life, it will be impossible for me to
come to a knowledge of the truth." With tears, he left
Isan and went to Nanyang, where he settled down. One
day, as he was clearing the undergrowth, and sweeping,
a stone struck a bamboo. Bursting into a loud shout of joy
at the sound, he suddenly became enlightened. Returning
to his hut, he performed ablutions and offered incense,
and prostrating himself in the direction of Isan, said,
"Thanks to the deep kindness of the Master, I have returned to my parents. If, at that time, he had explained
things to me, this would never have happened!"

The most enlightened person has still weaknesses and
blind spots, unresolved associations of ideas. These, it may be
said, do not affect the will, where Zen works. This is not so.
There is no single isolated activity called the will, any more
than there is a certain specific state of mind to be called Zen.
The strength of the chain which each person is, lies in the
weakest link. Tennyson says:

> It is the little rift within the lute,
> That by and by will make the music mute,
> And ever widening slowly silence all.

*

Taohsin came and bowed to Sengtsan, and said, "I ask
you for your merciful teaching. Please show me how to
be released." Sengtsan answered, "Who has bound you?"
"No one," he replied. Sengtsan said, "Why then do you
ask to be released?" Taohsin immediately came to a profound realization.

*

A monk said to Shifuku, "I have not finished even one
summer seclusion in the monastery, and I do not ask for
your teaching,—but help me please!" Shifuku pushed him
away and said, "Since I have been living here, I have never
once blinded a monk."

I have myself blinded many people with my explanations.
I am still at it.

*

Hyakujō came back one day from wandering in the mountains, as attendant upon Baso, and suddenly began to
weep. One of his fellow monks said, "Are you thinking of
your father and mother?" No," said Hyakujō. "Did somebody slander you?" "No." "Then what are you weeping
for?" "Go and ask the Master," said Hyakujō. The monk
went and asked Baso, who said, "Go and ask Hyakujō."
The monk came back to the room and found Hyakujō
laughing. "You were weeping a little while ago; why are
you laughing now?" he asked. Hyakujō said, "I was weeping a little while ago, and now I am laughing."

We laugh and weep at the same thing,—according to?
According to our free will. But neither to laugh nor weep is
to be dead.

*

VI | GOD, BUDDHA, AND BUDDHAHOOD

The story of the Buddha, Siddharta Gautama, also known as Gautama Sakyamuni, is well known but let me capsulate it here: he was born at Kapilavastu in the foothills of the Himalayas in 566 B.C., and after his enlightenment in 531 B.C. became known as the Buddha, which means the Awakened One, and also as Sakyamuni, the Sage of the Sakyas. As the scion of a patrician family he lived in comfort and affluence, protected by his doting parents from all contact with poverty, disease, illness, the ravages of aging, and death. But once confronted with the afflictions of the human condition, he left his family, and at age twenty-nine abandoned all possessions and set out on his spiritual quest seeking a solution for the human predicament of inescapable sorrow. He subjected himself to the most austere disciplines until "like a row of reed knots my backbone stood out through lack of sustenance," but failed to find the means to heal life's sorrow. Seeking mental clarification instead of self-punishment, he practiced an ever-deepening meditation which was to make him into a lamp for countless others. He became "a being not liable to delusion, for the welfare of the many, for the happiness of the many, out of compassion for the world." And soon after, in the Deer Park near Benares, he proclaimed the Four Noble Truths and the Eightfold Noble Path, which have become the Way of Perfection for all Buddhists. The Four Noble Truths are: Sorrow is universal and inescapable. Desire is the cause of sorrow. Extinction of desire is the extinction of sorrow. The way to extinguish desire is by following the Eightfold Path: right view, right intention, right speech, right action, right livelihood, right effort, right mindfulness, right concentration. This is not the place to elaborate on Buddhist teaching and history; suffice it to say that the Buddha never presented himself as a Saviour—he was a teacher; and that in Mahayana Buddhism, of which Zen is a development, the historical Buddha has assumed secondary importance to the Buddha Nature, the True Nature, the core in every human being. This Unborn, which is the existential core of every child, has to be realized if life is not to be wasted in primal ignorance and suffering. Bodhidharma, who brought Zen to China, expresses this realization as "attaining Buddhahood" in his famous gata. Bodhidharma (Dharma) is named Daruma in Japan. The question "Why did Daruma ever come from India to China?" always implies: "What is the Buddha-Nature? Who am I? What is a Buddha? What is Suchness?"

—*Editor*

Just as Western philosophy is said to be nothing more than footnotes to Plato, so all that Ōbaku says are paraphrases of the line of the *Kongō Kyō* which triggered the (second) enlightenment of Enō: "Arouse a mind resting upon nothing!" If you feel the pull of this command, you like Zen; if you don't, you don't.

Haikyū asked, "Does the Buddha save living creatures, or not?" Ōbaku answered, "In actual fact there are no living creatures for the Buddha to save. There is no I, how can there be any not-I? Neither Buddha nor living creatures exist."

Christ as the Saviour disappears. Haikyū's questions are never answered because Ōbaku denies the terms of them, the suppositions behind them, the questioner himself, and the answerer.

People do not dare forget their own minds; they dread falling into Emptiness with nothing to cling to.

All creeds and dogmas, even assertions such as I am making now, are an expression of weakness. The creation of the universe itself was such.

*

"The Mind is not the Mind, and becoming enlightened is not becoming enlightened."

This kind of statement, which Ōbaku repeats again and again, is not an intimation of the inadequacy of words and phrases; after all, the statement itself consists of words and phrases. "The Mind is not the Mind" means that the Mind is both the Mind and not the Mind. The word does not correspond to the reality because the reality does not (only) correspond to itself. A thing is itself and at the same time transcends itself. A word corresponds to the thing and at the same time the word transcends itself just as, and to the extent that the thing does. So also enlightenment is enlightenment and is not illusion, but at the same time it is not merely enlightenment but illusion also.

*

"We teach the Law by not teaching it."

Literally, "The Law is not to be taught; this is called teaching the Law." Here again it is not that words are misleading or insufficient. They are so only if the receiving mind is misleadable and inadequate. The Law is not something fixed, to which we approximate in time. The Law itself is changing and growing, in so far as we change and grow. So when we don't catch the butterfly, we reveal its nature.

*

Isan said to Kyōzan, "The *Nirvana Sutra* has about forty chapters of the Buddha's teaching; how many of these are devil teachings?" Kyōzan said, "All of them." Isan said, "From now on, nobody will be able to do what he likes with you." Kyōzan asked, "From now on what should be my mode of life?" Isan said, "I admire your just eye; I am not concerned about the practical side of the matter."

This anecdote shows how strongly the Zen masters felt about the creeds and dogmas. The more true and useful the sutras were, the more dangerous, the more devilish. So with societies and groups; the loftier their object the more they are to be shunned. Isan's last remark is not correct. The "minute details" are more important than the general principles. A just eye is of prime importance, but so is a steady hand and so are well-made tools. "Love God and do as you like" is quite correct, provided that the love of God is 100%. When it is only 60 or 70, we must not do altogether as we like.

*

One day while Gensha was thinking, he heard the voice of a swallow, and said, "How well it has explained the Buddhist Truth, speaking profoundly of the Real Nature of Things!" and came down from his seat. Afterwards a monk, wishing to get some profit from his words, said to Gensha, "I didn't understand what you meant." Gensha retorted, "Be off with you! How can anyone trust you!"

I have been asked many questions in my life about poetry, religion, life, and I have given precisely the same number of answers, but I have never, I repeat, *never*, satisfied a single interlocutor. Why was this? Because all questioning is a way of avoiding the real answer, which, as Zen tells us, is really known already. Every man is enlightened, but wishes he wasn't. Every man knows he must love his enemies, and sell all he has and give to the poor, but he doesn't wish to know it,—so he asks questions. Gensha's reply to the questioner is too kind; he should just say, "Liar!"

*

Haikyū asked Ōbaku, "How do all the Buddhas activate the Great Mercy and Compassion and preach the Law for the sake of all creatures?" Ōbaku replied, "The Buddha's mercy and compassion is causeless, so it is called 'Great' mercy and compassion. 'Mercy' means Buddha's not becoming Buddha. 'Compassion' means people's not being saved."

This interpretation by Ōbaku of Great Mercy and Compassion would have been as incomprehensible to Buddha as the Athanasian Creed would have been to Christ. But this does not mean that either is wrong. And in fact Ōbaku's explanation is more human, closer to our daily experience than the orthodox Buddhist one. What makes a thing great is its poetry, its cause-and-effect-lessness. As Lawrence says, "To know (intellectually, psychologically) the mind of a woman (or a man, for that matter) is to end in hating her." The mercy and compassion which we extend to all things (including ourselves) is the will for things to be as they are and to become as they will become. What seems, on the relative plane, to be our powerlessness to change the world closer to the heart's desire, is in the absolute realm the will, and this will is a compassionate will. This is the meaning of Jōshū's answer when he was asked by an old woman how she could escape the "Five Hindrances" of a woman. He answered, "May all human beings be reborn in paradise! May this old woman sink for all eternity in the sea of pain!" Intuitively Jōshū realises that this is "the best of all possible worlds, that the Five Hindrances are at the same time Five Helps, that Lady Macbeth and Medea and Mrs. Gamp and the Wife of Bath and Cleopatra and all the lesser ilk are inevitable, and desirable.

*

The aim of the Buddhist is Nirvana, a state beyond description and in this sense non-existent, for what cannot be expressed has never been experienced, and what has not been experienced has (so far) no existence. But Bach tells us explicitly what Nirvana is, or rather his music is Nirvana, in the same way as much of Beethoven's tells us what Heaven and Hell are. Bach's music never stops; it never begins and never ends. Huineng says:

> If the feelings are not fixed upon That which flows
> ever unfixed.
> This lively activity is the Buddha's eternal Samadhi.

When it is hot, we are to be as hot as it is, no hotter. The end of a gatha by Chang Hangchang runs:

> I do nothing meritorious,
> But the Buddha-nature manifests itself.

> This is not because of my teacher's instruction,
> Nor is it due to any attainment of mine.

In Christian parlance, he gives God all the glory.

*

"God is not a God of the dead, but of the living, for unto Him all live." This is true, but not the whole truth, because unto God the dead are also dead, and the living living. There is not a relative truth, *and* an absolute truth. The relative is the absolute, the absolute is the relative. According to the Bible, man was made in the image of God, but if we take this as Eckhart's Godhead, how can we be an image of the un-imageable? Mumon wants us to answer this unanswerable question by being ourselves the abyss, by being ourselves image-less, thought-less, emotion-less, beauty-less, morality-less, truth-less,—but also nothing-less, and indifference-less.

*

A monk said to Useki, "Who is the teacher of the God-head? Who is the master of the Absolute?" "I won't say," said Useki. "Why not?" asked the monk. "If I say," said Useki, "my tongue will shrink; if I don't say, I'll become dumb." This monk went to see Tōzan, and told him about this. Tōzan spread out his *zagu* widely, and bowed on it and said, "An Ancient Buddha! An Ancient Buddha!"

A monk asked Tōzan, "What is the Buddha?" He replied, "Three pounds of flax."

What is the Buddha? In Buddhism we have a trinity, trikaya, which is also a unity, but the correspondence to the Christian trinity is difficult to make out. There is first, the Dharmakaya, Immutable Truth, represented by Dainichi Nyo-rai, Vairocana, the chief object of worship of the Shingon Sect. The Daibutsu at Nara is his image. This corresponds to the Godhead. Second, the Sambhogakaya, represented by Amida Nyorai, glory in Heaven. This corresponds to the Father. Third, the Nirmanakaya, the apparitional body, represented by Shaka Nyorai. This corresponds to Christ the Son, but also to God walking in the Garden of Eden in the cool of the evening, and the "angels" of the Old Testament.

Taking the correspondence in reverse, The Father corresponds to No. 1, and No. 2, the Son to No. 3. The Holy Ghost has some similarity to No. 1. ("And when the Comforter is come he shall teach you all things") since in early Mahayana the Dharmakaya was the body of truth taught by Sakyamuni, his mind and spirit. In some ways, however, Buddhism is far closer to the emanations of Gnosticism than Christianity.

What the Buddha is, is the most difficult question man can ask. What is God? What is Truth? What is Life? What is the Universe?—these, all these together make up the monk's question. Tōzan's answer comes then as a kind of anticlimax, too absurd to be serious, and if it does not make you laugh when you hear it, you are in a bad way indeed, for as Blake said, "No man can see truth without believing it," and who can see truth without joy and laughter?

*

What is wrong with "Our Father which art in Heaven" is not the anthropomorphic vocabulary, "Father," but the separateness of "Which art in Heaven." Even if we say "Which is in earth, in me, in the stone and the stream," we still have "in." Evil is separation, an "in" is separation, even "is" is separation, "equals" is separation, all affirmation of identity is separation, all denial of difference is separation.

As for answering the question "Who is He, She, or It?" before we answer it, it must be truly asked. "Show us the Father, and it sufficeth us." "No man hath seen God at any time." The disciples were not sincere in asking to see God. They were not, that is, willing to pay any price to see him. Christ answers, "You see what you want to see, and almost no man really wants to see God, though he may cut himself with knives, and throw himself into the fire in his pretending to. And anyway, only God can see God. "A cat may look at a King, but it can't really see him." But at the same time, "The Son, he hath declared him," and we also must reveal in everything we may say and do Stevenson's "Unseen Playmate."

*

Sozan said to his monks, "Before the year of Kantsu, 860 A.D., I had already understood an approximation of the Dharmakaya. After that year I understood the absoluteness of the Dharmakaya." Ummon asked him, "I have heard that you understood the approximation of the Dharmakaya before Kantsu, and the absoluteness of it after it. Is this so?" "It is so," said Sozan. "What is the approximation to the Dharmakaya, Buddhahood?" asked Ummon. Sozan answered, "A withered paulownia." Ummon asked, "What is the Absolute Buddhahood?" Sozan answered, "Not a stake." Ummon said, "May I, a learner, explain the rationality of this, or not?" Sozan said, "All right." Ummon asked, "Doesn't a stake express the approximation to Buddhahood?" Sozan said, "It does." Ummon asked, "Not being a stake,—doesn't this express the Absolute Buddhahood?" "It does," said Sozan. Ummon asked, "Does the Dharmakaya include all things in it, or not?" Sozan replied, "How could it not include them?" Ummon asked, pointing to a water-pot, "Is this included in the Dharmakaya, or not?" Sozan said, "Do not understand the matter with regard to the approximation of a water-bottle!" Ummon bowed to him.

The point of this anecdote is in the last remark of Sozan, his warning Ummon against thinking or asserting that a material thing is the Law-body,—not that it isn't, but when we say it is, it isn't, because two things are not one, and one thing is not two. Two things are one and two, and one thing is two and one simultaneously, and the assertion of any of the statements, and the consecutive assertion of the one after another cannot help falling short of the truth.

*

Haikyū said, "Illusion obstructs the Mind; how can illusion be got rid of?" Obaku said, "Creating illusion, getting rid of illusion,—both these are Illusion, for illusion has no root; it appears by reason of descrimination. If you do not think of contraries, such as ordinary and superior, illusion ceases of itself, and how can you then get rid of it?"

*

Nō: waki actor

Nansen said to the assembled monks, "The Buddhas of the Three Worlds—we know nothing of their existence. What we know is the existence of cats and oxen."

We don't know Buddha or Buddhism or Zen or such-like things. We don't know heat or cold, but only this hot water and that hot water, and these things are nameless; this knowledge is unspeakable. When we talk about Buddha this is not merely second-hand, but damaged goods, with as much relation to a fish in the sea as a fish on a fish-monger's slab. What we know is things, not the Super-Essences described in the Hermetic books.

*

Hōgen was a great exponent of the Avatamsaka, the Buddhism of the Kegon-Avai. The Kegon School was founded in China by Tojun, who died in 640. The Sutra was first translated by Buddhabhadra, who arrived in China in 406. The Sect went to Japan in the 8th century. The Kegon teaching is that the real world is timeless and placeless, yet not static. Here is everywhere, but not undifferentiated. Logic, consistency, verisimilitude and relativity are all transcended. Love (compassion) makes the world go round. By interpenetration, every single thing is itself, a single limited thing, and all other things, and all things. "This world" and the real world are not-two.

An example of Hōgen's philosophical Zen.

A monk said to Hōgen, "The teaching [of the Sutras] is that all things have their origin in the Impermanent; what is this 'Impermanent Origin'?" Hōgen said, "Form arises from the not-yet-qualified; the name arises from the not-yet-named."

*

A monk asked Kyōzan, "Can you explain the explanation of the Law Body?" Kyōzan said, "I can't, but there is one who can." The monk asked, "Where is this one who can explain it?" Kyōzan pulled forward the pillow. When Isan heard of this he said, "Jaku is using the blade of the sword."

"Things speak so loudly I cannot hear what you say."
This is the reason why Christ spoke in parables, not so as to
make things easier. Things are indeed trenchant; they cannot
swindle or be swindled. But we must not ask, "What does the
pillow mean?" It pillows. It is the everlasting arms.

*

A monk asked Sozan, "Who is the Teacher of all the
Buddhas?" Sozan answered, "Why don't you ask Sozan?"

We can take this in two ways. First, that Sozan is himself
the Teacher of All the Buddhas, which is of course a fact.
Second, and more interestingly, Sozan means, "Why don't you
ask me a QUESTION, instead of asking me a question?" The
man who can ask a QUESTION is the Teacher of the Buddhas.
He who knows the Question is greater than the he who knows
the answer. What is the Question? It is: "Who is the Teacher
of All the Buddhas?"

*

A monk had come and was already going. Kisu said,
"Where are you off to?" The monk replied, "I'm going all
over the place learning the five flavours of Zen." Kisu
said, "Yes, there are the five flavours of Zen in various
places, but here I have only one." The monk asked, "And
what may be your one-flavour-Zen?" Kisu struck him.
The monk said, "I understand! I understand!" Kisu said,
"Tell me what! Tell me what!" and as the monk began to
speak, struck him again.

Kisu dislikes the monk's nonchalance, Buddhology, and
talkativeness. The universe has one taste only. According to
Kierkegaard and Kisu, it is pain.

*

Rikukō Taifu said to Nansen, "I have a piece of stone in
my house. Sometimes it moves and has its being, sometimes it lies down. I would like to make it into a Buddhist
statue; can it be done?" "It can, it can!" said Nansen.
Rikukō asked, "It can be done; is that certain?" "It can't,
it can't!" said Nansen.

Psychologically speaking, we can do what we think we can do,—within certain narrow limits, of course. We can't do what we think we can't do, within different limits, wider perhaps. But religiously speaking, that is, from the Zen point of view, the problem is a different one. Being a Buddha or not is a question of will. When Christ said, "Be ye perfect as your Father in Heaven is perfect," he meant that perfect obedience is the nature of God,—obedience to what is a question which must not be asked in the case of man just as it must not be asked concerning God. Nansen's yes-no answer points to the fact that each man is himself and all other men, and the same-and-different from every other man, and the Buddha he can-and-cannot become is the same-and-different from every other Buddha. This is the religious, the poetical realm we must accustom ourselves to live in.

*

Jōshū said to his monks. "A clay Buddha won't pass through water; an iron Buddha won't pass through a furnace; a wooden Buddha won't pass through a fire."

This does not mean that the Buddha is something spiritual. It does not mean "Lay not up treasures for yourselves on earth, but lay up for yourselves treasures in heaven." It does not mean put your mind nowhere, on nothing. It means that you must be the changeless water, the furnace, the fire, through which all things must pass and change. It means that you must be clay, the iron, the wooden Buddha, and change with them.

I was once riding with Mr. Warner, who saved Kyōto from bombing. He said he was thinking of becoming a Roman Catholic. I said to him, "Mr. Warner, don't believe in anything which you have to defend."

*

A monk asked Kokusei, "What is the Great Meaning of Buddhism? He answered, "Shaka was an ox-headed lictor of Hell; the Patriarchs were horse-faced hags."

As in all jesting remarks, what Kokusei says is half true. As we see especially in European history, religion has caused more suffering (or shall we say more exactly, has been the excuse for it) than anything else in the world. But in every and any case, religion is a painful and disgusting stage between the simplicity of primitive man and the enriched simplicity which is the aim of Zen. Mankind is at present wallowing in a kind of lagoon, a morass of superstitious vulgarity.

*

A monk asked Dankū "What is the mind of the Ancient Buddhas?" Dankū answered, "Ears had they, but they heard not." The monk said, "Kwatz!" Dankū said, "One-eye!"

The aim of Zen, opposite to that of Confucius and Christ, is that of Eckhart,—not to "hear."

To listen without discrimination, to hear a violin played out of tune without cursing the violinist, to hear praise and blame with delight at one's indifference to it,—this is part of Zen.

*

A monk asked Dankū, "What is Dankū's Zen?" Dankū answered, "Dust and dirt all over the face,—and all the more a shower of rain makes it feel fresh!"

This makes us think of a kind of harpsichord Zen, in which every note is bright and clear. The world is seen without emotion, without desire or loathing.

*

A monk asked Sanshō, "What is the meaning of Daruma's coming from the West?" Sanshō answered, "Stinking meat attracts flies." The monk brought this up to Kōke, who said, "I wouldn't have said that." The monk asked, "What is the meaning of Daruma's coming from the West?" Kōke answered, "There are enough bluebottles on a broken-down donkey."

Kōke, a brother monk with Sanshō, and in the direct line of the Rinzai Sect, bewilders the monk still more by suggesting to him that Sanshō was wrong, and then saying the same thing in other words. A is different from B, and C is different from B but C = A. It is this kind of thing which we must swallow in theory and in practice; or rather it is this kind of thing, which we do all day long, which we must do knowingly and willingly.

*

A monk asked Kisu, "What is the Buddha?" "If I tell you," said Kisu, "Will you believe me?" The monk replied "The master's words are so momentous, how could I not believe them?" Kisu said, "Simply, You are it." The monk asked, "How can we maintain this state?" Kisu said, "If your eye is just a little clouded, flowery illusions are rampant." The monk was enlightened at this.

This is very explanatory, it is a mistake to suppose that Zen is not explanatory! Kisu's question, "Do you believe in me?" shows the monk's state of mind, ready to believe, ready to believe, not anything, but everything. Kisu said to the monk, "You are the Buddha!" This is not true (and it is not true that he is not), but that doesn't matter. The important thing is to believe without reservation. We must not say, "I love you, but . . ." We must say, ". . . , but love you."

Mumon tells us that we are the Buddha,—only we mustn't say so! Why not? Saying so makes the Buddha something apart from ourselves, just as the words in the dictionary are apart from things. When we can speak a language, we don't need the book of words. When we live the Christian, the Buddhist, the Zen life, such phrases are meaningless. Telling us that our mind is the Buddha is like going out with someone who insists on telling us all the historical anecdotes of places and the botanical names of all the pretty weeds.

*

Fugyūzai, a disciple of Baso, ascended the rostrum and declared, " 'The mind is the Buddha',—this is the medicine for sick people. 'No mind, no Buddha',—this is to cure people who are sick because of the medicine."

This is very good. We think the Buddha is outside us. To cure this disease of false humility Baso gives us the medicine, "You are the Buddha." Then we suppose that we and the Buddha are the same thing, and become bumptious. To cure this, caused by the medicine, Baso tells us "No mind, no Buddha!"

*

One day Rekison was making tea, when a monk asked, "What is the meaning of Daruma's coming from the West?" Rekison held up the tea-spoon. The monk said, "Does this meet this case, or not?" Rekison threw the spoon into the fire.

Daruma came from India to tell people what they already knew, that each thing, each movement of each thing, is of infinite, and equal importance. The Assumption of a spoon or of the Blessed Virgin are religious activities and are to be done or viewed with the utmost seriousness and the utmost lightness.

The throwing of the spoon in the fire was not (we must suppose) due to Rekison's exasperation at the monk's denseness, nor done as a whim, nor to symbolise the finality and absoluteness of his previous action of holding up the spoon, but as one more acting of the uselessness of things. A spoon is something to ladle out tea-powder with. But it is also something to throw into the fire or beat a tattoo with,—it has every use. Every use is no use, no use is every use.

> When they are not two things,
> They are not one thing,
> And the wind
> In the Indian-ink picture
> Is cool indeed.

When we think that the intellect is dichotomous and divides things into two, we suppose that the One is the reality. But this is not so. Things are empty in their self-nature, and therefore neither divisible into two nor reducible to a unity. When we "know" this, (and how seldom we do!) things are cool or warm, good or bad, according to the "picture" in our minds.

*

Bokushu said to the assembled monks, "If you are not yet clear about the Great Matter, it is like the funeral of one's parents; if you are already clear about it, it is like the funeral of one's parents."

This is very good. According to Buddhism, Buddha is always in his abode of bliss. The gods drink and play in their celestial abodes. God created the world and found it good. But Christ was and is a man of sorrows and acquainted with grief. Kannon becomes a fish-seller for our sakes. Prometheus is always bound to the rock, a vulture tearing out his liver.

*

A monk said to Baso, "What is the meaning of Daruma's coming from the West?" Baso replied, "At this moment, what is this 'meaning'?" Again the monk asked, and Baso struck him, saying, "If I didn't strike you, people would laugh at me."

What is the meaning of "mean"? When you say, "What is a blanket?" you don't know what a blanket is, but you must know what a "what" is? What do you mean by "what"? Is God a person? But what do you mean by "person"? In other words, the fundamental question is simply, "How deep are you and your words?" If they are shallower than mine, you can't understand my answer. If they are deeper than mine, why ask a question?

Striking the monk is just like smacking a child. It is useless and foolish, but there is nothing else to do, and if we don't do it we shall be adjudged indifferent parents.

*

Mayoku asked Tangen, "Is the Twelve-faced Kannon holy or not?" "Holy," said Tangen. Mayoku struck Tangen once. Tangen said, "I knew you hadn't reached that state of mind!"

At first we think certain things or places or persons are holy. Then we understand that this is superstition, and know that they are not holy. Finally we realise that all things are holy, and some things especially. Mayoku thought Tangen was in the first state, but Tangen says he is in the third, and that Mayoku is still in the second.

*

The monk asked, "What is the Godhead?" Enkan said, "It is the passing of a bottle with all your soul."

The monk was wrong in not listening to Enkan with all his soul. To pass a bottle requires the whole universe, plus our whole soul.

*

Haikyū asked, "What is the Way? How shall we do religious practices?" Obaku answered, "What do you mean by 'the Way'? Do you really want to do religious practices?"

People always do this kind of thing. They ask, "Do you believe in God?" without thinking what "belief" is, what "God" is, what "you" is. The Way has no existence in itself, apart from those walking on it. And are not religious practices simply masochism? We should be better occupied in some more positive mischief.

*

Another disciple of Tōzan's, Yusei, about whom nothing seems to be recorded, was asked by a monk "What is the Buddha?" Yusei said, "You don't believe (he is) all living things." "I believe it deeply," said the monk. "If you explain it in a 'holy' way," said Yusei, "you will involve yourself in a cloud of errors."

"Believing" is not with the head so much as with the senses. We must touch and smell and taste and hear and see the Buddha, and even sometimes think about him and ask questions about him and answer them.

Attaining Buddhahood means attaining manhood, being a citizen of the world, of double sex; besides this Shakespearean state, it means attaining childhood, beast-hood, flower-hood, stone-hood, even word-hood and idea-hood, and place-hood and time-hood.

*

A monk asked Yakusan, "Did the essence of Buddhism exist before Daruma came?" "It did," said Yakusan. "Then why did he come, if it already existed?" "He came," said Yakusan, "just because it was here already."

This *Alice in Wonderland* conversation is a remarkable escape from the scientific world of cause and effect. Five centuries before Daruma came to China, Christ had died to save sinners who were already saved by the eternal love of God.

*

A monk said to Nan-yin, "What is the Great Meaning of Buddhism?" Nan-yin said, "The origin of a myriad diseases." The monk said, "Please cure me!" Nan-yin said, "The World Doctor folds his arms."

This is unusually poetical, and of a melancholy grandeur. It also happens to be true. Buddhism is both the cause and effect of an unsound mind in an unsound body. Note that greediness, stupidity, maliciousness and so on are not illnesses, for animals have them. Illness means thinking you are ill. And who can cure the illnesses which Doctor Buddha and Doctor Christ have caused?

*

One day Jōshū was in the Buddha Hall when he saw Bun-on bow to the Buddha. He gave him a blow with his staff. Bun-on said, "It is a good thing to pay one's respects to the Buddha!" Jōshū said, "It is better still not to do something good."

Evidently Bun-on had a slightly sanctimonious air as he bowed to the Buddha. There was a sort of holy "smell" about him which offended Jōshū's spiritual nose.

*

A monk was taking leave of Jōshū, who said to him, "Where are you off to?" "To Seppō," the monk replied. Jōshū said, "Suppose Seppō asks you what words I have lately, how will you answer?" The monk asked Jōshū to tell him what to say. Jōshū said, "Tell him, 'Winter is cold, summer is hot,' and if he suddenly asks further about the Essential, what will you say?" The monk was silent. Jōshū went on, "Say, 'I have come from Jōshū intimately; I'm not just a messenger.'" The monk went to Seppō, who asked him, "Where have you come from?" "From Jōshū." "Does he have any words?" The monk told him what Jōshū had said. Seppō said, "This must be the first time I got something from Jōshū."

Jōshū's gnomic saying "Winter is cold, summer hot," is an example of Christ's "Judge not!" for if we think that winter is unpleasantly cold or the summer pleasantly hot, Nature will judge us to be self-loving jackanapes. When we are further badgered about the meaning of life or the atomic bomb, or such-like (supposedly) important things, we should answer, "I am a friend of God, not His interpreter." God never apologizes, and we must not apologize for Him.

*

A monk asked Sekisō, "Is the meaning of Daruma's coming from the West contained in the Buddhist teachings?" "It is," replied Sekisō. "What is the meaning of Daruma's coming from the West taught there?" "Don't look for it in the sutras!" said Sekisō.

This is very good and clear. The truth is in the Bible, the Holy Bible, but don't look in the Bible for it! As Thoreau said, "When you visit God, don't ask to see one of the servants."

THE TRANSMISSION OF MIND

This is a collection of the sayings of Ōbaku (Huang Po) made by Haikyū, otherwise known as Haishōkoku, a great admirer of Ōbaku. In his Preface, 858, he tells us how in 843 and in 849 especially he questioned Ōbaku intensively and recorded his answers. The following are a few extracts and comments on them.

*

Banzan said to the monks, "It is like a sword flung up into the sky. We can discuss whether it has reached there or not. There is no scar left on the sky, and the sword itself is not diminished."

What is "it"? It is Zen; it is poetry; it is love; it is God; what is not it?

> Walking is Zen, sitting is Zen;
> Talking or silent, moving, unmoving,
> the essence is at ease.
>
> —Chentaoke

*

Banzan said to the assembled monks, "In the Three Worlds not a thing exists; where shall we search for the mind?"

If there is no object, there is no subject. If it be asked what remains, we must parody Emerson and say that when the (two) half gods go, the (whole) gods arrive. Another sermon of Banzan's.

Banzan one day went to the market and saw a man buying wild boar's flesh. The customer said to the butcher, "Cut me a slice of good meat!" The butcher threw down his chopper, folded his arms and said, "Your honour does not know that this is all good meat?" Banzan was greatly enlightened on the spot.

The best comment on this is the never-to-be-forgotten saying of Wordsworth:

> All that we behold
> Is full of blessings.

*

To realise that religion is eating, that every mouthful is the flesh of Christ, that when we walk we walk with Christ's legs, when we sit we sit with His buttocks,—this knowledge is the most exhilarating thing in the world. Every smell is the smell of God, every death is the death of God,—to know this is indeed to be at ease.

*

VII | ZEN, SIN, AND DEATH

Zen cannot assert either the mortality or the immortality, the existence or the non-existence of the soul. Buddhism may do so, for it is a religion; Christianity may do so, it is a religion; Zen cannot do so, because it is religion itself, which deals with the infinite in this finite place, eternity at this moment of time, and cannot make general or abstract statements about any world to come or not to come. What answer shall we give then to the question, "Is there an after-life?" Thoreau's is the most concise: "One world at a time!"

To come to the second point, there is nothing American (Christian) about this answer, and when a Japanese rōshi replies, he should reply in the same unjapanese way. Above all, we do not want the casuistry and sophistry of the double answer, that from the absolute point of view we are unborn and undying, as far as our real self is concerned; and from the relative viewpoint we are blessed or cursed with a succession of rebirths and redeaths. If I am asked the question, I will say that, upon dispassionate inspection, the life of man looks like that of the plants, that grow, reach maturity, decay, and disintegrate into their various elements. This is doubtless the law for the so-called spiritual world, which actually is not separate from or even correlated with the material world, but is a mere aspect of it, just as the material world is a mere aspect of the spiritual. This answer, however, is not the kind of answer I give when asked about Bach's *Art of Fugue,* or Bashō's *Furu ike ya,* or Shakespeare's "Never, never, never, never, never." It is only an opinion, and per se no better than anybody else's.

(Perhaps the most difficult examination of oneself is to be told, not that one is a fool or a knave, or even a hypocrite, but that what one says is not interesting or useful.)

*

Death is a fearful thing because of its irrevocableness, but at times, when perhaps least expected, or even unwanted, the realization comes to us that what has never existed, the individual soul, the ego, has not gone and cannot go out of existence. What was born, immediately ceased to be. At every moment, neither existence nor nonexistence can be predicated or denied,—yet what a world of difference between a living child and a dead one!

Consider the following sentence of Thoreau's, put into the form of a haiku:

> Over the old wooden bridge
> No traveler
> Crossed.

This no-traveller, like deserted roads, empty chairs, silent organs, has more meaning, more poetry, solidity and permanence than any traveller. "No traveller" does not mean nobody, nothing at all; it means everyman, you and I and God and all things cross this old rickety bridge, and like the bold lover on the Grecian Urn can never reach the goal.

*

The aim of Buddhism is of course enlightenment, but enlightenment is not a state; it is an activity. The other shore is actually never reached. If reached, we drop dead. The omnipotence and omniscience of God would be his undoing. The great illusion is that we are enlightened. That is the reason Christ is greater than Buddha. His life ended with "My God, my God, why?" The Buddha said that these "why"'s were unprofitable, which is another way of saying he had given up the problems.

If all this seems depressing to an ambitious mind, ambitious in the sense of desiring the progress of mankind, we may think of time,—backwards. How can all the madness and sadism and vulgarity be undone? How can past torture and heart-break be annulled?

We are not human beings of the dead, but of the living dead, for unto us all live. And for the present and for the future that we shall never see, no less than the past that is almost unknown to us, we must have, not mercy and compassion, but The Great Mercy and Compassion.

> If at the end of our journey
> There be no final resting place,
> How can there be
> A way to lose ourselves in?

There lies concealed in this verse the paradox that when we realize that our sins are not real, we cease to do those very things which appeared to be sins.

In Zen, sinning is to think that we have committed sin. In mysticism, sin and its immediate consequence, or rather, coincidence, Hell, is the soul's separation of itself from God by self-love. Sin is egoism, not the egoism of Zen, which is given up to gain the enlightenment of egoful egolessness, but the egoism of supposing that we can be saved from our egoism.

*

> All the sins committed
> In the Three Worlds
> Will fade and disappear
> Together with myself.
> —Ikkyū

"The Three Worlds" are the past, present, and future. If there is no good, there is no bad. If there is no sinner, there is no sin. What we call "our" life belongs to the universe, and what we call our good and bad deeds also.

& rock preaching...

> Of Heaven or Hell we have
>   No recollection, no knowledge;
> We must become what we were
>   Before we were born.

If there is Heaven or Hell for us after death, there must have been Heaven or Hell for us before birth. But we have no recollection of such a condition. Therefore all we can say is that into that state we came from, we go once more.

> Since the journey of life
>   Is little but grief and pain,
> Why should we be so reluctant
>   To return to the sky of our native place?
>   —Ikkyū

Ikkyū quotes a waka of Musō Kokushi, 1271–1346, composed when he was enlightened:

> Born like a dream
> In this dream of a world,
>   How easy in mind I am,
> I who will fade away
> Like the morning dew.

> Better than flattering
>   And living pleasantly,
> Is not to flatter,
>   And rest at ease in poverty.

Perhaps Ikkyū was thinking of Tōenmei, 365–427 A.D., one of the most famous of those who would not "bend their backs" to obtain office or fame.

and:

> Though you practise virtue,
>   Do not grieve that misfortune arises;
>   The guilty Karma
> Of the previous world
> Is vanishing away.

*

Grief and pain in this world is explained by the theory of reincarnation as the atonement for sins committed by us in previous lives. This explanation, which seems to stand or fall by an unacceptable doctrine of rebirth, has yet some independent validity in human experience, as we see when we compare it with the Christian doctrine of the vicarious suffering of Christ, and the members of the Church together with him. In other words the Christian idea is a mystical form of the Buddhist pseudoscientific notion.

*

Whatsoever it may be,
    It is all part of the world of illusion,
Death itself
    Not being a real thing.

Ikkyū calls the above verse "the medicine of Unborn-Undying." If death is not something real, why should we fear it? And what else is there to fear? "Death once dead, there's no more dying then."

*

When Sozan was about to die he made a verse:
    My road is beyond the blue sky;
    The clouds never make any commotion.
    In this world there is a tree without any roots;
    Its yellow leaves send back the wind.

After saying this, he passed away.
    Sozan's world is very much like what the real world must be, beyond thought, beyond even imagination, beyond and beyond, and yet this world all the time.

*

When Tōzan was dying, a monk said to him, "Master, your four elements (earth, water, wind, fire) are out of harmony, but is there anyone who is never ill?" "There is," said Tōzan. "Does this one look at you?" asked the monk. "It is my function to look at him," answered Tōzan. "How about when you yourself look at him?" asked the monk. "At that moment I see no illness," replied Tōzan.

The absolute, that is our real self, is neither well nor ill. He is always looking at us, but it is our job to look at him, and when we do, as St. Juliana did at the "wrath of God," we say as she did, "I saw no wrath, but on man's part."

*

Nan-yin had two well-known disciples, Eikyōan and Fuketsu. Eikyōan (Ying-ch'iao-an), dates unknown, was sitting by the fire when Shō, an official, asked him, "How can we get out of the burning in the Three Worlds?" Eikyōan picked up the incense-tongs and showed him some embers, saying "Officer! Officer!" Shō was enlightened.

We live in a burning world, in which we are ourselves burning. How are we to deal with the fire that we cannot bear to touch? Clearly, we need some tongs. What are the tongs?

*

When Daibai was about to die, he said to his monks, "What comes is not to be avoided, what goes is not to be followed." A little afterwards he heard a flying-squirrel screech and said, "This is just this, and nothing else. You all keep this faithfully. Now I must depart."

This is my idea of Zen, I mean listening to the cry of the animal, and knowing and saying that this is this, and nothing else. This is the truth, the whole truth and nothing but the truth!

*

> "We come into this world alone,
> We depart alone,"—
> This also is illusion.
> I will teach you the way
> Not to come, not to go!
>
> —Ikkyū

Ikkyū wishes us to live always in the spaceless, timeless world, where there is no birth and death, no coming and going, for these are unknown in the universe as a whole.
and:

> More frail and illusory
> Than numbers written on water,

> Our seeking from the Buddha
> Felicity in the after-world.
>
> —Ikkyū

To ask the Buddha to help us, in time, is foolish for two reasons. First, because he will not do so. Second, because we are by nature unborn, undying, timeless, eternal, omnipotent.

*

> We are born, we die.
> All are the same,
> Shakamuni, Daruma,
> The cat and the ladle.

This is the real democracy, the democracy of nature, the democracy of death.

*

> We pray for our life of tomorrow,
> Ephemeral life though it be;
> This is the habit of our mind
> That passed away yesterday.
>
> —Ikkyū

This waka expresses one of the oldest Buddhistic ideas, that each person is a succession of fleeting selves, with the illusion of continuance and permanence that makes us "look before and after, and pine for what is not." Where Buddhism makes its great mistake is in asking for eternity without time. As Blake said:

"Eternity is in love with the productions of time."

*

> The morning dew
> Flees away,
> And is no more;
> Who may remain
> In this world of ours?

We feel in this verse the sadness of Buddhism which brought out of the pleasure-loving Japanese the melancholy that was latent in their hearts. And this sadness is part of our inalienable heritage, the human tragedy which makes *The Divine Comedy* look cheap.

Why are people called Buddhas
After they die?
Because they don't grumble any more,
Because they don't make a nuisance
Of themselves any more.

—Ikkyū

By this humorous verse Ikkyū seems to imply that if we merely live and let live even in this life we shall be Buddhas.

*

A monk died, and Chōsa stroked his body and said to the assembled monks, "This monk is an example and an evaluation of truth for the sake of you monks," and made a verse,

Before your eyes, not a thing!
In this place, also, not a person!
The vast Kongō body
In neither illusion nor reality.

The Zen attitude to death is remarkably unsentimental. The problem is how to reconcile this with common humanity, just as we have to reconcile the Zen view of death with grief at it.

The same problem comes in Christianity with God's tears at the death of Lazarus, further complicated by the fact that He was going to raise him from the grave, and then kill him once more.

*

A man said, "All my life I have killed cows, and enjoyed it; is this sin or not?" "It is not," said Kōkō. "Why not," asked the man. "One killed, one given back," was Kōkō's answer.

Apart from the (accidental) fact that this was the best way to treat the cow-slaughterer psychologically, we may say that morally speaking the sin of killing the cows lay with the meat-eaters, including the monks who would have gladly eaten meat if they had not been monks, or nuns. From the (orthodox) Zen point of view, however, to be or not to be is not the question.

To kill is all right, not to kill is all right. Killing is one half of life, which is giving life by killing, and giving death by not killing. Even from the commonsense point of view, a cow can live only if cows are killed. A world full of cows only is not possible. But Zen cannot omit the moral element, for that would be to omit part of humanity itself, that is part of Buddha Himself. A man is to live killing as few cows, directly and indirectly, as possible. Not to kill cows at all, as Buddha suggests, is impossible, if human life is to continue. But to find pleasure in it,—is wrong, *because I am the cow*, and as Christ did not say, we should do unto ourselves even as we wish to do unto others.

*

Gutei's dying words are of deep meaning: "It was not finished." What is true is always new.

> New every morning is the love
> Our waking and uprising prove.

New every morning is the sun, like Gutei's finger, like the Nembutsu, like Bach's solo violin sonatas.

*

> I shan't die, I shan't go anywhere,
> I'll be here;
> But don't ask me anything,
> I shan't answer.

This is said to be Ikkyū's death verse, but whether so or not it is very good, expressing as it does, so concretely and simply, the contradictions that make up our life and death.

*

When Goei was on the verge of death, he made his ablutions and burned incense, then sat in the proper way and said to the monks, "The Body of the Law in Nirvana shows birth and death; the thousand Holy Ones are all the same basically; the ten thousand spirits all return to one. I am now disintegrating; why should I be foolish enough to grieve at that? Do not trouble your souls. Keep a true mind! If you obey these demands you are truly showing your gratitude to me. If you do not, you are not my children." At this moment a monk asked, "Where is our teacher going?" Goei answered, "I am going to No-place." The monk said, "Why shan't I be able to see you any more?" Goei said, "That place is not one to be seen with human eyes," and passed away.

This No-place is not annihilation, any more than it is heaven. It is not a no-place, but a No-place, a Place, not a place, a placeless place. "I shan't go away, but I shan't be here," he might have said.

*

Kassan and Jōzan were going along talking together, when Jōzan said, "If, within life-and-death there were no Bud-dha, there would be no life-and-death." Kassan said, "If the Buddha were within life-and-death, there would be no delusion with regard to life and death." They both argued back and forth, and there was no end to it. They climbed up the mountain to Daibai and asked him about it. Kassan said, "Of these two opinions which is the more 'familiar'?" Daibai said, "One is familiar, one is distant." "Which is the familiar one?" asked Kassan. "Go away now and ask me again tomorrow," said Daibai. The next day Kassan came again and asked. Daibai said, "A familiar one does not ask. One who asks is not familiar." Kassan afterwards said, "At that time, when I was with Daibai, I lost my Buddha-eye."

*

A monk said to Tōzan, "A monk has died; where has he gone?" Tōzan answered, "After the fire, a sprout of grass."

I take this to mean, "He is as dead as a door-nail. He has gone nowhere. He has ceased to exist. At the same time, life, in some form or other continues, at present anyway." This question of the after-life, which is mixed up with the notion of reincarnation, does not often arise; the most interesting reply is the following. Seppō said to Gensha, "Monk Shinso asked me where a certain dead monk had gone, and I told him it was like ice becoming water." Gensha said, "That was all right, but I myself would not have answered like that." "What would you have said?" asked Seppō. Gensha replied, "It's like water returning to water."

*

When Kassan was about to die, he called the chief monk, and said to him, "I have preached the Way to the monks for many years. The profound meaning of Buddhism is to be known by each person himself. My illusory life is over; I am about to depart. You monks should go on just the same as when I was alive. You should not blindly make ordinary people miserable." Having said this, he immediately passed away. Kassan seems to have been a nice sort of chap.

*

Rinzai's death was typical of the man. When he was about to die, he said to his monks, "After I am gone, do not destroy my Treasury of the True Eye of the Law." Sanshō said, "Who would have the temerity to destroy it?" Rinzai said, "Afterwards, if someone asks you a question (about it), how will you reply?" Sanshō said "Kwatz!" Rinzai said, "Who would think that a blind donkey would destroy it?" He then died doing zazen.

*

When Banzan was about to die, he asked his monks to bring him his portrait, but he was not satisfied with any of them. At that time Fuke had one. Banzan said, "Why don't you show it to me then?" Fuke turned a somersault and went out. Banzan said, "This lunatic will pervert the true way from now on."

Zen has not lacked (Zen) lunatics to remind people of the demonic and insane character of the universe . . .

*

VIII | ZEN AND POETRY

Zen is poetry and poetry is Zen. The word poetry, or poetical, may be used in three ways: verse, as opposed to prose; deep meaning in verse, that is Zen in words of regular rhythm; deep meaning, that is Zen, in verse or prose or sound or acts or states of mind. "Poetry" is used here with the second meaning.

From earliest times thinkers must have perceived that on the one hand they could not think without words; on the other hand, words expressed only half the whole truth. This experience may be verified logically. If a thing is all things, if each grain of sand is the universe, its sensuously perceived hardness, yellowness, smallness, lifelessness and so on must be accompanied by all the contrary qualities, softness, non-yellowness, bigness, liveliness, and so on, all equally present though invisible etc. to the senses. Words are thus as harmful as they are useful, and the early Zen monks naturally inveighed against the dichotomy of words. Literature became suspect, and this in a country, China, where letters and words and books and even paper, were regarded with a superstitious awe.

*

"Poetry" is a term usually employed in connection with words. "Musical thought," Carlyle called it. One of the mistakes of Zen is to assert that Zen is beyond thought, beyond words, wordless. This is like saying that no impression should be followed by an expression, which is the more foolish in that expression must always begin at the very moment of the commencement of impression. Words are not separate from things, any more than form is from matter or body from soul. This fact was well understood by the Shingon Sect. According to the Shingon Sect, more exactly, the Shingon Himitsu Shu, "The True Word Mystery Sect," there are Three Secrets, that of Activity, that of Word, and that of Meaning. The sect is called Shingon, "true word," to emphasize the underrated importance of the second of the Secrets. "In the Beginning was the Word," but just as the doctrine of the Trinity reunites the never-divided Father, Son, and Holy Ghost, so Activity, Word, and Meaning are in reality only one. That is to say poetry, most deeply considered, is the True Word. Even when written down and printed in a book, it still lives in the same way and to the same degree that the man who spoke the words lived, and it is still living, and is inseparable from him.

*

Poetry, like Zen, though incapable of definition, that is, of limitation, of isolation, can be exemplified. The trouble is, however, that what is shown is not necessarily what is seen, and *vice versa*. Nothing is foolproof (but then again, in case you are discouraged, nothing is sage-proof or saint-proof or poetry-proof or Zen-proof). Instead of defining Zen, and then defining poetry, and somehow or other twisting the definitions until they approximate, it may be better to point to a common element in both,—and this common element is perhaps we are all really looking for,—I refer to humour. The humour of Zen is almost too obvious. The *Mumonkan* in particular (and the *Hekiganroku* to a lesser degree because it is so garrulous) is simply a collection of cosmic jokes. Enlightenment is always accompanied by a kind of sublime laughter. It is an odd and significant thing that Zen began, or what is much more deeply true, is supposed to have began with Mahakasyapa's smile.

To bring out the meaning of the word "humour" as used here, we may say that Mark Twain has little, if any, but that every sentence, even the saddest, of Thoreau's writings is impregnated with it. The real humour, like the real poetry and the real Zen, can never be separated from the whole, can never be pigeon-holed, can never become an illustrative anecdote. Herein lies the danger of such books as the *Hekigranroku* and the *Mumonkan* and magazine articles on Zen. By ceasing to be poetry, by being a collection of stories and essays they cease to have any Zen at all,—unless we can make these dry bones live.

*

Poetry is a meaningful activity, whether it appears visibly in walking or flying (in an aeroplane) or (bull-) fighting; or invisibly, as in thinking. The question what it means is not to be asked, or to speak more severely, the question itself arises from that secret desire we spoke of before, the will not to know, not to be. Poetry is the will to exist, the will of long things to be long, and soft things to be soft. This is the will to mean, the poetical activity *per se*. But coming closer to the ordinary usage of the word poetry, literature being poetry in verse or prose, we will now use the word poetry in the restricted meaning of literature in verse, that is to say, deep experiences expressed in rhythmical language, in repeated forms, for example the parallelisms of thought in Hebrew verse, or the repetitions of stress and line and stanza in modern European poetry.

*

There seems to be a great difference between Japanese and Chinese poets on the one hand and European poets on the other. Chinese poetry is devoid of romantic love; however, marital love and a sort of platonic(?) homosexuality are found. In Japan, some of the waka poets were, or pretended to be, Don Juans, for example Narihira, but the haiku poets seem quite sexless, both in their lives and in their writings. Without thinking of Sappho and Catullus and Goethe and Baudelaire, and confining ourselves to English poetry, the English poets were a pretty sexual bunch of people. Beowulf was quite a gentleman, but Chaucer was guilty, it seems, of rape. Shakespeare, unexpurgated, is not fit to be read in schools (see Eric Partridge's *Shakespeare's Bawdy*). Milton shows a strong interest in women everywhere, not least in his choice of Samson (and Delilah) as a subject in his old age. Wordsworth was always surrounded by women, had an illegitimate child, but probably was not guilty of incest with his sister. Keats' violent passion for a young lady, Shelley's "feminated" life, and Byron's which stinks of women,—all these show that a poet must be a fully if not over-sexed person. The sexual respectability of both Tennyson and Browning is not unconnected with their dullness and verbosity.

If we make a comparison of the poetic form of Japanese (and to a lesser extent, Chinese) verse and that of Europe, we see the same difference. Japanese verse is in form excessively spiritual, almost mathematical, being alternations of five and seven syllables. European verse is far more physical; it dances with the trochaic and dactylic rhythms, or at least strides with the iambic. Poetry, dancing, music, sex, religion, sacrifices (human and animal), eating, hunting, and so on,—these were once a single activity, and even now traces of the rest can be seen in poetry alone. Japanese and Chinese verse, even if connected with religion, is related to the pantheism and cosmic animism of the *Upanishads,* or the purification ceremonies of primitive Shintō. European poetry has blood, purgation, the agony of unfulfilled desire, Job's cursing of God. Sex and will are deeply related, at bottom the same thing perhaps. The most profound line of Shakespeare's plays is Lear's

>   Never, never, never, never, never.

It expresses a despair beyond despair.

Lear's enlightenment, his realisation that pride of power is nonsense, is followed by Cordelia's death, by his realisation that what he loved had become nothing, and that the loving soul of Cordelia has been annihilated, is as if it had not been. But Sir Walter Raleigh has another "never":

>   True love is a fire
>   In the mind ever burning,
>   Never sick, never old, never dead,
>   From itself never turning.

>   *

Love and death have no connection with each other. One cannot have the victory over the other, for they exist in different worlds, one poetical, timeless, the other scientific, timeful. Lear's love, Cordelia's love are transcendental things, about which despair is impossible. There is yet one more "never" in English literature, the most tremendous of all. Blake says:

> And can he who smiles on all
> Hear the wren with sorrows small,
> Hear the small bird's grief & care.
> Hear the woes that infants bear,
>
> And not sit beside the nest,
> Pouring pity in their breast;
> And not sit the cradle near,
> Weeping tear on infant's tear;
>
> And not sit both night & day,
> Wiping all our tears away?
> O, no! never can it be!
> Never, never can it be!

This asserts the supremacy of the individual will over all the apparent factuality of things. It is the final sexual thrust, the masculine orgasm in which the world is abolished. Nature exists no more to tantalise us with her female charms.

To join, to separate, to re-join, to re-separate,—this sexual, centripetal centrifugality is the essence of life, the essence of Zen. A word is a (real) word because it is not a word, because it is a thing, a thing which is a real thing only when it is not a thing, when it is a word. The charm of language, that charm without which, as Emerson says, nothing can conquer me, consists precisely in its separate-inseparate character. In the Shingon Sect the separateness, the intrinsic power of words is declared. The Jōdo Sect also rides us safely to Paradise on the word *Namuamidabutsu*. In the Zen Sect words are publicly denounced as being, like men themselves, "deceivers ever," but the truth is that both are right. The Word, the Logos is God, and yet not God.

Admitting then that Zen and poetry overlap to some extent, let us ask the question, is there anything which is poetical but has no Zen in it? Are there some non-poetical elements in Zen? Zen may seem to be pragmatic and practical, but it is also wildly fantastic. It gives us the "sermons in stones and

books in the running brooks," but it also has "magic case-
ments opening on the foam of perilous seas forlorn." The
words of Euripides are pure Zen: "At high tide the sea, they
say, leaves a deep pool below the rock-shelf; in that clear
place the women dip their water jars." But Zen also sees "the
floor of heaven thick inlaid with patines of bright gold," and
hears the stars "still quiring to the young-eyed cherubins."
The enemies of poetry,—vulgarity, sentimentality, romance,
indifference, lack of humour,—these are the enemies of Zen.
Yet Zen, like poetry, like humour, turns our stupidity into
interest, our falsity into a revelation of truth, our motiveless
malignity into meaningful "love," our defeat into victory. Thus
are confirmed the paradoxical words of Socrates, "Think this
certain, that to a good man no evil can happen, either in life
or in death." This "good man" is the man of Zen, the man of
Poetry.

The word "poetical" as used here is more difficult to define
than the word Zen, since it includes Zen, but goes beyond it.
Arnold said, "Poetry is a criticism of life," and this creative
judgement is what I also intend by the word "poetry." The
poetical attitude, or rather, activity, is something like the
poems of Shenhsiu and Huineng put together. The Mind is
both a mirror, and an ever-expanding eye which creates what
it sees, and destroys what it does not. I clear my mind of cant.
I learn all I can of the culture of the past, and remove my
prejudices of rank and nationality. I desire nothing but what
has been, is, and will be. I hold the mirror up to nature, and
the good and evil, wise and foolish, beautiful and ugly pass
before it, and leave not a wrack behind of remorse, pride,
loathing, or possessiveness. *But*, at the same time, I violently
object to the vulgar and the superficial; I yearn towards Bach
and Bashō; I am excited by Beethoven and Shakespeare; I
judge, with extreme finality, that bull-fighting is bad, and
newspapers worse. The mirror reflects all, equally, but as the
witty saying goes, some more equally than others. This is the
poetical spirit. It is an agony of mind which finds itself in
complete solitude, yet does not desire either company or comfort. The beauty of nature is intolerable, the heroism of human
nature unbelievable, the power of art overwhelming, the sufferings of animals unforgivable, the creation of the universe

Dragon on a purification basin

by God inexcusable. For such a mind, the poetical mind, Zen is the only possible "philosophy of life." It gives us the lack of support that we need; it takes away the unwanted words; it removes the non-existent bonds. At last we have timelessness in time and placelessness in place. But as said before, the spirit of poetry actually goes beyond Zen, which is: "All that we behold is full of blessings." The poetical mind does not want blessings, does not want Nirvana.

*

Ummon said, "Within the cosmos, within the universe there is a Treasure. It hides within the body. We pick up the lamp and take it into the Buddha Hall. We take the Great Gate and put it on the lamp."

The word "in," which Ummon uses, is misleading. Is the soul "in" the body? If so, it must have the shape of the body, which it fills completely. What is the Treasure? Is it the Buddha nature, or God, or the universal soul, or Zen? I would rather say it is the *poetical* nature, which enables us to do all things, ordinary and extraordinary,—if there be two kinds of things, as Ummon suggests by his two examples of what the enlightened man can do.

*

Zen is energy, the energy by which we rejoin what is separated, and separate what is joined. Zen is not tranquillity. Peace of mind is something we are always just going to have. If and when we actually have it, it has been attained by some insensitiveness, resignation, laziness, deathliness, stupidity, blindness, obstinacy, comfort-lovingness, self-satisfaction, emptiness. Poetry is the exact opposite of these. Tranquillity is there, but swallowed up in activity; the immovable must move:

> Sumer is icumen in;
> Lhude sing cucu!

Science aims at a unity which is achieved in madness and mysticism, in love, and in poetry, but it is not correct to speak of "Buddhahood, in which all the contradictions of the intellect are entirely harmonised in a unity of a higher order," for Zen is harmony *and* disharmony. It is disunity just as much as unity. When Shakespeare wrote *Hamlet*, he became Hamlet. This is true, but at the same time he remained Shakespeare, for without this paradoxical condition no drama, no poetry, no *Hamlet*, is possible.

*

The (orthodox) Christian, the Buddhist, the scientific will is towards symmetry, but the Zen will is towards asymmetry.

The sayings of Christ are to be taken neither literally nor figuratively, but in the Zen, that is, the poetical way.

Mechanical people think that the universe is a machine like themselves. The poet, full of life and joy himself, sees it just so full of life and joy. Which is "true"? It all depends upon oneself, but it may be laid down that something is better than nothing, and a machine is precisely nothing, whether it is a cosmos (the flower) or the cosmos. We are thus placed in a dilemma; either the world, including ourselves is a meaningless chain of cause and effect, or, daffodils dance, skies weep, stones shout hosannah, and so on. Is a river flowing, H_2O+gravity,—or is it "Thou wanderer thro' the woods"? The humour of the whole business is the contradiction between the dead truth of science and the living truth of poetry, between the sense and use of ordinary life and the value and uselessness of art. Literature is the struggle between poetry and science, the struggle of life and death, death in this case meaning nothingness, no-meaning.

*

The poetic experience is not wordless, any more than the soul is bodiless. In the original poetical experience the words are not yet separated from the experience. They are not yet printed in a book by a mechanical machine that takes us farther even from the first, undifferentiated state, perhaps a kind of primaeval will.

The naturalness of (good) poetry comes out clearly in its balance of form and matter. It seems possible, at first sight, to have a poor form for rich matter, and vice versa, but perhaps this is an illusion arising from the shallowness of our judgements. In theory at least, the profoundest words of

Shakespeare have an equally (or even more) profound rhythm and sound.

There is an old senryu, it is true, which says rightly enough:

> The cough
> Is used
> In many, many ways.

The differences of meaning however depend very much upon the circumstances of the case, and the persons coughed at, and we must try to hold fast to the truth that form is not the mere appearance of some abstract matter, but that form and matter are two different aspects of the same thing, just as "the soul is that portion of the soul perceived by the senses in this world." In other words, form and matter both derive from the (supposedly) formless, matterless, incoherent original experience.

*

Prepositions are mortally dangerous, for example "in." "To see a world in a grain of sand,"—has this "in" the physical or the spiritual meaning? It should be taken physically, and then we get the Tendai philosophy of "All in one, one in All," but most people take "in" to mean "by means of," "taking (a grain of sand) as a symbol." It is necessary always to understand poetry and religion literally, not literarily. Perhaps the most important preposition is "like," because this involves simile, a weakened form of metaphor, which is an experience of identity of different things, the more different the better.

*

Just as comedy must include tragedy, so agedness should have youth involved in it. Mere age is dryness and a declining of life and energy. "Agedness" means all of youth with none of its stupidity, insensitiveness, egoism, and cruelty. It is age without its cynicism and obstinacy and pride of power. What is wrong with age is that it has no youth in it. What is wrong with youth is that it has no age in it. Tichborne, executed in 1586 at the age of twenty eight, tells us his age:

I sought my death and found it in my womb,
I looked for life and saw it was a shade,
I trod the earth and knew it was my tomb,
And now I die, and now I was but made;
My glass is full, and now my glass is run,
And now I live, and now my life is done.

*

The function of poetry is to save the world from meaningless pain, but no less, perhaps more, to save it from meaningless pleasure. Pain has some hope of enlightenment, pleasure none. Joy then is Nirvana, is blessedness.

One day a monk asked, "What is the Great Meaning of Buddhism?" Seike answered, "The wooden crane flies on the post of the gate of the grave."

The essence of Buddhism cannot be grasped without jumping out of sense into non-sense. That is why musicians and poets and madmen and lovers (different names for the same thing) understand Zen so well, and find something repulsive about ordinary, unpoetical Zen.

The rain has drubbed us in his cold laundry,
The sun has parched us blacker than a crow,
And kites have made each eye a cavity
And torn out beards and eyebrows even so.
There is no resting place where we may go,
But here or there, just as the wind may blow,
We dangle at his pleasure to and fro,
Pocked more by birds than thimble surfaces.
Be not therefore of our fraternity,
But pray God's mercy upon all of us.
   —*Ballade of the Hanged Men*, Villon

Now having washed and cleansed the robes of stain,
They spread them out in rows upon the shore,
Where most the breakers wash the pebbles clear,
Then the girls bathed and rubbed them well with oil,
And took their meal upon the river banks,
And waited for the clothes to dry in the sun.
   —*The Odyssey*

Some eat the countries; these are kings;
The doctors, those whom sickness stings;
The merchants, those who buy their things
And learned men, the fools.

The married are the clergy's meat;
The thieves devour the indiscreet;
The flirts their eager lovers eat;
And Labour eats us all.

—*The Panchatantra*
c. 200 B.C.

What is the common element in all these lines? It is the nature of things, which is speaking with the voice of a man, the thingness of things in Homer, the deathliness of life in Villon, the liveliness of death in Fielding, the life of apparently lifeless things in Hebrew poetry, the eating eatability of things in the *Panchatantra*.

Chōshūsai interviewed Seidō, and asked him "Mountains and rivers and the Great Earth,—do they really exist or do they not really exist? Do all the Buddhas of the Three Worlds exist, or not?" Seidō replied, "They all exist." Chōshūsai told Seidō that Hyakujō always answered "They do not," to such questions. Seidō said, "Let's wait till we come to be like our senior Hyakujō, and then everything will *mu*."

The world exists, it does not exist, it both exists and not exists. That it exists, or that it does not exist can be asserted by science and common sense. Only art can express the third. Seidō's conclusion is admirable, combining loyalty and independence with humour.

*

Freedom means freedom from emotion, from thought, from beauty, from law, from self, from God. Does anything remain? According to the Zen experience, only when all these half-gods go do All Things remain, does poetry remain. Art submits itself to law in order that freedom may be brought out by contrast. Further, it takes every advantage of (un)lucky accidents, turning its loss to glorious gain. When Wordsworth began to write *To My Sister*, apparently in April, he said,

It is the first mild day of March.

Why this lie? Because "April" won't rhyme with anything, and apparently there was a larch near the house he had rented in Alfoxden. But also, by accident, the sequence of vowels gives just the mood he was in at the time. Also the m's of "mild" and "March" have the same function as the six m's of the third verse, the same function of love, "the spirit of the season." The two l's coming together in "tall larch" is also a lucky accident. They increase the height of what is already high. Freedom thus means making use of fixed fate, (really) liking what you do instead of doing what you (think you) like.

*

Why should anything be hidden? Is it not a mere trick? Why much in little? Why not much in much? Is not understatement a kind of cowardice, or at best miserliness? It is no use talking about suggestiveness or imagination, for this begs the question, which is, why should we (be forced to) imagine what might just as well be displayed in full? When we eat Christmas pudding we are not asked to imagine the raisins.

The answer is that the question is based on a false conception of truth, which is not static and perfect, but dynamic and imperfect; it is growing, otherwise dead, and mere factual, scientific truth. Strictly speaking, the artist or the poet does not select the most significant part of the whole so that, in some miraculous way, the part may be greater than the whole. He chooses all that is living and moving and changing of the mixture of life and death in the object or circumstance. It is this living and growing of the "truth" of a thing which we refer to as its latency. It is its will, its existence-meaning.

As said before, a hippopotamus is more poetical than a butterfly, because its beauty is almost entirely latent. However, on a starlit night just rising above the water of an African jungle, the profound poetry, that is, the agedness of a hippopotamus is clearly visible.

IX | THREE ZEN POETS

HANSHAN (Japanese: *Kanzan*)

It is perhaps not possible to have a clear picture of Hanshan (Kanzan) a Zen fool. Was he a Taoist? a Buddhist? a Zen monk? an eccentric? a natural? a poseur? or a little of each? The Japanese have turned him into a kind of Zen madman, and artists especially, for example Mincho, Indra, Liangk'ai, show him together with Shihtê as a couple of poetical lunatics, with matted hair and a perpetual grin on their faces. Shihtê, whose name means "picked up," was an orphan, and as a baby was picked up by Fêng and given to someone to rear him. Shihtê was far from being a poet, but wrote verses; the following is an example:

> Hanshan is of himself Hanshan;
> Shihtê is of himself Shihtê.
> How can the common or garden man really know
> them?
> (But Fêng knows them through and through.)
> If you want really to see them you mustn't just look
> at them.
> When you want to find them, where will you seek for
> them?

I ask, "What is the relation between them?"
And hasten to answer, "They are men with the omnipotence of doing 'nothing.' "

Fêng was head priest of Kuoch'ing Temple in Tient'ai
(Tendai) Mountains, and Hanshan and Shihtê often visited
the temple and were on very good terms with him.

Fêng also wrote verses, of an equally mystical character,
for example:

Hanshan came specially to see me,
Shihtê too, a rare visitor.
We spoke unaffectedly and without reserve of the
    Mind,
How vast and free the Great Emptiness,
How boundless the universe,
Each thing containing within itself all things.

The poems of Shihtê and Fêng are usually printed together
with those of Hanshan.

The famous poet-monk Ch'anyüeh (Zengetsu) 832–912,
speaks of Hanshan in a poem sent to Shutaoshih, of Ch'ihsung,
which is fairly near Mount T'ient'ai. This suggests that Hanshan must belong to about the 8th century A.D.

Perhaps Blake's "madness" is the closest to Hanshan's
alleged preposterousness, but there is a human joy in Blake
which contrasts with the rarefaction, isolation, and other-
worldliness of Hanshan. Clare's love of nature in its minute
variety, and hatred of (Wordsworth's) mysticism distinguish
him distinctly from Hanshan, but they are alike in misanthropy and failure to be loved by women. This was also the
case with Thoreau, who has the same perversity but not the
eccentricity, uncouthness, deliberate mystification and wanton
wilfulness we sometimes feel in Hanshan. A certain amount of
(womanly) poise, the insensitivity of nature, the "enlightenment" of Zen is necessary not merely for the lowest, but for
the highest life. A supersensitive God would go out of his
mind; perhaps He has.

The following are the most poetical of Hanshan's verses,
and (therefore) those with most Zen in them. They are in a
kind of chronological order.

My mother and father left me enough to live on,
I have no need to grudge others their lands and fields.
My wife works at the loom; creak! creak! it goes.
My children prattle and play;
Clapping their hands, they dance with the flowers,
They listen to the song of the birds, chin on hand.
Who comes to pay his respects?
A woodcutter, occasionally.

This seems to have been written before Hanshan left his home to become a wanderer, until he settled at Hanshan, the Cold Mountain from which he took his name. Such an earthly paradise as he describes here is not possible in this world. Heaven is a room for one person.

Beams with a thatch over them,—a wild man's dwelling!
Before my gate pass horses and carts seldom enough;
The lonely wood gathers birds;
The broad valley stream harbours fish;
With my children I pluck the wild fruits of the trees;
My wife and I hoe the rice-field;
What is there in my house?
A single case of books.

This also is Hanshan's pre-Robinson Crusoe life. It is the ideal life of everyman; ideal, not real, not realisáble.

I live in a village;
And everybody praises me to the skies,
But yesterday I went to the town.
Even the dog watched me suspiciously;
The people don't like the cut of my coat,
Or my trousers are too long or too short for them.
If an eagle is struck blind,
The sparrows fly openly.

The real difference between the town and the village is not so much that the villagers are all trusting and true-hearted fellows, and the townsfolk mean and suspicious, but that the town is bigger than the village. We cannot be known in a crowd. The point of the last two lines seems to be that Hanshan has no economic or social power, and the townsfolk behave to him like the vulgar and stupid people they are. We are irresistibly reminded of Kierkegaard.

> I was pretty poor before,
> Today I am wretchedness and misery itself.
> Everything is at sixes and sevens.

> I meet suffering everywhere I go.
> I often slip about on the muddy roads;
> I get belly-ache when I sit with my neighbours.
> When the tabby cat is lost,
> Rats occupy the rice-chest.

Here he shows us his grumbling Zen. On some days everything goes wrong, and life hardly seems worth living; energy (sexual?) is at a low ebb. However, it is not that some days must be dark and gloomy. It is that darkness and gloom are good in themselves, not as contrasted with bright and cheerful days, nor as a chance for resignation. It is rather

> The Devil's in Hell,
> All's wrong with the world!

> Here's a fine chap, strong in mind and body,
> He has the Six Accomplishments;
> But when he goes South he's driven North,
> And when he goes West he's sent away East,
> Always floating like duckweed,
> Like "flying grass," never at rest.
> You ask, "What kind of man may this be?"
> His surname is Poverty; the first name is Extremity.

> Last night I dreamed I was back home again,
> And was looking at my wife weaving.
> She stopped the loom, and seemed deep in thought.

This poem would not ordinarily be quoted as an example of Zen, but I wish to take it so. Zen is not medicine for the spiritually afflicted, nor a tonic for the potential hero.

Hanshan has a yearning for his old life. And this is as it should be, because it is as it is. Illusion is (a form of) enlightenment. To forgive (one's own erring) is divine.

> The way to Hanshan is a queer one;
> No ruts or hoof-prints are seen.
> Valley winds into valley,
> Peak rises above peak;
> Grasses are bright with dew,
> And pine-trees sough in the breeze.
> Even now you do not know?
> The reality is asking the shadow the way.

The last lines, as usual, are suddenly difficult. The meaning is perhaps that the reality is ourselves, and it is useless to question outward things, these "vanishings," for the reality. "Hanshan" is of course the mountain, the man, and reality.

> Quietly I visited a famous monk;
> Mountains rose one after another through the mist.
> The master pointed out my way back;
> The moon, a circle of light, hung in the sky.
> My hut is beneath a green cliff,
> The garden a wilderness;
> The latest creepers hang down in coils and twinings,
> Ancient rocks stand sharp and tall.
> Monkeys come and pick the wild fruits;
> The white heron swallows the fish of the pools.
> Under the trees I read some Taoist books;
> My voice intones the words and phrases.

This is both ideal and real, like Thoreau's life at Walden, but has a faint undertone of something else in it, however skilfully hidden.

> I dwell below boulders piled one upon another.
> A path fit for birds! It only prevents people from
>   coming.
> The garden,—can you call it a garden?
> The white clouds embrace ineffable rocks;
> How long have I lived among them all?
> How many times have I seen spring depart, seen win-
>   ter come again?
> But avoid the dinner bell and banquets galore,
> Beware of names empty and profitless.

Pinetree, Imperial Palace Gardens, Kyoto

> I live in a nice place,
> Far from dust and bustle.
> By treading the turf, I have three paths;
> The clouds I see I make my four walls.
> To help Nature express itself there are the voices of
>   birds;
> Here there is nobody to ask about Buddhist philoso-
>   phy.
> The Tree of the World is still growing;
> My short span of spring,—how many years will it be?

This is the ideal life, but even here there is a pervasive melancholy.

> These past twenty years!—thinking of them,
> How I have walked quietly back from Kuoch'ing
>   Temple,
> And all the people of the temple
> Say of Hanshan, "What a nincompoop he is!"
> Why do they call me a fool, I wonder?
> But I can't decide the question,
> For I myself don't know who "I" is,
> So how can others possibly know?
> I hang my head; what's the use of their asking?
> What good can thinking about it do?
> People come and laugh at me.
> I know quite well what they think of me.
> But I am not foolish enough to retort to them,
> Because they do just what I want them to do.

This reminds us of Blake's *Proverbs of Hell:*

> Listen to the fool's reproach! It is a kingly title!

And this is not to be taken in a cynical or scornful way but more philosophically. It takes a great man to know a great man, and a fool sees only fools. If a fool saw a wise man as wise the wise man would be a fool.

> People ask the way to Hanshan,
> But there is no way to Hanshan.
> The ice does not melt even in summer,
> And even if the sun should rise, dense vapours
>   clothe it round.

As in Kafka, the road, the way, The Way, is "No Thorough-fare!" Hanshan, as said at the beginning, is a very mixed character. His Zen is mingled with a spirit of despair, even desperation, which is the antithesis of Zen. But as Thoreau says, it is wrong to systematise our thought and our experience. Let it be as it is, contradictions and all, and we shall then become even more real, more human than Hamlet and Hanshan.

IKKYŪ

Ikkyū's life and character are full of contradictions. He is a Buddhist priest, obeying all the Buddhist rules; but he is also a Zen priest, breaking any law freely. He was a son of the Emperor; but lived in the direst poverty for many years. He had very great political influence; and yet he was not given any office until made head of Daitokuji Temple in his eighty-first year. He was an enlightened man in the true and religious sense; nevertheless he twice attempted suicide, once in his youth, once in his old age. He has more contradictions in him than Hamlet, and yet, he is, in the words of Hazlitt, "always, amid every fluctuation of feeling, every shifting of intelligence, one and the same man of genius."

Ikkyū Zenji is the most remarkable monk in the history of Japanese Buddhism, the only Japanese comparable to the great Chinese Zen masters, for example, Jōshū, 778–897; Rinzai, d. 867; Unmon, d. 996. But he is different from these, and from all the other Zen Masters in that he does not deny, by his silence, the existence of sex. Just as the moon does not make a hole in the water, so enlightenment, real enlighten-ment, does not rid a man of his human nature. Thoreau says in his *Journals*, 1857, "I see that the infidels and skeptics have formed themselves into churches, and weekly gather together at the ringing of a bell." Ikkyū is as free of Zen and zazen and the 1700 koans as Thoreau is of churches and church-going and dogmas, and thus has no position in the so-called "History of Zen." Ikkyū reminds us also of the 19th century clergyman Sydney Smith, in his being anti-priest, careless of dignity, and a believer in the saving power of humour. He is unlike Bashō or Ryōkan; he has no "quietness" in him, and inclines to vulgarity. Ikkyū is closest to the Zen priest Sengai, 1750–1837, who also associated with all classes of society, and painted some of the best Zenga (Zen pictures) in existence. The real Ikkyū is difficult to grasp; there is a pureness that is elusive, a lack of back and front which escapes our paradoxes. He is indeed the cloud in the sky, the foam on the water, the shadow of the bamboo on the palace steps, the sound of the wind in the picture.

Ikkyū was born on New Year's Day 1394, six years before the death of Chaucer, his mother being a Lady in Waiting to the Emperor Go-Komatsu, the 100th Emperor of Japan. She seems to have waited too much or too long on various occasions, and became pregnant, to the displeasure (as it is said) of the Empress, who had her dismissed. When he was in his twenties he heard of Kasō Zenji in Katada, endeavoured to enter his temple, and at last succeeded in doing so. Kasō's temple was in a very poor condition, the food being rather less than the minimum to sustain life. When food and clothing ran out completely, Ikkyū would go to Kyōto, make some incense, sell it, and come back with the pittance thus gained. Six years passed in a sort of duel between the sullen teacher and the desperate novice. In the evening of the 20th of May, 1420, Ikkyū became enlightened on the hearing the caw of a crow. In 1428 Kasō died; Ikkyū was now 34. Kasō had given him a certificate of his enlightenment, but Ikkyū only threw it on the ground. Kasō wrote another, and later, this document fell into his hands, and he shed tears as he read it:

> When you were enlightened, Jun-zōsu (Ikkyū), I gave you a paper of Buddhist words. You asked me why I wanted a stake to tie the ass to, and went off, dusting your sleeves. . . . When the True Law of Rinzai is lost, you must bring it back again. You are my child; keep this in your heart; think of it.
>
> May, the 27th Year of Oei,
> Kasō

Ikkyū's life from now on was spent in teaching the people, and condemning the sham monks of his (and all) time, but whether he lived alone in a poor hut or in Daitokuji Temple, he was surrounded by zealous disciples. In 1467 civil war broke out, Kyōto was devastated, and Ikkyū spent a wandering life in Yamato, Izumi, and Settsu. In 1475, Ikkyū was asked by the Emperor to become the head of Daitokuji Temple. He was unable to refuse this position of great honour, but expressed his feelings in the following verse:

> The disciples of Daitokuji have extinguished the guttering
> lamp;
> It is difficult for them to understand the poetical feeling
> of an icy night;
> For fifty years I was a man wearing straw raincoat and
> umbrella-hat;
> I feel grief and shame now at this purple robe.

"Dōka" are didactic waka, moralizing, and usually Buddhistic, seldom if ever of great poetical value, and usually of easy popular comprehension. Ikkyū wrote about a hundred and fifty of these poems, many of which are well known. Ikkyū's dōka, unlike his Chinese poems, often give us the ancient melancholy of primitive Buddhism, the same feeling that life is suffering which we find in the *Hōjōki* and the *Sarashina Diary*. But many others are full of the contradictions of Zen, yet portray for us a man of deep sincerity, too honest perhaps to be a great lyrical poet:

> If we say, "There is not,"
>   People think "There is not,"
> Though it answers,
>   The mountain echo.

*

When we say that every thing is "empty of self-nature," people think that there is really nothing at all. An echo is something non-existent, yet it is always "there," ready to answer to our calling.

> If we say "There is,"
> People think "There is";
>   But though it answers,
> It is not,
> This mountain echo.

> The lovingkindness we feel,
>> The merciful deeds we do in this life,
> Are the seeds of the spring flowers
>> Of the future Third Meeting.

The "Third Meeting" means the appearance in the infinitely distant future, of Miroku Bosatsu, Maitreya. There seems here some implication that in our creation of goodness we are the masters not of our own, but of All Fate. Without us, the flower of eternity will never bloom.

> A mind to search elsewhere
>> For the Buddha,
> Is the foolishness
>> In the very centre of foolishness.

Our mistake is to look for truth outside, or inside ourselves. The great mistake is to look at all, for what we always were, and always will be, is not to be found or attained. In some supremely odd way, we are the Buddha, and this place is the Earthly Paradise.

> If you break open
> The cherry tree,
>> Where are the flowers?
> But in springtime,
> See how they bloom!

*

> Deeply thinking of it,
> I and other people,—
>> There is no difference,
> As there is no mind
> Beyond this Mind.

*

> Pitiful are
> People who do not know
>> Nirvana and its eternal felicity!
> How they grieve
> At life, death, and mutability!

In our deepest nature, we are unborn, undying; but we do not know or forget this, and our life is one long endeavour to escape from the inevitable, to remain changeless in a world of change.

> Rain, hail, snow and ice
> Are divided from one another;
> But after they fall,
> They are the same water
> Of the stream in the valley.

Rain, hail, snow and ice are different forms of the same thing; so with enlightenment and illusion, goodness and badness, beauty and ugliness, truth and error. To know this in the head is to have knowledge; to know it in the body is to have wisdom.

> The figure of the Real Man
> Standing there,—
> Just a glimpse of him,
> And we are in love.

Home again. But what was home? The fish has the vast ocean for home. And man has timelessness and nowhere.

> Shaka, and Amida too,
> Were originally human beings;
> Have I not also
> The form of a man?

We see in the verse a rather deep difference between Christianity and Buddhism. According to the former, we are sons of God. According to the latter, we are God, not a part of God, not a slice of the cake, but the whole cake.

> The mind:
> Since there is really
> No such thing as mind,
> With what enlightenment,—
> Shall it be enlightened?

Enlightenment means knowing that there is no illusion, that is, it means knowing that there is no such thing as enlightenment.

> Though it has no bridge,
>   The cloud climbs up to heaven;
> It does not ask aid
>   Of Gautama's sutras.

Kudon is the transliterated form of Gautama. We, like the clouds, may climb to heaven by our own lightness, without asking the help of any words of wisdom.

> To harden into a Buddha is wrong;
> All the more I think so
> When I look at a stone Buddha.

It is the nature of man, (that is to say his biological nature,) to harden into something or other. Eternal life means having it without hardening, having it abundantly and over-flowingly.

> To write something and leave it behind us,
>   It is but a dream.
> When we awake we know
>   There is not even anyone to read it.

This verse is the conclusion of *The Skeleton*. It is in this transcendental spirit that Shakespeare wrote his plays, careless, so it seems, whether after all that labour and ecstasy they should survive in the form he wrote them, careless even whether they should survive at all.

> Our mind,—
> Without end,
>   Without beginning,
> Though it is born, though it dies,—
> The essence of emptiness!

> The mind remaining
>   Just as it was born,—
> Without any prayer
>   It becomes the Buddha.

This verse expresses in gently poetic words what is coldly and philosophically stated as: All men have the Buddha nature.

Look at the cherry blossoms!
Their colour and scent fall with them,
Are gone for ever,
Yet mindless
The spring comes again.

Here again we have the same lesson. When the flowers
fall, scent and hue disappear with them, but the next spring
some unseen, unthinking, unthought power makes them bloom
again with the same perfume and colour. Emily Brontë says:

When it blows,
The mountain wind is boisterous,
But when it blows not,
It simply blows not.

When the wind blows, it blows mindlessly; when it does
not blow, it is mindlessly calm. Nothing comes into existence
or goes out of existence. Things *simply* happen or *simply* do
not happen.

The mind,—
What shall we call it?
It is the sound of the breeze
That blows through the pines
In the Indian-ink picture.

There are other phrases which express the nature of the
mind, for example, the sound of one hand clapped, the sound
of the voice of a crow that does not crow on a dark night, a
man's shape before he is born. All these are to convey the idea
that the mind is not something, though it is not nothing, for
after all, we do see and feel something in the picture of the
pine trees.

He fell ill and died suddenly on the 21st of November
1481 at the age of eighty-eight. His death poem is said to be
the following:

Dimly, for thirty years;
Faintly for thirty years,—
Dimly and faintly for sixty years:
At my death, I pass my faeces and offer them to
Brahma.

> Whenever we see them, all are
>   Just as they are:
> The willow is green,
>   The flower is red.

The willow is green. But in reality, we say, it is colourless. This is so. But at the same time, it is green. When we know it has no colour, then for the first time we see how deeply green it is.

> The crescent moon
> Becomes full, and wanes,
>   And nothing is left;
> But still, there in the dawn,
> The crescent moon!

> The mind cannot become the Buddha;
>   The body cannot become the Buddha;
> Only what cannot become the Buddha
>   Can before the Buddha.

Ikkyū asserts here the unqualifyability, the indefinability, and yet the reality of the Buddha.

> The vast flood
>   Rolls onward
> But yield yourself,
>   And it floats you upon it.

When we realize that we do not live, but *are lived* by some "power, not ourselves, that makes for righteousness," we float down the stream of time never submerged, because we always do what Stevenson tells us to do, "travel light."

> On the sea of death and life,
> The diver's boat is freighted
>   With "Is" and "Is not";
> But if the bottom is broken through,
> "Is" and "Is not" disappear.

To get rid of the relativity of the outer world is impossible. What we can do is to break through the bottom of our own desiring and loathing.

> As Ikkyū does not think of his body
> As if it were his body,
> He lives in the same place,
> Whether it is town or country.

It is a mistake to live in solitude, whether it is a city or a mountain recess. We are alone with our closest friend; even Robinson Crusoe was not alone on his island.

> How marvellous,
> How god-like the mind of man!
> It fills the whole universe!
> It enters every mote of dust!

Emerson says:

> There is no great and no small
> To the soul that maketh all,
> But where it goes all things are,
> And it goeth everywhere.

but Ikkyū:

> I would like
> To offer you something,
> But in the Daruma Sect
> We have nothing at all.

This verse, so witty, so true, is one of Ikkyū's best. It might be used at a feast, or at a funeral.

RYŌKAN 1758–1831

The Japanese have no genius for religion, in the ordinary sense of the word. They can drink tea religiously, arrange flowers religiously, write poetry, paint pictures, build shrines religiously, even kill people religiously and go to the lavatory religiously, but they can't be just religious. In a church or a temple they look and feel hypocrites and dastards.

Ryōkan is not to be found in *Zenshu Jiten*, the Dictionary of Zen, or in the great Buddhist dictionaries, but appears quite prominently in Japanese literature and in the history of calligraphy. Indeed, not knowing otherwise, one would suppose that he belonged rather to the *tariki* side of Buddhism, to Jōdoshū or Shinshū than to Zenshū, and it is precisely this anti-social or rather non-social aspect of Ryōkan which is most interesting. However, it is not the scorn of the world of Tao Yunming or Yoshida Kenkō that we find in him. Ryōkan felt himself to be inferior, not superior, to ordinary people, and this was not due to any inferiority complex, but to the fact that he was, in fact, inferior to them, in everything but self-knowledge. He was actually a kind of fool. Sōma Gyofū, who has not only written many books about Ryōkan but really understands him, calls one of them *The Great Fool Ryōkan*, and this word "fool," if we grasp the significance of it, is the key to Ryōkan's life, and to his value as a human being. In the first chapter of the first *Epistle to the Corinthians*, Paul approaches to this meaning of foolishness, particularly in verse twenty five, where he says, "The foolishness of God is wiser than men; and the weakness of God is stronger than men." During the Middle Ages fools were much appreciated in Europe, and the fool in *King Lear* approximates, in his weakness, pathos, truthfulness, and understanding of the tragic nature of human life, to Ryōkan. But unlike the fool in *Lear*, Ryōkan had no desire to teach royalty its duties. Being himself a child of God, a child of Buddha, a child of nature, Ryōkan was in his element with children:

> How happy I am
> As I go hand in hand
> With the children,
> To gather young greens
> In the fields of spring!

He often reproached himself, but never for his way of life. He did not hold up either, however, as a model for others. Each man, Ryōkan probably thought, must (and anyway does) live according to his own nature. The only thing is, what is this particular man's nature? Ryōkan: A poor weak creature who did nothing for mankind but lived a life as humble as that of woodlouse,—how is it that this simpleton, this simple Simon can touch our hearts so deeply in this age of power and pride of service? He did not, like Thoreau, work even three days a week:

> The wind brings enough
> Of fallen leaves
> To make a fire.

We may wish to think of him as an artist, as a poet, as (what he was) a great calligrapher, but he himself says:

> There are three things I dislike: poems by a poet, handwriting by a calligrapher, and food by a cook.

Ryōkan never preached, never tried to push anyone into Heaven. Like Christ in Lawrence's *The Man Who Died*, he could say, "The teacher and saviour are dead in me." He never did any good deeds, and lived freely as he wished, yet he was admired and beloved by all the villagers. No one wanted to poison or crucify him.

> What a happy thing it is
> To listen to the frogs
> In the mountain fields,
> Stretched at full length
> In my thatched hut!

But on the other hand, he could not forget the misery of the times, the decay of the Military Government of the Tokugawa, the decadence of people, the suicide of his own father, the vulgarity, the scoffing (even senryu itself was now degenerating). He could not help grieving for the world outside.

On the one hand the life of Ryōkan was that of quietness and purity, and it had its profound pleasure, just like that of Wordsworth at the cry of the cuckoo, or the sight of the glow-worm.

> Though I think
> Not to think about it any more,
> I do think about it,
> And wet my sleeves
> Thinking about it.

As he grew older his soul became more lucid (full of light) more selfless, more unseparated from nature, more serene. His last poem:

> What shall I leave
> As a memento?
> Flowers in the spring,
> The *hototogisu* in summer,
> Tinted leaves of autumn.

We see then that Ryōkan was after all living by the Zen that he never spoke about, never even thought of. He lived in Zen just as the fish lives in the water or the bird in air. To the good, goodness is invisible; to the truthful (in action) there is no truth and untruth to be contrasted to each other, nor to be equated Ryōkan could have said as Thoreau did on his deathbed when asked if he had made his peace with God: "I have never quarrelled with Him." Ryōkan had much in common also with Hanzan, the Chinese hermit, but closest of all is the man described by Wordsworth in *A Poet's Epitaph:*

> He is retired as noon-tide dew,
> Or fountain in a noon-day grove;
> And you must love him, ere to you
> He will seem worthy of your love.

> But he is weak; both Man and Boy,
> Hath been an idler in the land;
> Contented if he might enjoy
> The things which others understand.

X | ZEN AND THE ARTS

An eminent Japanese art critic and devotee of Zen once said to me that there could be no Zen in Western art or literature since the word itself did not exist in any European language. This opinion betrays both an exclusiveness and an excessive respect for words which Zen itself deprecates. A thing, for example a physical or mental disease, or art itself, may exist while there is as yet no word for it; and many words in the dictionary, for instance, "unnatural," "divine," "purity," have practically no objects corresponding to them. Further, the word Zen is not Japanese; it is borrowed from China. But Zen is not a Chinese word; it was imported from India. Where did the Indians get it from?

*

Eastern Zen art always portrays *satori*, enlightenment, either in the person depicted or in the object as seen by the eye of the enlightened man. Western Zen art, on the contrary, very often shows us *mayoi*, illusion, irresoluteness, the divided mind, the unsatisfiable desire, that of *Faustus* and *Hamlet*. Such is the Greek statue (bronze) of the Boxer Resting, 3rd Century B.C. The strength and weariness, the hairy brutality and the pitiless pity (of the sculptor), the broken nose and thongs round the hand and arm, the powerful body and frown of stupidity,—it is the universe itself, and concentrated in the very turn of the head. Should this, and other examples of *mayoi*, seem strange to Japanese "Zenists," let them remember the most difficult doctrine of Zen, that illusion *is* enlightenment, enlightenment *is* illusion.

According to Shinichi Hisamatsu's recent book, *Zen to Bijutsu*, "Zen and (Chinese and Japanese) Art," Zen has seven characteristics as seen in painting, pottery, calligraphy, Nō, the tea ceremony, and so on; they are:

1. Asymmetry (avoidance of the geometrical and perfect; unsaintly saints)
2. Simplicity (black and white preferred)
3. Agedness (finished before it is begun; Wordsworth's "bare trees and mountains bare")
4. Naturalness (innocence; thought-less-ness; no compulsion)
5. Latency (the gentleness of the warrior; the subdued but not gloomy light of the tea-room; much in little)
6. Unconventionality (indifference to contradictions; no "Idea of the Holy")
7. Quietness (inner, not outer)

We should use these terms flexibly; they may include their apparent opposites. Quietness is heard in the roaring end of a Bach fugue, with *organo pleno*. It is seen in the writhing of a million maggots in rotting fish-heads. Unconventionality may be expressed in the wearing of a silk hat and frock coat. Zen has latency (*yūgen*) but is not symbolic. It is deep, but easy. Zen is natural, but there is little Zen in children and none in animals, which are near-machines. We must become children, but a man who has become a child is not merely a child.

Each of the above qualities is necessary; none can be omitted, because they are different names of the same nameless thing which is not a thing. When one is absent, all are absent. To these seven I wish to add four more:

8. Freedom (absolute freedom—to be symmetrical if we want to)

9. Humour (includes paradox and contradiction, and the blessedness which we attain to in their perception)
10. Sexuality ("Eternity is in love with the productions of time"; this sexual relation between man and the world is Zen, and enlightenment is its orgasm; "All nature is my bride," says Thoreau. Those human and necessary elements, sadism and masochism, are included here.)
11. Joy (youthfulness, Blake's *Glad Day*; the early Wordsworth's universe)

Applying the last four qualities, prominent in Western art, to some alleged examples of Zen in Eastern art, we may say that Liang K'ai *Sakyamuni Coming Out of the Mountains* looks at first sight quite sexless, but when we examine his eye we see a subdued passion in it like that in the eye of Bach. Again, where is the humour? Look at his feet. On the other hand, the famous Zen garden of Ryōanji Temple, consisting of sand and huge stones only, seems to me too deathly, sexless, joyless; it is the universe as a machine. These stones are not "deep in admiration." Again, Hiroshige's landscapes are not Zen because they are too good, too poetical; nothing is left to the imagination. The Ise Shrines, with all their purity, simplicity and quietness, lack freedom,—and lack one, lack all. Zen art is the primitivism and unselfconsciousness of the savage together with the timelessness and cosmic consciousness of the saint or sage. Zen is religious, not moral; poetical not beautiful; intuitionistic, not intellectual; significant, not emotional; sensual, not philosophical; youthful, not world-weary.

Zen is not "an Oriental thing," but again Western Zen is not Eastern Zen. A man's Zen is not a woman's Zen. My Zen is not your Zen. It is the same, yes, but it is different. We must be on our guard against oneness, against the absolute. We must protect the individual. We must protect ourselves. We shall find the last four qualities far more in evidence in Western than in Eastern Zen, but they should be present (if only as No. 5, latency) in Eastern Zen also. These eleven characteristics are not necessarily visible and tangible; but they cannot be absent. Any work of art, therefore, which is a-sexual, or anti-sexual, which is completely without any cos-

Nō: "Okina", the black masked Sambasō

mically comical elements, which is joyless, or is limited, or stinks of Zen, lacks Zen. Further, the judgement of a work of art is, however often repeated or revised, an immediate, single, unified act, a unifying of the perceiver and the thing perceived. These seven or eleven or sixty-five qualities, or what not, are thus only so many separate intellectual justifications and confirmations of a single artistic unity. In this sense Zen is momentary, or rather momental, or more strictly speaking, non-successive, not cumulative, because timeless. (Da Vinci spent four years on *Mona Lisa*, trying to get woman's Zen into it.)

*

We say, "There is Zen in this picture, no Zen in that," but this is not really correct. If we, and the picture or words or whatever it is, are undivided, there is Zen, and not otherwise. Or to speak more exactly, when I am it and it is I, and at the same time I am I and it is it, there is Zen. Thus, "There is no Zen in this picture" is really the judgement that it was painted for and with money or fame or imitation or habit or stupidity, not with Zen, and it is therefore difficult to get Zen into or out of it. Also, to say, "This has some Zen," or "more Zen" is absurd because Zen is not a thing, not a principle, not a force, not a cause or an effect of anything. What we really mean then by saying, "There is Zen in Rembrandt's self-portrait (that of 1658), in Hogarth's *Shrimp-girl*," is that Zen is easily seen in that face, that eye. It sinks into the mind effortlessly, the mind that "watches and receives."

*

The idea of sacred and profane art, of religious and secular literature, is a preposterious one, only to be entertained by those who have no idea of what religion and poetry are. The question, "Can art be a substitute for religion?" is simply saying, "Can religion be a substitute for religion?" And if it is pointed out that many artists were dissolute men, then let us answer firmly that Christ and Buddha were fanatical, pettifogging, women-hating, fig-tree-destroying people. When sacred really equals profane, we have Zen.

Tolstoy, in *What is Art?* 1896, declares that what is incomprehensible to the majority of men is not real art. The indifference of the mass of people to aesthetic matters is more justified than many suppose. We wonder today at the profundity and beauty of Shakespeare's plays, written for a mixed Elizabethan audience. The *ukiyoe* of the 18th century were made for and sold to a public that now seems hardly to exist. I believe that this condition of affairs today is due not so much to the spoiling of popular taste by commercialism, as to the false values and dead artificiality of the high-brows. Lawrence speaks of those "directing all their subtle evil will against any positive living thing, masquerading as the ideal in order to poison the real." But after all, you can't fool all the people all the time; goodness, like murder, will out.

*

The enemies of culture are many; art for art's sake, dilettantism; cynicism and facetiousness; ordinary stupidity and superficiality; sensationalism; infatuation with society, inability to be alone; lack of balance between the new and the old; artistic snobbishness; above all, sentimentality. Culture is on the one hand the most delicate thing in the world; on the other hand it is what enables a man to endure all the slings and arrows of outrageous fortune.

*

"Vulgarity" is perhaps the most difficult word in the language to define; it is almost equally difficult to illustrate, and this shows how near it is to culture itself. Heaven and hell are but a hair's breadth away from each other; there is no neutral ground. It may be said that the greatest writers have no vulgarity or sentimentality; they are not to be found in Homer or Shakespeare, in Milton or Wordsworth, in Bashō or Buson. In Goethe, Cervantes and Dante, however, I find some insensitiveness and cruelty at least. Nevertheless, one cannot say what vulgarity is, for it is vulgar to do so. It is not exactly insensitiveness or stupidity, for animals may have these, but they are never vulgar. It is in the will, in the choosing of what is low, loving the worse rather than the better, quantity than quality. We feel this vulgarity deeply and painfully, for it makes us doubt the ultimate goodness of the universe.

*

In European painting, Picasso's *Head of a Faun* on a plate is subject to the suspicion that it has received some indirect influence from Zen, but anyway it has all the eleven elements of Zen without being in the least imitative of Oriental art, or tending to abstraction; it has always given me an extreme joy. The same objection, that he may have been affected by Chinese and Japanese painting, can be made to Klee, who is full of Zen, so let us take Rousseau, who is so realistic and minute, his materials so individual and even provincial, that his Zen is different from anything we find in the Zen paintings of China and Japan. The jungle pictures are all excellent, especially the *Charmeuse de Serpents* and *Eve*, both of 1907, the feeling of age being given in the former by the wooden face and rope-like hair of the naked woman; in the latter by the old-world flamingoes and the snakes, and the dark color of the right half of the picture. But it is in *La Bohémienne Endormie*, 1897, that we see Rousseau's Zen most vividly. This will be quite clear if we simply repeat the list of eleven points; asymmetry, simplicity, agedness, naturalness, latency, unconventionality, quietness, freedom, humour, sex, joy. This picture has the only good kind of mysticism, that which does not stink of religion. The Zen is in the lion's tail, which stretches out in the Void (*kū*), just like Gutei's finger (*Mumonkan*, No. 3). The eye of the lion is that of Mu Ch'i's *Bull-headed Shrike on a Pine Tree*. The eye sees through us into the universe. "*Tiere sehen dich an.*"

*

For the Zen artist, the problem is how to make manifest the meaning of the empty space in a picture. *Mousehold Heath* by Crome in the National Gallery in London is a fine sky which too often in European landscape painting is filled with trees, or at least with clouds. The earth exists to give meaning to the sky, which again has no significance without the withered stretch of ancient heath, the path over it, the shepherd and the animals. The small sketch by Girtin reproduced in *Zen in English Literature* has a Zen-less Zen that leaves us with nothing to say about it.

To see this same Zen in Goya's *Los Proverbios* and *Los Desastres de la Guerra* needs some courage, some energy of mind. The Chinese and Japanese are too sentimental (in art) to have anything like the truth of these sketches. Oriental artists have to the full the willing acceptance of Marcus Aurelius and Epictetus, but not enough of the Greek loathing of death, not sufficient appreciation of pure violence, of motiveless malignity. The ancient Central Americans and the Spaniards excelled in this latter. Zuoaga, a modern painter, who died in 1945, never made a sketch for any of his pictures. *The Dwarf* is full of Zen. We see the Divine Ugliness, the Cosmic Bestiality in this hideous, under-sized creature carrying two over-sized dead hogs. But he is not rejected by us. Under him also are the Everlasting Arms. And has not a pig, dead or alive, the Buddha-Nature? El Greco has this Spanish Zen. His *View of Toledo* is really a View of the Universe. Bridges leap, roads wind, houses rise, churches soar, above them a mild and whirling sky. In all this we invisible human beings are irresistibly and inveterately involved. There is no union of man and nature, for there was never any division. The still small voice and the thunders of this Sinai are the deafening silence of Vimalakirti.

*

The Zen of Blake's paintings seems at first sight somewhat eccentric, but upon closer and deeper examination we see they have also the general Zen characteristics. God is white-haired, but has no wrinkles. Satan is as handsome as the best of them. All of Blake's figures have both poise and energy. They fly without wings. Joy is felt in every line. Everything is strange and new, but nothing is distorted. The trees and flowers, the sun and moon are as sexual as the human beings, who also are naked and unashamed. Nothing is fixed or dead, "for unto him all live."

*

Claude Lorrain, born in 1600, was apparently an uneducated and ignorant man, who got others to draw the human figures in his landscapes, but the *Liber Veritatis*, which Turner tried so vainly to surpass in *Liber Studiorum*, has drawings of trees and hills (pen and wash) in which we feel all nature involved. His regular paintings are overlaid with romance and mythology, but these sketches show his earthy feeling for

Archer, Sanjusangendo, Kyoto

earth, fiery for fire, airy for air, watery for water. Indeed it is in the sketches by Girtin, Crome, Rembrandt, Ruysdael and others that we often find Zen, smothered by externals and details in completed pictures.

Let us take a picture in the Louvre, No. 1322, by Ghirlandajo, *An Old Man and His Grandchild*. The realism of the old man contrasts with the formality of the landscape, and with the poor painting of the child's hand. The Zen is in the nose of the old man, or rather, in the eye of his grandchild, who gazes at it with the greatest simplicity. He really sees it, and, "All that we behold is full of blessings." The ugly excrescences on the nose, beloved by the child, "spoils the picture," according to an English art critic. "Listen to the fool's reproach, it is a kingly title!" Zen is indeed what spoils. It spoils beauty, it spoils morality, intellectuality, emotionality, abstract truth, religion, art, literature, science.

*

Going farther back, Piero della Francesca's *Nativity*, in the National Gallery, has the serene inner power of symbolic Christianity. God lies on the cushion in the form a a babe. Statuesque but graceful maidens sing a solemn but joyous song. The ground is dry and sandy, the stable ruined, grass grows on the roof, but,

> All's right with his heaven!
> God's on the earth.

We feel Zen in the benignant severity of Giotto, the greatest concentration of it being in the kiss of Judas in the garden of Gethsemane (the fresco in the church of Maria del Arena). Christ and Judas went at each other with the same intentness and intensity with which the monk looks on as the two cocks fight in the pictures by Liang K'ai and Niten (Miyamoto Musashi).

*

One of the elements of Zen in Christianity is the God-man nature of Christ. With the Flemish school Christ becomes indeed too human. Blake says:

> Thou art a Man, God is no more,
> Learn thy own Humanity to adore.

This is Zen; adoration also is necessary. Some of the best examples of Zen in Christian art, especially that greatest of all subjects, the Crucifixion, are found in Byzantine churches from the 6th to the 11th century. At this time Roman naturalism was being blended with Near Eastern methodology; the material and the spiritual attained a temporary balance.

We must not confuse Zen or *Zen-mi*, the taste of Zen, with Zen taste, *Zen-teki na shumi*. There is a tendency for people to like quietness and solitude as they grow older. But age is not in itself good, any more than youth is. It is the perfect combination of both which gives us the excellence of *Don Quixote* and the Parthenon. The East is more passive, the West more active. But passivity, as Wordsworth said, must be "wise," and activity that of "unmoved mover."

There remain many problems still unsolved: Is there any relation between Zen and the creation or appreciation of art? Does one increase the other? Can a man go to (be in) Heaven who has bad taste? Is Zen itself good taste? Is Zen perhaps God's Taste?

ZEN AND MUSIC

Primitive music was heard as something magical, and this is already Zen, for Zen is magic, what Emerson called "charm," that makes the sun forgotten. And from the beginning, we must suppose, both in the rhythm of the dancing and the rise and fall of the sounds, the magic was the sound-silence, the motionless movement, the difference sameness. There is no other magic. All the rest is bunkum. We do not know anything of ancient Greek or Chinese music, but when we think of Plato's ban on tragedy, and of what Confucious and the Tang poets said of music, we can guess how much we have lost,—in Zen rather than music in the ordinary sense of the word. Greek music was all melodic, with a similar value perhaps to that of a Bach solo violin or cello. Chinese music, like Korean, was harmonic in a philosophic sense, the clay, metal, wood, and instruments of other materials giving us literally the music of the spheres.

The most remarkable thing about real music, by which I mean polyphonic Zen, is the change from melody to harmony, that is, from horizontal to vertical. It is said that two-part singing was practised in the 9th century in Europe. In England part-singing was already popular in the 12th century. To say two things at once is not possible in words, but it can be done both in painting and in musical polyphony. It is interesting to note the Spenglerian fact that when three-part organa and three-part motets were being written in the 13th century, there was also a combining of the religious and secular, a mixing of the hymns of the church and the songs of the jongleurs. When sacred really equals profane, we have Zen.

The music of Palestrina, 1525–94, has an excessive purity and other-worldliness. It lacks earthiness, and joie-de-vivre. (It is odd, by the way, how many qualities are necessary for Zen. And if one is missing all are missing.) In England, the madrigals of Morley, Wilbye, and Weelkes have a Shake-spearean naturalness and at the same time ingenuity, but they lack the German mysticism of Scheidt which led to the Zen of Bach. Byrd and Purcell have not only mysticism, but Zen also, especially in some of their lighter, purely instrumental works. The chorale is of the essence of Zen. Zen in music can be tested to some extent by the importance of the bass. The *basso ostinato* of the 17th century, the passacaglias of Bux-tehude and Bach are particularly important in this respect. It is a pleasure to play the accompaniment only, even the left hand only, of Bach's viola da gamba sonatas; this "pleasure" is Zen. Handel's bass is strong, but often merely pom-pom-pom.

*

The opera, which more or less begins with Monteverdi's *Orfeo*, 1607, has not a spark of Zen in it, even when Mozart writes it. The operatic element in *The Messiah* makes it odious, and it even spoils the *Matthew Passion*. Music is not emotion. Music is Zen. A certain amount of emotion and thought and beauty may be added to music, as we put salt in cakes to bring out the sweetness, but salt and sugar are different things.

Bach is Zen itself. Like Zen he absorbed everything. Like Zen, everything he wrote wrote itself. The only way to de-

scribe this naturalness, the self-full selflessness of Bach's music
is to quote from *A Week on the Concord* concerning literature:

> As naturally as the oak bears an acorn and the vine a
> gourd, man bears a poem, either spoken or done. . . .
> Homer's song is a vital function like breathing, and an
> integral result like weight. . . . He is as serene as nature,
> and we can hardly detect the enthusiasm of the bard.

Bach is more full of contradictions than Hamlet. Classic and
romantic, abstract and pictorial, traditional and original, ancient and modern, introspective and impersonal, calm and
poignant, he is like Shakespeare in that every work is a self-
portrait, yet he remains an enigma; others abide our question.

The Zen of Bach, however, does not lie in these paradoxes
or in the mystery of his character. It consists in the fact that
everything he wrote is faultless. He has the ear that never
sleeps, the hand that never slackens; he is never weary in
well-doing. His Zen is adumbrated in Cecil Gray's rhetorical
question in *The History of Music:*

> Was he a musical alchemist who had discovered a kind
> of philosopher's stone, some formula of construction
> which enabled him to transmute the basest material into
> purest gold?

The Art of Fugue is pure Zen from beginning to end.
When we hear it first it seems dark and gloomy, dry and lifeless, but if we play it often, at last it loses this character, and
we hear it as we see the rising and setting of the sun, the
procession of the seasons, life and death, men coming and
going on the earth. *The Art of Fugue* means free necessity, a
willed necessity.

*

Any man who thinks Handel "stands as little below Bach
as Bach is below him," has no understanding of Bach, in other
words, knows nothing of Zen, that is, of music. Handel has
no Zen. He has the solidity which Telemann lacked, due to
his respect for the bass, but he has no poetry, no depth, no
complexity; he is only, musically speaking, "a jolly good fellow." For the same reason, Haydn has no Zen. Mozart is full

of it, and yet sometimes, when we come in at the middle of a quartet or early symphony, we can hardly tell at first whose it is. As far as the form goes, Haydn, Mozart, and Beethoven adopt the new kind of solo melody in their sonatas, with alterations of it between the instrument and the piano. The world was growing cheaper, more vulgar, sensational, sentimental, romantic. People were tired of listening to contrapuntal music; they were tired of Zen. They wanted their ears tickled, their heart-strings pulled, their lachrymal glands squeezed. An example is Haydn's Emperor's Hymn used in a set of variations for a string quartet. Another example is the Fugues of Wilhelm Friedrich, Bach's eldest and most gifted son. They have all the sentimentality which Bach had not, and lack all the poetry which Bach had. The Zen of Mozart by which he defied the times, and which caused his death, is not in the violin concertos, or even the piano concertos, but in the trio for piano, clarinet, and viola, the quintets for strings, the oboe quartet, where inexorable fate moves slowly or swiftly, but never unwillingly. We feel that Mozart died before he composed each piece of music. Beethoven's Zen is almost always smothered by his emotion, by his strong will, by the crudeness of his thinking. Beethoven alternates between war and peace, the male and the female, joy and grief, but sometimes his anger is just, and his sweetness is piercing.

*

The romantics fell lower still, though not so low as we. Schubert never wrote a line of music. It is all feeling, either bombast or self-pity. His songs are truly wild roses and garden roses, but a rose has no Zen. Schumann, who admired Schubert so much, has moments, in some of his symphonies, when a valiant spirit raises him above emotion into a heroic world that is selfless. Selflessness is Zen. Mendelssohn has no asceticism, but also has a few moments, as in the *Hebrides Overture* and in the beginning of the *Scotch Symphony*. The *Midsummer Night's Dream* music is only the chattering of monkeys. It has little of the pseudo-poetry of Shakespeare, and none of his real magic, the fairy world of living creatures. Weber is cheap, with the breathless mysticism of the German forests, and a gorgeousness that wearies in the end. Zen is always homely and friendly, in spite of its sternness. Bizet has some Zen in him. Carmen is in the line of Medea and Lady Macbeth. It is a woman's Zen, beyond passion. The "I am I" is so strongly expressed that we find it the counterpart of the Upanishad "I am you." It is not Zen, but it is Half-Zen. Most so-called Zen is this Half-Zen.

Liszt is wallowing in emotion, like Rachmaninoff, but Berlioz has something in him. He follows himself, and owns no other kin. He has the fault of exhibitionism, but his programme music is often music when the pure music of others is classical dullness. Wagner is all that Zen is not. A false simplicity, a bulging, over-sexual grandeur, a unity gained by combining all the values except Zen, masochism and sadism, the devotedness of woman, the sinfulness of man, eternity and infinity, false tragedy, fantastic mythology, cabbalism, Catholicism, Buddhism,—what a pot-pourri it all is! and "pourri" is the right word, for what he who is not for us is against us, and what is not Zen has a pernicious, a poisoning effect upon the world.

XI | ZEN AND NŌ

Any kind of life whatever, may rightly be called an escape; the question is whether we escape from reality to unreality, or from unreality to reality. The tea ceremony, landscape gardening, Nō, the composition of 31-syllable verse were 14th century examples of the latter type of escape. The feudalistic system, the Communist, the Christian, the Buddhist systems are all forms of unreality (as systems) from which we must flee into the real, the poetical world, that is, the world of everyday poetical life of our own creation.

Nō was time seen as eternal, history glorified yet saddened by the Buddhist thought of impermanence, "battles long ago" remembered in the pitying heart. Nō combined three forms of culture, music, dancing, and poetry, but by the genius of two men, father and son, Kan-ami and Zeami, it was lifted out of the triviality of opera. The "dancing" enabled the spectators to see the past as present, the distant as near, the impersonal as personal, the existent as nonexistent. The Nō-actor walks as though not walking; the mask smiles and weeps without the slightest change of expression. This is God-like; this is Zen.

In speaking about Zen, especially in its relation to forms of culture, it is necessary always to bear in mind the difference

Nō : "Okina", Sambasō's dance

between Zen as a "system" of paradoxes evolved in India and China during a period of three thousand years, and Zen as Zen, that is, the spontaneous, individually created timeless-activity-in-time of an undivided mind-body. This is the substratum, the continuum, the *basso ostinato* of the former, the historically developed consciousness of Zen.

"Zen is not a religion; it is religion . . ."

The actual historical connection between Zen and Nō is extremely difficult to make out, and not so charming when we do so. Kan-ami and Zeami were patronised by the 3rd Ashikaga Shōgun, Yoshimitsu, and it is asserted and repeated that Yoshimitsu's interest in and knowledge of Zen were somehow or other communicated to them. It is doubtful whether the understanding of Zen on the part of Kan-ami and Zeami, both theoretical and practical, was very much wider and deeper than that which Shakespeare displayed in *King Lear* of the ancient Druidic religion. Moreover, Yoshimitsu seems to have been a pretty awful sort of chap, and his interest in Zen may well have been because of its non-moral character, justifying the antisocial arts of sculpture, the tea-ceremony, Nō and such, as well as the slaughter, of family and opponents by which a shōgun attained or retained his power.

The Zen of Nō is the movement of the body-mind of the actor, especially visible in the (apparent) slow-motion, where eternity shows itself in love with the productions of time. On the Nō stage the illimitable is freely and perfectly limited. How is this done? As said before, in the mind-body of the performer, who travels from one province to another in a single step; who lives in the past more fully than we do in the present, who is more Hecuba than he is himself. "The mind is its own place." As literature also, Nō plays are full of Zen, not only in the poetry, and the inevitability of the outworking of the simple plot, but even in the word-play common throughout these dramas. As Herbert said, "by mere playing we go to Heaven." Christ is said to have founded his Church on a pun, and word-play is justified by the Zen notion that any word (thing) may mean anything because all words (things) are equal just as all men are, being infinite in (poetical) meaning.

The Buddhism of the Nō plays is of several kinds. There is the mystical, or rather symbolic and shamanistic Buddhism of the Shingon sect, seen in the priests in *Sotoba Komachi*, and the *yamabushi* of *Tanikō* and other plays. Then there is the ordinary popular Buddhism of the Amida sects, whose aim was salvation and the Western Paradise. The dramatic value of *karma*, rewards and punishments in the next life (lives) was fully and rightly utilised in a great many of the Nō plays. (Rightly, because every heroic or villainous life is felt as extending beyond the limit of physical death.) The paradoxical views of the Zen sect seem to be taken as detrimental to the holders of them (with the possible exception of Komachi in *Sotoba Komachi*), as for example Shunkan in the play of that name, and Nobutoshi in *Hokazō*. It is odd, by the way, that Komachi, whose Zen is so brilliant and poetical, is a woman. She belongs to a remarkable group. Medea, Cleopatra, the Wife of Bath, Lucy (Wordsworth's), and Mrs. Gamp. We cannot help feeling, however, that there is something dangerous about her Zen also—she is in fact a kind of murderess of her lover—and her arguments are amoral and destructive. She is therefore victorious as women always are and as Zen always is.

Nō plays themselves have something either lacking or excessive in their nature, too much seriousness, or too little humour for example, too much heroism or too little humanity. (You can't have too much Zen. You can't relieve the strain of Zen by reading a detective story. The only alternative to Zen is nothingness, sleep or death.) If a Nō play cannot stand by itself, it must be called lacking in Zen, that is, in some kind of perfection, totality.

The Zen of kyōgen [the comical interludes which alternate with Nō plays] is that of the Artful Dodger in *Oliver Twist*, of Master Bailey in *Martin Chuzzlewit*, of Mr. Pepys; a certain shamelessness as opposed to the excessive contrition of Nō. According to Nō, the universe is a tragedy, in which certain values are thereby made possible. For kyōgen the world is a comedy, and this comicality, when perceived-created, is itself a value. Kyōgen criticises power and rank, though usually everything comes out all right for the Lord in the end,

Nō : the orchestra and masked Shite

as it does in the actual world. It criticises Buddhism as being superstitious, and the monks for the flagrant contradictions between their precepts and their practice. Above all it is critical of Nō for supposing that because some people are virtuous there shall be no cakes and ale; in other words, it objects to the religious idea that happiness is incompatible with blessedness. Zen never weeps, it always laughs, laughs at the wonder of the world, its fantastic nature. Thus Zen is in a way closer to kyōgen than to Nō, but kyōgen lacks the depth of Nō. It was therefore an act of genius on the part of the founders of Nō to alternate it with kyōgen. Zen is indeed not alternation; but in the world of time alternation is inevitable. In the absolute world there is no alternation, but Zen is not in the absolute world. It belongs to the absolute relative world, so that a performance of five Nō plays with three kyōgen between them is the nearest that art can get to Zen,—as far as the question of tragedy and comedy is concerned. It should be noted further that women, who are so conspicuously omitted in Zen, that is, the Zen of the Zen sect, play an important part, play their important part in both Nō and kyōgen. Nō is as far from being sexless as Zen should be; we see this in *Sotoba Komachi*, which is both a love-story and a Zen debate.

The gorgeous costumes, the ceremonious diction, the aristocratic, unworldly atmosphere,—what have these to do with the simplicity, austerity, democracy, and everyday-ness of Zen? The costumes are a concession to human weakness and insensitivity. When we see a man in his underwear, or naked, we have the illusion that he is a poor forked radish, fantastically carved about the head. When we see a king in his robes, we perceive the richness, the dignity of every man; the purple without reminds us of the royalty within. In Zen itself we often get examples of the florid and flowery expressing the state of enlightenment. On the other hand, the extreme simplicity of gesture and dancing is the same thing in reverse. It is but one activity . . .

What is the relation of Nō to Zen? In the light of all that has been (unnecessarily?) already said, we may now restate the question: What is the relation between the value of Nō,

Nō: "Kumasaka": the demon exorcized.

that is, the Zen of Nō, and Zen? Clearly, the second "Zen" must refer to what was termed at the beginning of this essay, the Zen of timeless-activity-in-time. The Zen of Nō is indubitable. It comes in the poetry, in the Buddhist teaching and atmosphere (Zen is supposed to be the essence of Buddhism). It derives also from the fact that Kan-ami and Zeami were not only dramatic authors but actors; Zen is meaningful activity. The real question then is this: What is the relation of Nō to the Zen *sect*, and its non-teachings? And this is part of a larger problem: are the highest forms of culture (real culture is another name for Zen) related to historical Zen, the Zen which has its beginnings 3,000 years ago in the *Upanishads* and still continues in the works of Suzuki Daisetz? Does not Zen spontaneously appear in the choral preludes of Buxtehude, *Alice in Wonderland*, the paintings of Rousseau, the Nō plays? In all these it may not be possible to trace the devious and unsuspected routes by which the Zen of the *Upanishads* was carried to Asia and Europe via Buddhism and gnosticism and mysticism generally, but it seems probable in every case, as with *Cha no Yu* and *Ikebana* and *Bushidō*, that some external stimulus aroused that Zen which we must believe to be latent in every man. The doctrines of Zen were necessary to produce the doctrine-less Zen of the Nō plays.

But these two "Zens" are not really two. There is no Zen in a principle or a dogma, but Zen is not wordless. There is no Zen in mere silence. Zen is meaning, so that when silence and stillness really mean something, and voices and flutes and drums really mean something, in any place, at any time, there is Zen.

*

XII | ZEN, SEX, AND LOVE

The least admirable part of Buddhism is its attitude to sex. The Buddha accepted women into the Sangha with the utmost unwillingness, and indeed prophesied that they would be the ruin of his system. It is said that in this matter the Buddha "should not be judged by the standards of the twentieth century." This is not so. He should be judged by the standards of the thirtieth. If a man's views of half the world are wrong, his view of the other half must be so too. In actual fact one of the reasons for the decline of Buddhism in India was the resurgence of Tantrism with its female deities and esoteric eroticism. The same thing has happened in modern times to Christianity, only the sex-worship is extra-church.

Zen is the infinite meaning which finite things have by virtue of their potential oneness with humanity, this "things" including the fifth leg of a horse, and the Middle of Next Week. Sex is the great driving power of the world; it is what causes men and women to re-unite physico-spiritually. It is part of the larger cosmic urge to join and to separate, the centripetal and centrifugal forces of the universe. Love has a three-fold character, Eros, Agape, and Philia. Eros is self-seeking, Agape self-renouncing, Philia mutually self-fulfilling. The combination of all three is the meaning of "God is love."

Zen and sex and love are similar, in their universality, unavoidability, and omnipotence. They are different, in that the aim of sex, or rather sexual intercourse is physical relief, but the aim of love is not psychical relief, except in so far as loneliness is unbearable. The aim of love is to love more, to be in closer and closer contact with the thing or person loved. The aim of sex is pleasure; the aim of love is blessedness; at the same time they are aimless, intrinsic value. Zen is aiming, when the aim is love or blessedness, that is, when there is no aim, no no-aim.

Modern psychology, psychology since Freud, has debunked love, and will soon debunk Zen; sex never needed debunking anyway. According to Reik, one of Freud's best disciples, love arises from envy, an envy which is the obverse of admiration. We "love" a person conceived as superior to ourselves, our "enemy," as a means of conquering him or her. This reduces love, both of and by man and God, to a mere egoism, but there is something fundamental and satisfying in this rational explanation which is lacking in religious rant about love.

When we look back over the history of Zen, we find not so much an antipathy to sex or a perversion of it such as we see in (monastic) Christianity, but rather a sublime indifference to it. Women do not appear in the anecdotes of the *Hekiganroku* or the *Mumonkan*. A book entitled *Zen for Women* has yet to be published, and as far as I am concerned is not yet in manuscript. What claim can Zen possibly have to universality when it ignores one half of humanity, and assumes sexlessness, that is halflessness, in the other? There used to be much talk of "sublimation," the transformation of the energy of sex into some other form, for example aesthetic. But this explanation begs the question here, which is, is sex a means, or an end? The Zen answer, and anyway the correct one, is that sex is, like all other "things," an end in itself. Sex, that is the body-mind experience, is value and needs no metamorphosis. Thus sublimation is no way of escape from the problem. We must say then that there is and always has been something wrong with Zen in this respect, not that sex is perverted or repressed in the life of Zen, but that there is something vital lacking in Zen, and something unnatural in its (apparently real) indifference to the life of sex and love.

Zen cannot escape from sex, except by ignoring it, that is, by transcending it. But we cannot annihilate a thing by transcending it. Religion has always omitted women, as it has omitted nature, and human nature, but the result has been that religion has omitted itself.

The mistake which Zen has made is in wishfully believing that minds can be one though bodies are not. Body and mind are indissolubly united. They are identical. "That called body is a portion of soul discerned by the five senses"; Blake should rather have written, "Body is soul seen by the senses." If two bodies are two, the minds are two. Sexual intercourse is the vain attempt to break this law and unite what God hath put asunder.

We must never forget that the one thing in the world that is not a thing is Zen. International, transcendental, pure super-Zen has no existence. Buddha's Zen, and Daruma's Zen, and Enō's Zen and Rinzai's and Suzuki's and even perhaps Blyth's Zen, and certainly Mrs. Gamp's Zen, and the Wife of Bath's Zen,—but no Zen without them. Zen was produced, we say, in China, in other words and properer words, certain Chinese lived and moved and had their being in a way that we call Zen, a rather fish-like, loveless and sexless life. Fish-like Koreans and Japanese, and now Americans and Europeans are attracted to this Way of Life, a way that exists only in so far as there are travellers on it. The problem for us who are not fish-like, or wish we weren't, is—how shall we live a loving-sexual life of Zen? What is a sexual Zen? What is a loving Zen? These questions have yet to be answered in the experiences of living men and women; the answers must be "understood"; and they require further to be communicated from one person to another. Zen sex is like the other side of the moon, except that the latter is waiting to be discovered, the former to be created, if ever.

Is Zen unnecessary to women? Are they all born with it? How do women listen to music, read poetry, look at pictures? In these the timeless is seen in time, the spaceless in space, the

Mother and child, Otsu station

formless in form,—without being separated from time, space, and form. Can women do this? Women do not, I think, feel time so deeply; its dreadful inevitability. To that extent they cannot grasp the timeless, the timelessness of time, its time-fulness. When we listen to Brahms' *Alto Rhapsody*, with a *male* choir, do we hear what a woman knows of Brahms, or what Brahms knows of a woman?

The idea of retribution, the idea of law, of cause and effect is absent from her mind. Not only so, but the notions of guilt and remorse and atonement are very faint. There is no Emersonian doctrine of the instaneity of sin and its punish-ment by a feeling of transgression.

I asked a woman rōshi if the *satori* of a man and a woman are the same. "Of course!" she replied indignantly, but how could she know, an old woman of eighty who had never touched a man? How did she know what a man's *satori* is? Can a man know what another man's is? It is all guessing at best, and the superstition of oneness at worst.

In the history of the world men have used women, and women have used men, for their own purposes, so they sup-posed, but what really happened? It is possible to go from unrequited affection to Zen. Thoreau says, "All nature is my bride," and this means loving and being loved by Nature, which is a definition of Zen, but Thoreau also says something which sounds truer and deeper, "The only remedy for love is to love more," and "more" is qualitative, not quantitative. What I want to suggest now is the heterodox, not to say heretical idea, that the aim of Zen is to bring two people, preferably of the opposite sex, together, in other words, that the function of Zen is to remove the impediments to the mar-riage of true minds.

The theory of the matter is this. Two persons, hetero-sexual by (Nature's) preference, must have, or better, must be going to have the same feelings and thoughts about every-thing in the world, including themselves and one another. It should be noted that the feelings must be proper, and the thoughts right. It's no good having the same cruelty or the same stupidity. (What "proper" and "right" means is easy to explain. It is what I myself think is right and proper, today;

tomorrow of course I shall think differently.) To be more specific, these two imaginary people must love Bach and Bashō and Po Chüi and Eckhart and Cervantes and El Greco and animals and plants and the round ocean and the living air,— in the same way; this is the catch. Further, and equally important, they must hate the same things and the same persons, for the same reasons. I forgot to mention the most important part, the sexual parts. The two people must be in love with each other's bodies, the appetite growing with what it feeds on. All this is the ideal, and in the case of the real, each incongruity of attitude, every nuance of dissimilar feeling, all differences of judgement are to be felt as iron entering into the soul. A never-resting eagerness to enter into the other person's hopes and fears, a constant determination never to deceive oneself into seeing non-existent identities, and never to close the eyes to patent dissimilarities,—that is, the essence of such a pair.

The objection to this 50-year-plan are three: that it is impossible; it would be monotonous; and it is exhaustingly over-intense. As for its impossibility, this may be admitted; like peace on earth, and going to heaven, and the understanding of Zen, they are the heart's desire, and very easy not to achieve. But an ideal is something that however little we approach it, that little is what makes life worth living. The novels of the world are the accounts of the nonattainment of this union of souls.

The second objection, the monotonousness of such a condition, is also a valid one, but Nature kindly prevents all possibility of such ennui by making our span of life far too short to attain it. In addition, the differences of sex, nationality, environment, education and so on make the whole business so fantastic that monotony is the last objection to be made against it.

The third objection also, that it requires an enormous amount of nervous energy, that it is too conscious, too unnatural, involves us in ceaseless self-analysis and comparison, —this is only too true. Byron says that even love must have rest, and Thoreau that our best relations are buried under a positive depth of silence. But what is the alternative? Laziness, indifference, unloved, unloving loneliness, unknown, unknowing insensitiveness, infinity, eternity, happiness,—I had almost written Zen. What is the alternative to the alternative? Hours of anguish, moments of blessedness; mutual suspicion, mutual trust; withdrawal from the world.

A man's Zen is too talkative, too reasonable, even though it rightly generalises the particular. The woman's is too vague, but particularises the general. The answer then must be that both are better.

*

We may consider the question of women's Zen in a more technical, a more esoteric way. The most common kōan given to would-be Buddhas is that of *Mu*. What will a woman make of it? You may say, "The same as a man, for *Mu* is sexless," but this is a mistake, because a woman is not sexless, and a sexful person cannot grasp a sexless thing, any more than a sexless person can understand a sexful thing. A woman's mathematics is feminine, and a man's is masculine. A woman's man is female, a man's woman is male. This truth is a combination of Spengler and D. H. Lawrence, the idea that a person of one culture can never understand (the person of) another culture, and the idea that each thing has not only its own life and joy, as Wordsworth thought, but will and sex. But it may be asked, "Is there no such thing as transcending sex?" A man taught us to pray, "Our Father which art in Heaven." "The Church is the Bride of Christ." The angels in Heaven, who neither marry nor give in marriage—one would like to see them! . . .

*

Women are like nature; we can't understand them because there is nothing to understand. Zen is the same; we can't explain it because there is nothing to explain. The intellectual elements are completely dissolved in Nature and women and Zen. Only in men are they precipitated. The Zen of men also is inexplicable because the intellect is subsumed into the intuition. The Zen of a woman is inexplicable because she has no intellect. The Zen of women is a sort of pre-Zen. The Virgin Mary ascended into heaven, but she was not crucified. She never really died. The Zen of a man thus corresponds to

Western Zen, that of a woman to Eastern Zen. In some ways a man's Zen is better; it moves, and moves others. In some ways a woman's is better; it moves others without moving itself. A man must have a woman's Zen, and a woman must have a man's Zen. Impossible? All the better, for Zen is doing what is impossible, an imperfect human being doing something perfectly, and drinking up all the tea in the world out of one small cup.

*

People who love never speak of it,—and this goes for Christ too. Zen feels miserable when it is spoken about, and as for sex, "For God's sake hold your tongue and let me. . . ."

Material food must be spiritual; spiritual food must be material. "Man does not live by bread alone" is a mistake. "Man lives (also) by every word that proceedeth out of the mouth of God,"—this also is a mistake. We do not live half by this and half by that. We live by materio-spiritual bread. This is the teaching, though not clearly understood by the writer, of *Lady Chatterley's Lover*. The fact is that love, that is Zen, is psycho-physical, not partly body and partly mind.

We can judge Zen only by Zen, and from this point of view, that is, intuitively speaking, the woman's Zen is better. If a woman gives up her intuition and falls into intellectual dichotomy, she ceases to be a woman, she ceases to be anything. Women must avoid to ape men like the plague, but men must imitate women as far as possible. Of course a woman may pretend to think. In fact it is required in society and necessary in marriage, but it must be only pretending. A man must think, and believe that he is thinking, and his thought will remain to trouble him to the end of time. A women is *Mu* itself; she is submerged in it, suffused with it; this is her great power, her great attraction. She already is what man would attain to with his intellect. It is not possible, and that is why it must be done.

*

XIII | ZEN AND JAPAN

When Zen came to Japan (officially in the 12th century, but Buddhist sects also had of course Zen elements already in them), it continued at first to be a matter of monks and monasteries, of *zazen* and *kōans*, but the Japanese people were different from the Chinese, and also from the Indians, though there were common elements.

The chief common element was a lack of "rationality," and a corresponding lack of belief in its validity as a means of understanding a universe which is rational only in its rational and scientific aspect. Reason and logic, the Socratic method, were seen as correct, but as shallow, explaining nothing, only establishing a causal nexus which is totally unmeaning. Also common was the (dangerous and erroneous) idea or (falsely interpreted) experience that Truth, though not a thing in itself, is something once and for all attainable.

*

The Indians are soft, but somewhat sentimentally so, with their non-violence and ahimsa and excessively voluptuous or ascetic tastes. The Chinese are ruthless; without this violence of mind Zen would have been impossible. Sadism and Zen are deeply related, as we see also in Spain, for example in *Don Quixote*. The Japanese, however, (and this is a ticklish point) have no sense as the British have of a black and white justice, or abstract goodness. They can kill in a frenzy of fear, or (what is nearly the same) in a frenzy of patriotism, but mere killing, mere destruction, roughness, rudeness,—these are the antithesis of the Japanese spirit. Yet shininess, symmetry, slickness, Greek perfection, Chinese richness, are equally abhorrent. What the Japanese added to Zen was the most difficult thing in the world, simplicity; this was their own innate, potential Zen. Thoreau says that it (homeliness) "is almost as great a merit in a book as a house, if the reader would abide there." Japanese simplicity is seen most clearly in Shintō, which is a religion without a religious idea in it.

Zen, supposed to be the essence of Buddhism, is closest, not to the moralizing of Confucius or the philosophising of Buddha but to the silent bowing of the head before what is neither good nor bad, neither true nor untrue. To put the matter in another way, what happened to Zen when it came to Japan was that on the one hand it became aristocratic, in the artistic sense; Zen served poets and painters and sculptors in confirming their tastes, and deepest judgements of value. On the other hand, Zen spread among the common people, those who could not read or write, who were completely ignorant of the Mahayana philosophy, who did not and could not know, intellectually speaking, what Zen was, and had not heard even the word.

A native poetry and humor, these are what the Japanese added to Zen. The Chinese also had both, but their humour was too bucolic, too hard; their poetry was too Wordsworthian, too much concerned with mountains and skies, or with the vast sadness of

> Old, unhappy, far-off things
> And battles long ago.

Chinese Zen perhaps arose from, it was probably inspired, and certainly paralleled by the Taoism, the transcendentalism of Chuangtse and Laotse. But the 8th century Zen masters of China felt, rightly enough, that mysticism was as much a danger to the good life as Buddhist theology, and they emphasised the practice of Zen in daily life as against supernaturalism, as well as philosophising and verbal explanation.

Yet without abstraction and generalities, principles and dogmas, impossible ideals and ambitions, without, that is to say, the chance and the ability to reject these things, a man is not truly human. "Sell all thou hast!" is the command, and this applies to thought and judgement, idealisation, and the perception of truth, and goodness, and beauty. Only a rich man can become truly poor. Only an adult can be as a little child.

*

The Japanese wanted to make every detail of daily life significant, not so much beautiful as a perpetual blessing, so that flowers shall be arranged in the lavatory, and wither in the ammonia; a brush and a bowl should be a delicate pleasure to the fingers. Straight lines and the texture of the posts, the roughness of the walls, the silences between the tinkling of the wind bells, even in a poor man's house, are the pleasures of life.

But after all, even this requires a certain amount of wealth and leisure to enjoy it. Strictly speaking, Zen belongs to poverty, both material and spiritual. In Japan the hermits of China have always been admired more than in their native land,—yet one more example of the truth of Christ's words.

From this point of view we may hesitate in our appreciation of famous Japanese gardens, or Nō, or The Tea Ceremony, or even Flower Arrangement. A rabid objection to wealth of any kind, and to the culture connected with it, is not altogether commendable, but like Christ Zen (especially in Japan) always leans towards the small and lowly. Zen is seen at its best in those "Little unremembered acts of kindness and of love," not only towards other people and to animals but even more towards inanimate things, a stick or stone "which the best of us excel."

*

The other day I asked a rōshi what he would do for the rest of the day (it was about three in the afternoon) if he knew he was going to die that night. Before he had time to answer I suggested he might listen to Bach's music; or look at a collection of masterpieces of Occidental and Oriental paintings; or go next door and hold the baby while the mother went to the cinema. He answered that he would do zazen.

On my suggesting that he might do something for humanity before he left it behind in all its confusion and misery, he said that his doing zazen would be of inestimable value to the whole world, far more than any acts of virtue could be. In support of this idea he gabbled off something from Dōgen which I could not understand, but which I felt to be an argumentum ad baculum. This notion I had not heard before in Zen, though the Juzunembutsu, and the Protestant idea of the efficacy of prayer, and Roman Catholic prayers for the dead were of course familiar to me.

*

One other example, before I come to my thesis. I asked the rōshi, as I have asked several others, what was going to happen to him when he died. To make the answer easy for him, I told him how I had put the same question to a woman rōshi in Kyōto. She answered that she wasn't going anywhere, and when I said I would go with her, she was very pleased, partly perhaps because she was a spinster of eighty who had obviously never yet been anywhere with a man. The rōshi, the man, I mean, agreed with this, and I supposed that he meant what I did, that death is the end of all existence of a personal kind, in other words, "There is no knowledge nor wisdom in the grave, whither thou goest," but he then began to talk about transmigration, and how he would come back and go on doing zazen as before. Also, that Dōgen and so on still existed in some way or other, so we make offerings to their spirits and ask for their assistance when in any kind of difficulty, spiritual or physical.

*

There are two points I want to make: first, that Zen must have nothing oriental or occidental, Buddhist or Christian, masculine or feminine about it; second, that only satori, that is, deep experience, is true.

To begin with the second point, the mistake we all make is to confuse what we know with what we don't know. We know, for example, that the sun rose today, but we don't know it will rise tomorrow. In England thirty years ago, famous cricketers used to be asked their opinion about the existence of the Deity, the idea being that a man who could hit eight

Nō : Hashi Benkei

fours and three sixes in one innings must also have theological, not to say mystical intuitions. This kind of mistake, which everyone makes, is also made by Zen-enlightened people. They do not distinguish what they know by enlightenment, and what they (think they) know by education, custom, personal prejudice and so on. Enlightenment does not reveal to us anything which happened in the past or which will happen in the future. Enlightenment is being caught up in this moment which is both in time and beyond time. In being beyond time it partakes of the past and the future, and with regard to events of the past and future we can, or should be able to, make better guesses, think more clearly about them, but that is all. Zen speaks only of this moment. Indeed, Zen is this moment speaking. Thus, if we are asked what will happen to us after death, Zen does not answer,—let us be more courageous, and say that Zen *cannot* answer, just as God cannot tell a lie.

*

Zen theory distinguishes between *dai-ichi-gi*, and *dai-ni-gi*, between the absolute and relative, and we may speak from either. For example, absolutely speaking, men and women are the same, and their enlightenment is the same; but relatively speaking, they are different, and their enlightenment is different. But Zen means speaking from both at the same time, and we must speak from both at the same time all the time. Thus Zen cannot assert either the mortality or the immortality, the existence or the non-existence of the soul. Buddhism may do so, for it is a religion; Christianity may do so, it is a religion; Zen cannot so do, because it is religion itself, which deals with the infinite in this finite place, eternity at this moment of time, and cannot make general or abstract statements about any world to come or not to come. What answer shall we give then to the question, "Is there an after-life?" Thoreau's is the most concise: "One world at a time!"

When a Japanese rōshi replies, he should reply in an un-Japanese way. Above all, we do not want the casuistry and sophistry of the double answer, that from the absolute point of view we are unborn and undying, as far as our real self is concerned; and from the relative viewpoint we are blessed or cursed with a succession of rebirths and redeaths. If I am asked the question (and I never am), I will say that, upon dispassionate inspection, the life of man looks like that of the plants, that grow, reach maturity, decay, and disintegrate into their various elements. This is doubtless the law for the so-called spiritual world, which actually is not separate from or even correlated with the material world, but is a mere aspect of it, just as the material world is a mere aspect of the spiritual. This answer, however, is not the kind of answer I give when asked about Bach's *Art of Fugue*, or Bashō's *Furu ike ya*, or Shakespeare's "Never, never, never, never, never." It is only an opinion, and per se no better than anybody else's.

*

Japanese people must read *King Lear* with all the depth and tragic integrity and poetry they can summon up. English people are to read *Oku no Hosomichi* with all the sublime simplicity and purity and religiousness they can muster. In the same way, Japanese Zen is to be the experience of Japanese people of their humanity, that is, the sound of water, the taste of tea, the bending of branches, the look of food on a plate, the realisation that all's right with this terrible world. There is no superstition or dogma or provincialism, no wishful thinking, nothing that stinks of India or China or Japan here. The Zen which is the essence of Christianity must in the same way leave behind the Virgin Birth, the divinity of Christ, the existence or non-existence of God. These things may and should all be kept as symbols, not of ineffable mysteries, but of our own virginity, our own divinity, our own existence, and our own non-existence.

Zen is the poetry of life, and all poetry is the same, all poetry is different. The joy at the sameness, the joy at the difference, this is ZEN. And beyond this there is doubtless another Zen, but the printer can't print it, yet.

*

But is there really a Western and an Eastern Zen, just as Chinese and Japanese Zen differ to some extent? The deepest experience of the East is acceptance, acceptance of the universe without and within, and activity with it, activity *as* it. We can find this acceptance of and co-activity with the universe in the West, too, but we see also something else, something less or something more, resistance to it. To the Indian and the Oriental mind, resistance to Nature is inconceivable. Escape—yes, they can at least think of such an impossibility, but resistance,—that is a kind of egoistic madness, suicide, not even blasphemy, but mere pitifulness, though excusable. But in the European mystics even, we find man as the measure of all things. Herbert says in *Discipline:*

> Throw away Thy rod,
> Throw away Thy wrath;
> O my God,
> Take the gentle path.

"Man is the measure of all things" has its parallel in the Buddhist idea that without man there is no Buddha, but in this case, man is not so much the measure of all things, as the things themselves. Anyway, it is all a matter of experience, of depth of experience.

Eastern enlightenment is the full and perfect understanding that the stupidity, vulgarity, and hypocrisy of this world is quite all right just as it is. All the poems and pictures and music and significant architecture, all the natural beauty of the world may be forever destroyed,—but if so, it doesn't matter, nay, it is the best possible thing, "a consummation devoutly to be wished." This enlightenment is found in Christianity also; it is, "Thy will be done" in infinitely meaningless inanity. In the *Khuddaka-Patha* the Buddha denounces

> dancing, song, playing, music, seeing plays,

that is to say, he rejects Aeschylus, Palestrina, Shakespeare, Mozart. But this, together with the drama of the Crucifixion, is the Western Nirvana. Buddha was a self-proclaimed success, Christ a self-confessed failure, but the one who is defeated is always dearer to us than the conqueror; there is something cosmically significant here. Is it possible that there may be one day a Zen which shall include both the Buddha in eternal peace, and the Christ in eternal agony?

*

XIV | THE GREAT MASTERS

This section contains quotations and anecdotes connected with the lives and teaching of the Zen Masters of the T'ang period in China, as retold and commented on by R. H. Blyth, whom I can only see as a Master of the Hiroshima period of this world. (I do not disagree with anything he says, except perhaps where he judges Italian Baroque music in which he can't hear the Zen I hear!) This collection was completed shortly before his death and he unfortunately could not fulfill his wish to follow it up with a similar approach to the development of Zen in Korea and Japan.

Norman Waddell, who edited Vol. III of *Zen and Zen Classics*, quotes Blyth's remark on Hazlitt as applicable to Blyth himself, namely that he reminds us "of something we are likely to forget in these days of little men, of hypocrites and demagogues, that there is after all greatness and sublimity in the world, and to spend our lives in searching for it and embracing it is not to have lived in vain."

—*Editor*

SENGTSAN AND THE *HSINHSINMING*

The *Hsinhsinming* (Japanese: *Shinjinmei*) was one of the first treatises on Zen, at least, of those that remain to us. The author of this Buddhist "hymn," Sengtsan (Sōsan), the third (Chinese) Zen patriarch from Dharma, the first Chinese and the twenty-eighth Indian Zen patriarch, lived during the sixth century, dying in 606 A.D. Very little is known of him except that he also seems to have suffered persecution. However, his *Hsinhsinming* shows a less truculent attitude, and is in fact the most charming of all specifically Zen writings until we come to those of Dr. Suzuki Daisetz. The conversion of Sengtsan at the hands of Huike (Eka), the Second Patriarch, is recorded in the *Chuantenglu (Dentōroku)*, Part 3:

> Sengtsan asked Huike, saying, "I am diseased: I implore you to cleanse me of my sin." Huike said, "Bring me your sin and I will cleanse you of it." Sengtsan thought awhile; then said, "I cannot get at it." Huike replied, "Then I have cleansed you of it."

Sengtsan realized, not simply in his mind, but in every bone of his body, that his sinfulness was an illusion, one with that of the illusion of self. As soon as we are aware of our irresponsibility, all the cause of misbehaviour disappears in so far as the cause, (the illusion of self) is removed. If we have no self, it cannot commit sin. Yet, it must be added,

> "I can't see how you and I, who don't exist, should get to speaking here, and smoke our pipes, for all the world like reality." [Robert L. Stevenson, *Fables*]

And from another point of view, our self is a real entity, real in so far as we know (physically) that, as Yuima said, your illness is my illness. When one part of the body is diseased, all is diseased, for "We are members one of another." In this sense, there is no rest for anyone of us, still less for God himself, while one restless soul remains. But the real rest of God, the rest of "the man who has arrived," is something much deeper than this, which no simile or metaphor can express, lying as it does essential in the restlessness itself.

*

To go back to Sengtsan. He became the disciple or the Second Patriarch and practised austerities and led a life of devotion and poverty, receiving the bowl and the robe, insignia of the transmission through Bodhidharma, the First Patriarch (of China) of the Buddha Mind. At this time, one of the periodic persecutions of Buddhism broke out. Sutras and images were burned wholesale; monks and nuns were returned to the lay life. Sengtsan wandered for fifteen years all over the country, avoiding persecution. In 592, he met Taohsin (Dōshin), who became the Fourth Patriarch. His enlightenment was as follows:

> Taohsin came and bowed to Sengtsan, and said, "I ask you for your merciful teaching. Please show me how to be released." Sengtsan answered, "Who has bound you?" "No one," he replied. Sengtsan said, "Why then do you ask to be released?" Taohsin immediately came to a profound realization.
>
> —*Chuantenglu*, 3.

The title of the work may be explained in the following way. *Hsin* (*shin*) is faith, not in the Christian sense of a bold flight of the soul towards God, a belief in what is unseen because of what is seen, but a belief in that which has been experienced, knowledge, conviction. *Hsin* (*shin*), the mind, is not our mind in the ordinary sense, but the Buddha-nature which each of us has unbeknownst to us. *Ming* (*mei*) is a recording, for the benefit of others. The title thus means a description of that part of oneself where no doubt is possible. This is the same unshakable conviction that Shelley and Beethoven and Gauguin had. They too recorded what they saw with their eyes and heard with their ears, where no hesitation or indecision could enter. Especially noteworthy is the absolute faith in the value of the apparently trivial. It consists of 146 unrhymed lines of four characters a line, shorter than the general run of Chinese verse, which usually has five or seven. Perhaps the brevity suits the mood of Zen, and prevents any literary or rhetorical flourishes. There have been many commentaries on the *Hsinhsinming*, the first perhaps being by Chou Myōhon, 1263–1323, who quotes the *Chengtaoke* (*Shōdōka*), in illustration.

This *Chengtaoke* appeared a hundred years later than the *Hsinhsinming*, by Yungchia (Yōka Daishi), one of the chief disciples of (Huineng), the Sixth Patriarch. It is three times as long, and more flowery in style.

THE *HSINHSINMING**

("Inscribed on the Believing Mind")

There is nothing difficult about the Great Way,
But, avoid choosing!
Only when you neither love nor hate,
Does it appear in all clarity.
A hair's breadth of deviation from it,
And a deep gulf is set between heaven and earth.
If you want to get hold of what it looks like,
Do not be anti- or pro- anything.
The conflict of longing and loathing,—
This is the disease of the mind.
Not knowing the profound meaning of things,
We disturb our (original) peace of mind to no purpose.
Perfect like Great Space
The Way has nothing lacking, nothing in excess.
Truly, because of our accepting and rejecting,
We have not the suchness of things.
Neither follow after,
Nor dwell with the Doctrine of the Void.
If the mind is at peace,
These wrong views disappear of themselves.
When activity is stopped and passivity obtains,
This passivity again is a state of activity.
Remaining in movement or quiescence,—

* *Editor's Note:* R. H. Blyth's commentaries on the *Hsinhsinming* occupy fifty pages and far exceed the space available here. I shall therefore quote the treatise in its entirety in Blyth's translation and will have to choose some of the remarks, regretfully leaving out the others, all worth pondering . . .

How shall we know the One?
Not thoroughly understanding the unity of the Way,
Both (activity and quiescence) are failures.
If you get rid of phenomena, all things are lost.
If you follow after the Void, you turn your back on
    the selflessness of things.
The more talking and thinking,
The farther from the truth.
Cutting off all speech, all thought,
There is nowhere that you cannot go.
Returning to the root, we get the essence;
Following after appearances, we lose the spirit
If for only a moment we see within,
We have surpassed the emptiness of things.
Changes that go on in this emptiness
All arise because of our ignorance.
Do not seek for the Truth;
Religiously avoid following it.
If there is the slightest trace of this and that,
The Mind is lost in a maze of complexity.
Duality arises from Unity,—
But do not be attached to this Unity.
When the mind is one, and nothing happens,
Everything in the world is unblameable.
If things are unblamed, they cease to exist;
If nothing happens, there is no mind.
When things cease to exist, the mind follows them;
When the mind vanishes, things also follow it.
Things are things because of the Mind;
The Mind is the Mind because of things.
If you wish to know what these two are,
They are originally one Emptiness.
In this Void both (Mind and things) are one,
All the myriad phenomena contained in both.
If you do not distinguish refined and coarse,
How can you be for this and against that?
The activity of the Great Way is vast;
It is neither easy nor difficult.
Small views are full of foxy fears;
The faster, the slower.

When we attach ourselves (to the idea of enlighten-
      ment) we lose our balance;
We infallibly enter the Crooked Way.
When we are not attached to anything, all things are
      as they are;
With Activity there is no going or staying.
Obeying our nature, we are in accord with the Way,
Wandering freely, without annoyance.
When our thinking is tied, it turns from the truth;
It is dark, submerged, wrong.
It is foolish to irritate your mind;
Why shun this and be friends with that?
If you wish to travel in the True Vehicle,
Do not dislike the Six Dusts.
Indeed, not hating the Six Dusts
Is identical with Real Enlightenment.
The wise man does nothing;
The fool shackles himself.
The Truth has no distinctions;
These come from our foolish clinging to this and that.
Seeking the Mind with the mind,—
Is not this the greatest of all mistakes?
Illusion produces rest and motion;
Illumination destroys liking and disliking.
All these pairs of opposites
Are created by our own folly.
Dreams, delusions, flowers of air,—
Why are we so anxious to have them in our grasp?
Profit and loss, right and wrong,
Away with them once and for all!
If the eye does not sleep,
All dreaming ceases naturally.
If the mind makes no discriminations,
All things are as they really are.
In the deep mystery of this "things as they are,"
We are released from our relations to them.
When all things are seen "with equal mind,"
They return to their nature.
No description by analogy is possible
Of this state where all relations have ceased.

When we stop movement, there is no-movement.
When we stop resting, there is no-rest.
When both cease to be,
How can the Unity subsist?
Things are ultimately, in their finality,
Subject to no law.
For the accordant mind in its unity,
(Individual) activity ceases.
All doubts are cleared up,
True faith is confirmed.
Nothing remains behind;
There is not anything we must remember.
Empty, lucid, self-illuminated,
With no over-exertion of the power of the mind.
This is where thought is useless,
This is what knowledge cannot fathom.
In the World of Reality,
There is no self, no other-than-self.
Should you desire immediate correspondence (with
    this Reality)
All that can be said is "No Duality!"
When there is no duality, all things are one,
There is nothing that is not included.
The Enlightened of all times and places
Have all entered into this Truth.
Truth cannot be increased or decreased;
An (instantaneous) thought lasts a myriad years.
There is no here, no there;
Infinity is before our eyes.
The infinitely small is as large as the infinitely great;
For limits are non-existent things.
The infinitely large is as small as the infinitely minute;
No eye can see their boundaries.
What is, is not,
What is not, is.
Until you have grasped this fact,
Your position is simply untenable.
One thing is all things;
All things are one thing.

If this is for you,
There is no need to worry about perfect knowledge.
The believing mind is not dual;
What is dual is not the believing mind.
Beyond all language,
For it there is no past, no present, no future.

A SELECTION FROM THE *HSINHSINMING* WITH R. H. BLYTH'S OBSERVATIONS

There is nothing difficult about the great way,
but, avoid choosing!

We suffer, at one and the same time, from excessive pride and excessive humility. On the one hand, our intellect rushes in where angels fear to tread. On the other hand, we are too humble before the Buddhas and saints, not realizing that we too are the Buddha, as the *Avatamsaka* (*Kegonkyō*) declares:

The mind, the Buddha, living creatures,—these are not three different things.

Sengtsan attributes all our uneasiness, our dissatisfaction with ourselves and other people, our inability to understand why we are alive at all, to one great cause: choosing this and rejecting that, clinging to the one and loathing the other. There is a profound saying:

The flowers fall, for all our yearning;
Grasses grow, regardless of our dislike.

Other verses that express this fact of the life that comes from the death of self and its wants and distastes, are the following:

Just get rid
Of that small mind
That is called "self,"
And there is nothing in the universe
That can harm or hinder you.

In my hurt this spring,
There is nothing,
There is everything.
                              —Sodō

A hair's breadth of deviation from it,
and a deep gulf is set between heaven and earth.

A miss is as good as a mile. The slightest thought of self, that is, by self, and the Great Way is irretrievably lost. A drop of ink, and a glass of clear water is all clouded. Once we think, "This flower is blooming for me; this insect is a hateful nuisance and nothing else; that man is a useless rascal; that woman is a good mother, and she must therefore be a good wife,"—when such thoughts arise in our minds, all the cohesion between things disappears; they rattle about in a meaningless and irritating way. Instead of being united into a whole by virtue of their own interpenetrated suchness, they are pulled hither and thither by our arbitrary and ever-changing preferences, our whims and prejudices. We suppose this particular man to be a Buddha, ourselves to be ordinary people, this action to be charming, that to be odious, and fail to see how "All things work together for good." In actual fact, Heaven and Earth cannot be separated; one cannot exist without the other. Together they are the Great Way.

The two points to bear in mind are first the nearness of the Way and second, its corollary, the fact that we and the Way are not two things. It seems so far that we can never attain to it:

Far, far from here
Is the Heavenly Land,
    A million million miles away;
We can hardly get there
On just one pair of straw sandals.

The conflict of longing and loathing,—
this is the disease of the mind.

Something arises which pleases the mind, which fits in with our notion of what is profitable for us,—and we love it. Something arises which thwarts us, which conflicts with our wants, and we hate it. So long as we possess this individual mind, enlightenment and delusion, pain and pleasure, accepting and rejecting, good and bad toss us up and down on the waves of existence, never moving onwards, always the same restlessness and wabbling, the same fear of woe and insecurity of joy. So Wordsworth says, in the *Ode to Duty*:

My hopes must no more change their name.

In addition, the mirror of our mind being distorted, nothing appears in its natural, its original form. The louse appears a dirty, loathsome thing, the lion a noble creature. But when we see the louse as it really is, it is not a merely neutral thing; it is something to be accepted as inevitable in our mortal life, as in Bashō's verse:

Fleas, lice,
The horse pissing
By my pillow.

It may be seen as something charming and meaningful, as in Issa's haiku:

Giving the breast,
While counting
The flea-bites.

Not knowing the profound meaning of things,
we disturb our (original) peace of mind to no purpose.

When we are in the Way, when we act without love or hate, hope or despair or indifference, the meaning of things is self-evident, not merely impossible but unnecessary to express. Conversely, while we are looking for the significance of things, it is non-existent. Our original nature is one of perfect harmony with the universe, a harmony not of similarity or correspondence but of identity.

Neither follow after, nor dwell with
the doctrine of the void.

We are not to be beguiled by the senses, by the apparent differences of things.

> Rain, hail and snow,
> Ice too, are set apart,
> But when they fall,—
> The same water
> Of the valley stream.

On the other hand, we are not to fall into the opposite error of taking all things as unreal and meaningless. This is the basis of much of the poetical thinking of Swinburne, of Shelley and Byron. It tinges the poetry of Matthew Arnold, Clough, Christina Rossetti. It is the basis of all passive, quietistic thought. Both these extreme views are wrong; Yungchia describes the position in the following way:

> Getting rid of things and clinging to emptiness
> Is an illness of the same kind;
> It is just like throwing oneself into a fire
> To avoid being drowned.

If the mind is at peace,
these wrong views disappear of themselves.

> All the various
> Flowers of spring,
> Tinted leaves of autumn,
> Tokens in this world
> Untainted with falsity.

The ordinary world and the world of reality are here one; life and death are Nirvana. The great mistake of life and of poetry is the desire to get away from things, instead of getting into them, escaping from this world into a dream world. Yet even this world of day-dreams, or escapist poetry, Wagnerian music and pictures of Paradise, is also a way of life, is also, when we realize it, the Great Way. Thus it is again that enlightenment is ignorance, salvation is damnation, Heaven and Hell are one self place.

Not thoroughly understanding the unity of the way,
Both (activity and quiescence) are failures.

In other words, mere activity, activity without quiescence, mere quiescence without its inner activity, are no good, neither has its proper quality and function. Freedom is impossible without law, man is nothing without God, illusion non-existent except for enlightenment, this is this because that is that. But freedom and law, illusion and enlightenment, this and that are two names of one thing. Unless this is realized (in practical life) none of these is its real self. This is not this until and unless it is that; only when the two are one are they really two.

In practical life, this means that the composure we feel at home among our family, is only an illusion that is broken when we go out into the world and meet with vexation and disappointment, becoming irritated and depressed. Our activity when playing chess is not the true activity, as we see when we are beaten and our opponent's face and voice become hateful to us. It lacks the balance that preserves the mind from spite though we properly enough feel gloomy at losing.

In the poetical life it is equally important that we realize, through each all of the senses, that true diversity comes from unity. Even in the scientific world, the nature, for example, of a many-legged caterpillar is only understood when we know it is a six-legged insect. The nature of feathers, skin, hair, nails, scales, and so on is perceived when we find that they are all one thing. The poet delights in all the many names of things, because he knows in his heart that as Laotse said,

The name that can be named is not an eternal name.

Following after appearances we lose the spirit.

What is the "root" of the universe? Some say man, some say God. It is often convenient to have two names for one thing: spiritual, material; human, divine; free-will, determinism; relative, absolute. But if we think of the essence of things as the root, and the things themselves as branches and leaves, we are allowing these "thoughts" and "words," spoken of in the previous verse, to divide once more what is a living unity into a duality that is dead as such. For whether we look at things in their multifariousness, their variety and differences, or at the common elements, the "Life-force," the principles of Science, we are still far from the root, which is not either, not both, not a thing at all,—yet it is not nothing. Buddhists say the mind is the root of things—but it is not something inside us. Christians say it is God,—but it is not something outside us. But to know, to *realize*, the inside and outside as one, that my profit is your profit, that your loss is my loss, to make this fact, this dead matter-of-fact into a living, yea-saying Fact,—this is our own and our only problem. When this is solved, in our thinking and speaking, all is solved. When it is not solved, every thought is twisted, every word is sophisticated.

When we attach ourselves to this (idea of enlightenment), we
*   lose our balance:*
we infallibly enter the crooked way.

Our experience, our deepest experience has taught us something; we wish to convey it to others. When they question its validity, we become angry, losing our mental serenity by holding so firmly to what is after all more intangible than snowflakes or the rainbow. It is not merely calmness of mind that we have lost, however, but what is this and more, the Middle Way, the knowledge (and practice) that our profoundest interpretation of life also must be thrown overboard together with the sentimentality, cruelty, snobbery, and folly that make our lives a misery. The Crooked Way is not a morally distorted manner of life. It is composed of virtues as much as of vices, of ideals, religious dogmas, principles of freedom and justice, as much as of degradation and tyranny. The Crooked Way is over-grieving at inevitable sorrows, over-clinging to joys which must cease; it is regarding as permanent what is but transitory; always looking for the silver lining, desiring to be in the non-existent and impossible "Land beyond the morning star."

When our thinking is tied,
it is dark, submerged, wrong.

It is *dark*, so that we cannot distinguish the true nature of things; we see friends as enemies, strengthening trials as useless annoyances. We fail to perceive the so-called defects and errors of others as an aspect of their Buddha-nature. It is *submerged*; it does not float upon the waves of circumstances that can both drown or buoy us up. When all things work together for good because we love God, that is, we seek not to change that which is inevitable, the outside, but only the free, the inside, then we are as light as corks however low the billows descend, however high they mount aloft. It is *wrong*, because our nature is freedom. Perfect service, no task left undone or scamped, as best exemplified in a mother's unfailing, tender care, is right because not tied by duty or public opinion. When we look around and see odious people, a world of stupidity and spitefulness, the weather always too warm or too cold, all the elements conspiring to annoy us, death approaching nearer with its prophetic twinges and dull throbs, this is to be tied, pressed down by dark, mournful waves of thought.

Indeed, not hating the six dusts
is identical with real enlightenment.

This absence of hatred, of intolerance, disgust, righteous indignation, discrimination and judging, is itself the state of Buddhahood. This negativeness, however, is not that of the opposite of affirmation. It is not the passive condition it seems to be, neither can it be described by the words "love your enemies." It is not absence of feeling, or indifference, but some unnameable attitude of mind in which evil is accepted as such though not condoned.

Duality arises from unity;
but do not be attached to this unity.

It is the One that unites the Two; without It, the Buddha-Nature, the Void, the Mind, this and that yearn after the Ground of Existence. Things and circumstances are in themselves neutral, not meaningless, but *not* coloured intrinsically with the "opinions" we have of them.

> When we clap our hands,
> The maid serves tea,
> Birds fly up,
> Fish draw near,—
> At the pond in Sarusawa.

The clapping of the hands is It. The sound as interpreted by the maid-servant, by the bird, by the fish, is only half of It. But without halves there is no whole, just as without a whole there are no halves. As we endeavour to release ourselves from phenomena, the relative world, we become attached to something even more non-existent, the thing in itself, the noumenon.

If things are unblamed they cease to exist;
if nothing happens, there is no mind.

When we neither censure or praise anything, all things are devoid of censurable and praiseworthy qualities. When we do not judge things, things do not judge us. When things simply flow, every atom according to its nature, according to Nature, according to its Buddha-nature, there is no mind as something separate from what is not mind. Yungchia says:

> Walking is Zen, sitting is Zen;
> Whether we speak or are silent, move or are still,
> It is unperturbed.

Things are things because of the mind;
the mind is the mind because of things.

The aim of Zen, the aim of the poetical life, is to reach and remain in that undifferentiated state where subject and object are one, in which the object is perceived by simple introspection, the subject is a self-conscious object. Subject and object are to be realized as the two sides of one sheet of paper, that is one and yet is two. The one piece of paper cannot exist without the two sides, nor the two sides without the one sheet. This analogy fails to satisfy if taken in any other way but lightly and quickly, for to what should we compare the universe? How can anything be a true parable of the Essence of Being?

If you wish to know what these two are,
they are originally one emptiness.

This Emptiness is described in the following way: it is perfectly Harmonious, subject and object, Mind and Form are one. It is Pure and Undefiled; things are, just as they are, delivered from all stain of sin or imperfection. It is Unobstructed; all things are free, interpenetrative. That is to say it is age-less, non-moral, law-less. It is like light, containing all colours in it, but itself colourless. It is not a thing but contains all things; not a person but includes all minds; not beautiful or ugly but the essence of both.

Sameness and difference are also one thing, yet two things. At one moment we see the separate meaning of a thing, at another, its meaning as being all things; and at some most precious moments of all, incommunicable in speech but yet heard also through it, we know that a thing, a person, a flower, the cry of a bird, is both one thing and all things. Sameness and difference, and *their* sameness and difference are the same and yet different from our own non-existence.

Seeking the mind with the mind,—
is not this the greatest of all mistakes?

Clinging to the search for the mind is the last infirmity of the religious soul, and the most self-evidently absurd, for why should we search for the Buddha that we have already, why seek to release ourselves from bonds that are only fancied? But it is the greediness of our searching which invalidates it. This is beautifully expressed in the following:

> There is a treasure in the deep mountains;
> He who has no desire for it finds it.

Dreams, delusions, flowers of air,—
Why should we be so anxious to have them in our grasp?

These creations of the mind, so common and habitual that there seems to be some concrete reality behind them, are the protagonists of all tragic drama. Fixed notions of honour, propriety, faithfulness, conflict of necessity with the imperturbable, ineffable, and intangible truth that ultimately destroys them. Rigidity versus fluidity, the name versus the nameless; yet in this very willingness to die for some impossible creed we see once more that just as the ordinary man, as he is, is the Buddha, so these delusions are, as they stand, the truth, and without them there is no reality. What is wrong in the anxiety to get hold of them or the anxiety to reject them. Error or truth, profit or loss,—if we accept them readily, cheerfully, as in some sense ministers of God, remembering that even the devils fear and serve Him, these flowers of the air also have their beauty and value, for

> Every error is an image of truth,

and in every illusion there beats the heart of mankind that aspires for the truth that error masks. But the mask *is* the face.

Profit and loss, right and wrong,—
away with them once for all!

What Sengtsan means here, is that we are to give up the false idea that profit actually profits us, that there is any individual self to suffer loss or gain. Forgetting all moral principles, we are to "Dilige, et quod vis fac." (Love, and do as you please.) This abstention from choosing, from judging, does not mean that we do not choose as pleasant or judge as wrong. What it means is that God does it for us, God who is so often disobeyed, who turns the other cheek and forgives his enemies. When for example we give an order, as a teacher, or an official, it is to be given peremptorily without a thought of the possibility of its not being obeyed. But if it is not obeyed, there is no *personal* irritation and wounded vanity in the angry remonstrance we make. A law of nature, of human society has been broken and it is right that our emotion should be aroused by this.

The doctrine that in all our acts we are to be vice-regents of Nature is a dangerous one, but every truth is dangerous, for it liberates universal energies that may easily go astray. Religious persecution, megalomania, political fanaticism are all misuses of what the Third Patriarch inculcates. But we know them by their fruits; by the defects, the distortions, the hatreds of the dictators.

In the deep mystery of this "things as they are,"
we are released from our relations to them.

Things as they are, the coldness of ice and the sound of rain, the fall of leaves and the silence of the sky, are ultimate things, never to be questioned, never to be explained away. When we know them, our relations to them, their use and misuse, their associated pleasures and pains are all forgotten.

No description by analogy is possible
of this state where all relations have ceased.

Deity : Sanjusangendo, Kyoto.

Metaphors and similes, parables and comparisons may be used
to describe anything belonging to the relative, the intellectually dichotomised world, but even the simplest and com-
monest experience of reality, the touch of hot water, the smell
of camphor, are incommunicable by such or any means; how
much more so the Fatherhood of God, the Meaningless of
Meaning, the Absolute Value of a pop-corn, for in such matters, the unity of our own emptiness and that of all other
things is perceived as an act of self-consciousness, and nothing
remains to be compared with anything. In Chapter VII of the
Platform Sutra we are told of Nanyueh, 677–744, and his
meeting with Huineng, the Sixth Patriarch, who asked him
from whence he had come. "From Suzan," he replied. "What
comes? How did it come?" asked the Patriarch. Nanyueh replied, "We cannot say it is similar to anything."

When both cease to be,
how can the unity subsist?

There is no more a unity than there is duality; relative and
absolute are names of the nameless. Zen, that is to say, is a
word that is used like an algebraic sign, for all that is nameless, all that escapes thought, definition, explanation, yet
breathes through words and silence; is communicated in spite
of our best efforts to communicate it. Actions are either good
or bad; yet nothing is good or bad, but thinking makes it so.
That is to say, things are both good or bad and neither; relative and absolute; or, if you wish it, neither relative nor absolute, there is neither duality nor a unity.

Nothing remains behind;
there is not anything we must remember.

We are not bound by any "imitation of Buddha." There are
no snags, no undigested material, no fitting in with precon-
ceived notions, no formulae to follow in the way of our life or
manner of death. We may be confirmed or baptised if we feel
it is good for us, or die at the stake rather than submit to it.
And we extend the same privilege to everyone else. No one
need be converted to this or that religion. When we do wrong
or make mistakes, we go on with renewed vigour to the next

task; a faux pas cannot check us or make us dwell on it with self-torturing shame.

In the world of reality,
there is no self, no other than self.

To say this is easy, to believe it intellectually is not difficult. It has an emotional, a poetical appeal which few can withstand. With a full belly, a bank balance, when all is going well, such a doctrine will be readily adopted. But when food is scarce, when a man has lost his job, in hours of boredom, when children die, and our own death is not far off,—can we then rejoice with those that rejoice and mourn with those that mourn? In my own case, I must say that nothing makes me more contented with my lot than to see the sufferings of others, to find my children cleverer and prettier than those of my colleagues. How far indeed is this from the lines above.

When there is no duality, all things are one.
There is nothing that is not included.

When Thoreau lay dying, he was asked if he had made his peace with God; he answered, "We have never quarreled." In Thoreau's world, everything was included, nothing rejected and made into an enemy. Where there is no duality there can be no quarreling. When God lived for two years by Walden lake, Thoreau did not criticise, praise, or condemn Him. As St. Augustine says [Retractions i.1.]

To live happily is to live according to the mind of God.

The enlightened of all times and places
have every one entered into this truth.

This sounds rather depressing, as though ordinary people were excluded, but what Sengtsan means is that comparatively few know that they have entered into the realm of Buddhahood, where all men and all things without exception have their (unconscious and unwitting) being. Not a sparrow can fall out of God's care, nor can anyone, for all his hair-shirts and flagellations enter into His providence. It is only a question of becoming aware of our true condition, and this becoming aware is called "entering."

There is no here, no there,
infinity is before our eyes.

Here and there are dualities and therefore obstructions to the life of perfection. Infinity is under our noses, our noses are infinitely long. Yungchia says,

> The Mirror of the Mind brightly shining, unobstructed,
> Passes transparently through everything in the universe.

When this Mind is our mind, when we are not bored with here and longing to be there, when the life of things is breathed in and breathed out with every breath we take, when we live in the past of our world and into the unborn future without desiring to undo what is done, or avoid what must be, then we live a timeless life now, a placeless life here.

What is, is not;
what is not, is.

There is the most extreme form of expression of the Mahayana theory that corresponds to the Christian doctrine (mystical, and strictly speaking heretical) that God is above all qualities, all predications, even of existence. The "is-ness" of things is a fantasy of life's fitful fever,—but so is their "is-not-ness." Life is a dream, but so is this statement. This last fact is hard to catch. When we say that unreality is also unreal, in our normal moments, and especially when the mind is tired, this means nothing, or less than nothing. It irritates by its illogicality, and is repugnant because of the demand it makes that we are unable to supply. It is therefore necessary that we say such things, to ourselves or others, only when we are in a condition of mind to know what we are saying, otherwise by frequent vain repetitions we shall become as the heathen, unable to recognize moments of vision when they visit us.

Until you have grasped this fact,
your position is simply untenable.

Common sense is revolted by the above assertion that what is, is not, what is not, is, but in actual practice it is found to be the only valid one. The story of the monk who was praised for bringing a basket to catch the drips from a leaking roof illustrated this identity of what is and what is not. A bucket or a basket, there is no difference. One man's meat is another man's poison. A leaf of grass is a six-foot golden Buddha. Life is a perpetual dying. And if you keep to the so-called commonsense point of view (which is more elastic than supposed) you will find that your hard and fast divisions between right and wrong, profit and loss, useful and harmful, are inapplicable to all your problems and indeed to every circumstance of life that is deeply felt and profoundly experienced. So Blake says,

> Listen to fool's reproach! it is a kingly title!

and Yungchia says the same thing, a thousand years before him,

> Let me allow others to speak ill of me, trespass
>   against me;
> It is like trying to burn the sky with fire, only weary-
>   ing themselves out.
> Listening to them is like drinking the Nectar of Eternal
>   Life;
> All fades, and I am suddenly in the Wonderful World.

One thing is all things;
all things are one thing.

This expresses in an extreme form the state of Mind towards which things are constantly tending, called paradox by logic, metaphor by literature, genius or madness by popular consent. The humorist says, describing the beauty of a certain film actress. "When she comes into the room, the room comes in with her," and forget it, but another step has been taken towards the region where

> One sentence decides heaven and earth;
> One sword pacifies all sublunary things.

When you have really seen one flower, you have seen not only all flowers, but all non-flowers. One principle, one life, one animate or inanimate manifestation moves and upholds all things, and thus it is said,

> One sight, and all is seen,
> Like a great round mirror.

The believing mind is not dual;
what is dual is not the believing mind.

When we believe in *something*, this is not the believing mind. If we say we believe in ourselves, this again is a mistake, of experience or of expression. "The believing mind believes in itself,"—this, rightly understood, contains no error. The *Lankavatara Sutra* says,

> Believing in the truth of timeless life is called the Believing Mind.

Clearer still is the *Nirvana Sutra:*

> The Believing Mind is the Buddha-nature.

Here there is no danger of one thing believing in another thing. The Buddha-nature is the true nature of every thing and of everything. The believing mind is this Buddha-activity. A Haydn minuet or the Lord's prayer, or a kitten catching at the falling autumn leaves is a clear thought of this mind, a harmonious movement of the Buddha-nature. It is perfect because it is single, unique, complete, all-including.

Beyond all language,
for it, there is no past, no present, no future.

Language is vitally concerned with time, with tense. The Way is timeless and breaks through language, but does not discard it. Silence itself is a form of speaking, just as the blank spaces between the marks of the printing are as much part of the printing as the letters themselves. The Way is timeless yet it cannot dispense with time. Eternity and time are in love with each other, continually embracing in a divine union, yet always separate to the purely human eye.

*

HUINENG AND HIS SUCCESSORS

The history of Zen is the history of moments. It cannot be, like the history of ideas, or even the history of the freedom of thought, an account of development, systematisation, criticism, modification, replacement, and so forth. Zen seems to become deeper sometimes, shallower, broader, narrower sometimes, but there is no progress of the ordinary kind. It is a history only in the sense of being a list of names of great men in the attainment of greatness in words or deeds or manner of life.

I find no Zen in Buddha, and in Buddhism itself up to Daruma it is the Hinduism, the animism and pantheism of the *Upanishads* that keeps the universe alive.

Zen as zazen begins with Daruma, 6th century. Zen as a "philosophy of living" begins with Huineng (Japanese: Enō), 7th century. Huineng's Zen is not Indian, but neither is it Chinese. It is rather super-national, almost superhuman, though not supernatural. He reminds us a little of Hakurakuten; like him he would have been at home in Athens, Rome, Paris, or London. Zen as we now think of it, Chinese Zen, commences with Baso and his "wild and whirling words" and "pleasure in being mad." It attains its highest with Jōshū, 9th century, and Ummon, 10th century. (The Zen sect, in the sense of an organisation of monks with the purpose of gaining enlightenment, begins with Hyakujō [720–814]. It had its swan-song sung in the 11th century *Hekiganroku* and the 13th century *Mumonkan*.)

From the 4th Patriarch branched off Gozu Zen, and from the 5th Rōan Zen.

Gozu Zen showed the tendency towards strange behaviour which was to be a characteristic of Baso and his school. Eccentrics were attracted by the absolute liberty promised by Zen, and those who thus became free could not but be oddities. Rōan Zen also was characterised by wit and humour. Its adherents avoided imperial patronage, not unknown later. There were no doubt able and brilliant monks among them, but both Rōan and Gozu Zen did not last long enough to bring them fame.

When we think over the episodes in which the Zen master and his pupils play their parts, we can see that there are various types of minds, in both teacher and disciples, and the resolution of the doubts and difficulties fall into several patterns. It would be quite wrong and un-Zen-like for us to assume, as is invariably done, that there is one "truth," one enlightenment, one true state of mind, "one light that enlighteth every man that cometh into the world," one Zen, one Buddha nature . . . *and yet, of course, there is.*

Freedom from oneness is more important, in the long run, than the freedom from diversity which is the aim of all religion and science. Each anecdote, each question, each answer must be re-lived in its own way and in our own way. No system, no symbolisation, no tricks, no perpetual paradox or desire to astonish are to be allowed. Every blow has a different meaning, just as every shower of rain is different from every other. Praising or blaming, laughing or weeping, each case has its own unique meaning. "But at the back of all of them. . . ." As Goethe said to Eckermann, "Do not, I beg you, look *behind* phenomena."

There are, however, two ways in which we can prevent people from going behind phenomena, that is, separating (in life) the abstract from the concrete and thus spoiling both. According to Zen theory, A is A, and A is not A; further, A is A because it is not A (but surely A is not A also because A is A?). Thus the two ways are to show that A is A, and that A is not A.

The 6th Patriarch had many disciples, of whom five were the most important, Seigen and Nangaku; Kataku, Nanyō and Yōka, "the Five Great Masters of the Sect."

It is from Seigen and Nangaku that all the great Zen masters derive; from Seigen the Ummon, Hōgen, and Sōtō schools, and from Nangaku the Igyō and Rinzai, so that the present Rinzai and Sōtō schools come from the two chief disciples of Huineng: Nangaku and Seigen.

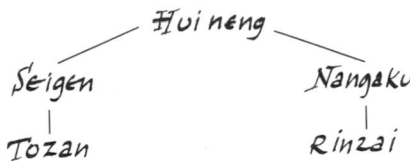

From Nangaku, it is Baso, Hyakujō, Ōbaku, Rinzai; and from Seigen, it is Sekitō, Yakusan, Ungan, Tōzan, and Sōzan, 840–901.

It is from the branch of Zen, beginning with Nangaku, who himself is not brilliant, that Zen makes its new development, to be precise, from Nangaku's disciple Baso onwards. Baso himself had two great disciples, Nansen and Hyakujō.

Nansen's disciple Jōshū and Hyakujō's disciple Ōbaku and *his* disciple Rinzai complete the list of the greatest Zen masters, and thus we get this (simplified) genealogy:

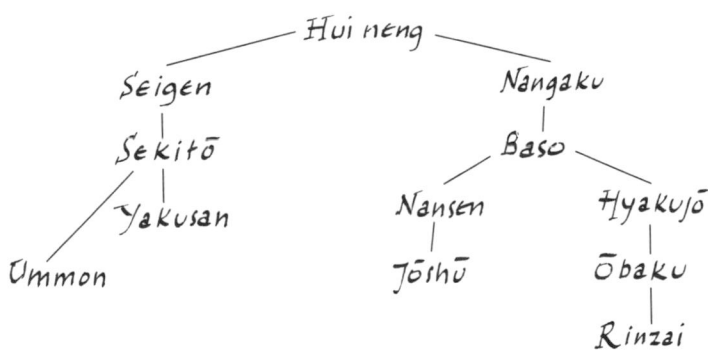

Ummon belongs to the Seigen, Sekitō, Seppō line. Sekitō has humour and wit, and ability to enlighten disciples in a practical way. Sekitō had two chief disciples, Tennō (Tienhuang) 748–807, and Yakusan (Yeuhshan), 751–834.

Tennō's chief disciple was Ryūtan. With Ryūtan begins
the idea of teaching by just not teaching, which is a development of Daruma's declaration that he did not know what Zen
was. But the famous blowing out of the candle by Ryūtan,
enlightening his disciple Tokusan by the darkness,—this is
orthodox Zen, that is, monkish Zen, at its best.

After his enlightenment by having the fire put out, Tokusan made a bonfire of his sutras. There is no account of any
Christian being converted into burning the Bible. The only
Bible that Christians have burnt is other people's. Nirvana is
the "blowing out" of the candle of life. Baptism is the Christian equivalent, but baptism is a prelude to resurrection, and
there is no resurrection in Nirvana. So in Daruma's wall-
gazing, nothing seems to have come of it. Even Enō's enlightenment was an end in itself.

Tokusan and disciples, Gantō and Seppō, have a liveliness
which shows that Zen was not nihilism. It had nothing to do
with the pessimism and escapism which drove so many into
Buddhism, but was an escape from this very escapism.

The anecdotes concerning Gantō and Seppō especially are
Zen at its most simple and most profound, so that we are
unable to distinguish their Zen from their activity in field,
forest, or temple.

Both the Ummon and the Hōgen Schools come through
Tokusan, who combined the doctrine of absolute emptiness
with the use of his stick, which was not used as an instrument
of punishment, but for both praise and blame, since "Whether
you manage to speak or whether you manage to be silent,
thirty strokes!" The other two sects, the Igyō and the Rinzai,
come through Nangaku.

Ummon Zen is the most brilliant of all, yet at the same

time quite physical in its spirituality. When for example Ummon was asked about the sword that cuts a hair dropped on it, that is, Zen, he answered "Tsu!," which is said to be the sound of a knife cutting into flesh. This does not "mean" something. It is the state of mind of Ummon, which he wants to communicate to the monk, the sensitivity to the danger and pain of life, a sensitivity which Zen should not dull. Another example was when Ummon was asked, "What is the True Dharma-Eye?" Ummon answered, "Universal!," which does not mean, as in Buddhism, that the Buddha-eye penetrates all things, but that the Buddha-eye is everywhere, seeing itself. When asked, "What is the Way?," he answered "Go away!," which means, "Go and walk on it! Don't stand there asking questions about it!"

Hōgen Zen was a very "kind" Zen, which tried as far as possible to meet the learner-monk half-way. This may have been partly because the Hōgen Sect was the last to appear, in the 10th century. The others belong to the 9th, except Ummon, who died in 949, nine years before Hōgen.

HUINENG AND
THE *PLATFORM SUTRA*

The Sixth Patriarch, Huineng, 637–1713, a man born en-lightened, was re-enlightened on hearing the *Diamond-Sutra* recited in a house to which he had just delivered some fire-wood, re-re-enlightened by the words of the same sutra when repeated by the Fifth Patriarch. Like Blake, he never went to school and did not need to go. Even if he had gone, like Thoreau, he would have suffered no ill effects. Huineng knows, and knows that he knows, just like Bach or Bashō. In the case of Huineng we can see that zazen was the result, not the cause of his enlightenment.

The history of Zen must always be as non-existent as Zen itself is, but when we look at the world with the scientific eye, the eye of time, of cause and effect, we see stages in human experience which correspond to the real progress, which is the deepening of life by (certain) men. Ideally, what seems to have happened is something like this.

1000 B.C.	The Upanishadic perception that the division of I and no-I is illusion.
500 B.C.	The Buddhistic denial of I and rejection of not-I; its identification of desire and illusion.
1 A.D.	The Mahayana conception of the Bodhisattva.
500 A.D.	The Bodhidharmic realisation that Zen is not a religion, not morality.
1000 A.D.	The (Rinzai) Zen of pure freedom from self and from otherness, in practical life.
1500 A.D.	The permeation of Zen into the life and thought of ordinary people in Japan.

Huineng's position in this schema, is his knowing and teaching that to see is the meaning of life, not to see something, but merely to see. He preached the gospel of impossibility, that the eye can see itself; the real actor is the action.

Huineng's *Platform Sutra* is—like every other sutra, including the *Prajnaparamitahridaya Sutra (Hannyashingyō)* which is the shortest—too long, and thus falls sometimes into superstition and nonsense, but it is not dull. The following are the passages which chiefly struck me on reading it again, for the how manyth time?

In Chapter I, Huineng says to the Fifth Patriarch at their first meeting, somewhat conceitedly:

> My barbarian body is different from your honour's, but what is the difference as far as our Buddha-nature is concerned?

This is not so. If the body is different, the nature is different; if the Buddha-nature is the same, they are the same physically. Take your choice. In the same chapter the Fifth Patriarch says something which is one of the chief tests in Rinzai Zen:

> A man who has seen into his Buddha-nature sees it whenever questioned about it.

Whenever circumstances seize us by the lapels we must show our Buddha-nature. The great rule is, speak first, and think afterward.

The best thing in the *Platform Sutra* are to me the two poems, by Shenhsiu and Huineng. Apart from the fact that a poetry competition, not to speak of a Zen competition, is of very doubtful validity and in very questionable taste, and despite the fact that the whole thing seems a cock and bull story like *Hamlet* or the gospels, what is interesting is the way in which the two poems embody the whole history of Buddhism. The booby's verse is:

> The body is the Tree of Salvation, (Bodhi Tree)
> The mind is a clear mirror.
> Incessantly wipe and polish it;
> Let no dust fall on it.

This is primitive Buddhism. It is the *Dhammapada* in four lines. It is the essence of morality and the good life. But then comes along Sam Weller out of the kitchen with a pert composition that knocks the whole thing to smithereens:

> Salvation is nothing like a tree,
> Nor a clear mirror;
> Essentially, not a "thing" exists;
> What is there, then, for the dust to fall on?

However, this apparent nihilism had two thousand years of spiritual endeavour behind it. The moralists we still have with us; they are the parliaments of the world, and the world parliaments, and the world is being ruined by them. But Huineng's verse gives us the feeling of absolute freedom, with the result that we gleefully wipe and polish the non-existent mirror and cherish that infinitely empty space inside the tiny seed of the Tree of Life.

> To see all the good and evil of humanity without being attracted or repulsed by it and without being engulfed by it, with our minds as empty as vast space,—this we may call greatness.

> To see the goodness of others without infatuation, and their badness without disgust is not so difficult, but to see their happiness without joy and their suffering without grief, —can we, should we do this?

Occasionally, as pointed out before, Huineng falls into the trap of comparison, which is always odious, and this is one of the most charming of his sayings:

> An ordinary man *is* a Buddha; illusion *is* salvation. A foolish thought,—and we are ordinary, vulgar, stupid. The next enlightened thought,—and we are the [exalted, poetical, and wise] Buddha.

What Huineng should have said, though it was suitable to the audience, which was exceedingly large and probable exceedingly philistine, was:

> A foolish thought,—and we become the Buddha.
> An enlightened thought—and we are again ordinary people.

Why? Because folly is wisdom, and salvation is damnation. We must avoid enlightenment like the plague, and do zazen to keep our minds in a constant confusion like that of nature, and be madly attached to infinite trifles.

A passage, from a gatha, which I feel as if uttered to me personally, is the following:

> One who walks the Way
> Sees not any faults in the world.
> Seeing others' faults
> Means that one's own faults are strengthened.

This applies not so much to our petty cavillings and criticisms of others, but to our low opinion of the universe, which comes from our own lowness and poverty of spirit.

Zen, when it came to, or reproduced itself, in China, lost all its misty and mystical Indian vagueness, and much of its escapism. It became as "heartless" as the Chinese, as the universe; it became sensuous, take-off-able and washable. Zen was now a comfortable old pair of shoes, the breaking of a rotten tooth, the smell of urine, a donkey's bray. Yet it was still a thing of monks and monasteries, something esoteric, communicated or at least stimulated from one enlightened monk to an as yet unenlightened one, and utterly incomprehensible to the uninitiated. However, the 6th Patriarch, Huineng, had already said something less miserly, deeper and broader:

> A thought of folly,—and one is an ordinary man; a thought of enlightenment,—and one is a Buddha.

Zen, after all, is simply the humanity of human beings, and cannot be restricted to monks and nuns, who are in many ways super-human, or rather sub-human, father-less, mother-less, wife-less, child-less creatures who tell us to be attached to nothing, like the fox that lost his tail in a trap.

The *Platform Sutra* is in some sense a polemic, or at least a partisan piece of writing. Huineng is always right, Shensu is always wrong. It seems doubtful if Huineng and Shensu, the leader of the Northern School, actually belonged to the same monastery under the Fifth Patriarch, so that the contest of the poems may be a purely manufactured affair. Of course the historicity of the matter has but little to do with the poetico-religious truth thus symbolised.

The autobiographical chapter at the beginning is suspiciously self-laudatory, and self-depreciating. The idea of the writer of this "sutra" seems to have been to exaggerate the Sixth Patriarch's lack of education and culture, in order to bring out his natural genius, or at least the non-intellectual character of Zen. He tells us what Shensu thought just as the evangelists tell us the private prayers of Christ.

Nevertheless, when we read the *Platform Sutra* we feel something new and fresh, a freedom from all talk of the accumulation of merits, initiation and confirmation, salvation and gratitude.

Shensu was Dr. Watson to Huineng's Sherlock Holmes, and by sticking to the factual Buddhist truth, that we must train ourselves in virtue, improve our characters and taste, he had earned the contempt of all subsequent generations, whereas Huineng, with his (also one-sided) transcendentalism and denial of anything obviously so, such as the necessity of polishing a mirror in order to make it reflect better, and by saying no when we expect yes, has become the pattern of all would-be Zen eccentrics. Another peculiarity of Huineng, more admirable, was his aversion to zazen. Huineng seems to have got his Zen first from cutting (and selling) firewood, and then after entering the 5th Patriarch's temple by pounding rice (and of course eating it). There are several anecdotes concerning zazen which pour contempt upon Shensu. One is that Shensu used to tell his disciples to concentrate their minds on quietness, to sit doing zazen for a long time, and not to lie down as far as possible. One of them went to Huineng and asked him about it. Huineng said, "To concentrate the mind on quietness is a disease of the mind, and not Zen at all."

At the beginning of the seventh chapter, which goes back to the life of Huineng before he became famous, we are told that the aunt of a Confucian scholar Chihlueh asked him how he could understand the meaning of the *Mahaparinirvana Sutra* though he did not know the meaning of the words. He answered:

> The profound meaning of all the Buddhas has no connection with words and letters.

It would be more accurate to say that it has little connection with dictionaries, which are produced by machines, even human machines, but the intoning of a sutra is certainly part of the meaning, even perhaps most of the meaning, and, if Buddha intones it, all the meaning. When we hear Othello speaking Russian, it has even more significance than in English, because our listening is the more physical and less grammatical. So in the same chapter Huineng said, in a gatha:

> The right way [to recite the sutra] is according to its
>   meaningless Meaning.
> To put a meaning into it is all wrong.

A gentleman with the delightful name of Fattat (in Wong Moulam's translation of the *Platform Sutra*) then confessed with tears that up to that time he had been quite unable to rotate the *Suddharmapundarika Sutra,* and had indeed been rotated by it. As Nichiren also said, we must read it, turn it over, with our body, not our lips.

*

When it is hot, we are to be as hot as it is, no hotter.

Zen has no gratitude, but at the same time it has no pride. This combination seems negatively attractive. The end of a gatha by Chang Hangchang in chapter eight runs like this:

I do nothing meritorious,
But the Buddha-nature manifests itself.
This is not because of my teacher's instruction,
Nor is it due to any attainment of mine.

In Christian parlance, he gives God all the glory.

One day the Patriarch said to the assembled monks, "I have something that has no head, no tail, no name, no character, no back, no front; do you monks know what it is?" Jinne came forward and said, "I will tell you. It is the origin of all the Buddhas. It is my Buddha-nature." The Patriarch said, "I told you it has no name or character, and yet you call it the origin of the Buddha-nature. You may afterwards become the master of a little temple, but you will never be anything more than a lecturer on Zen."

*

Yungchia walked round the Sixth Patriarch three times [without bowing] and merely shook his Buddhist staff with iron rings. The Patriarch said, "A Sramana embodies the 3,000 rules of deportment and the 80,000 minute moral rules. From whence does your honour come, may I ask, with your overweening self-assurance?" Yungchia replied, "Birth-and-death is a problem of great moment; all changes ceaselessly." Huineng asked, "Why not embody the unborn and grasp the timeless?" Yungchia replied, "To be unborn and deathless is to embody it: to be timeless is to grasp it." "That is so, that is so," assented the Patriarch. At this, Yungchia acted according to the prescribed ceremonial, and prostrated himself, then soon after bade farewell to the Patriarch. "Aren't you in a bit of a hurry to be off?" said the Patriarch, but Yungchia retorted, "Motion has no real existence, so how can there be such a thing as 'hurry'?" "Who knows that motion is unreal?" "You yourself are discriminating [in asking such a question]." The Patriarch exclaimed, "You have grasped birthlessness splendidly!" but Yungchia remarked, "Has the expression birthlessness any meaning whatever?" The Patriarch countered with, "If it had no meaning, how could anybody discriminate?" "Discrimination also has no meaning!" asserted Yungchia. "Very good indeed!" exclaimed the Patriarch.

THE SEIGEN BRANCH
OF CHINESE ZEN

Seigen (Chingyuan), who died in 740, had a very great number of disciples. His Zen teaching was minute and severe. An example: A monk came and asked him, "What is the object of Daruma's coming to China?" Seigen answered, "He went off again somewhere." The monk then said, "I ask you for one or two words of wisdom." Seigen said, "Come closer!" The monk went closer. "Write it down clearly," said Seigen.

Sekitō (Shiht'ou), 700–790, met Huineng when young, and studied under Seigen after his death.

A monk asked Sekitō, "What is the inner significance of Daruma's coming to the West?" Sekitō said, "Go and ask the outside post of the Hall!" The monk said, "I don't know what you mean." "Nor do I," said Sekitō.

An effect has a cause, but what is the (ultimate) cause of the cause? A cause has an effect, but what is the ultimate effect? God felt lonely, and created the universe. Quite possibly, but why did he (suddenly) feel lonely?

Tanka (Tanhsia), 738–824, was the disciple of Sekitō, and his conduct was strange, like that of Lear's Old Man.

Concerning Tanka's burning of the Buddhist images at Erinji Temple to warm himself, the universal opinion was that what he did was right, was Zen, but the action had further repercussions. Suibi (Tsuiwei), a contemporary of Tanka, was one day making oblations before the Rakan, the Buddha's disciplines, when a monk said to him, "Tanka burned the wooden Buddha, and do you hold a requiem mass before the Rakan?" Suibi answered, "Even though it was burned, it could not be burned up completely, and anyway, let me hold a service if I want to!"

*

Sekitō's disciples Tennō and Yakusan are important in themselves, and also as leading, respectively, to Tōzan and Sōzan, and Hōgen and Ummon.

Ryūtan (Lungtan) had been with his master Tennō three years, when one day he suddenly said to him, "I have been

with you all this time, and received no teaching from you!"
Tennō said, "Ever since you came here, when have I not
taught you?" "Taught me when?" said Ryūtan. Tennō replied,
"When you brought tea, I received it from you. When you
brought a meal, I received that too. When you bowed to me,
I inclined my head to you. When did I not teach you?"
Ryūtan stood there thinking. Tennō said, "When you look,
just look. If you wonder about it, you won't get to the point."
Ryūtan was enlightened.

> Tokusan's enlightenment was one of the oddest, for the
> immediate cause was "endarkenment," the blowing out of
> a candle by his master Ryūtan as he was about to take it.
> Later, Tokusan was asked by a monk "What is bodhi
> (salvation)?" He answered, "Be off with you! Don't bring
> your dung here!" Again he was asked, "What is the
> Buddha?" "Just an old monk of the Western World!"

When he was on a "pilgrimage," that is, visiting great
Zen Masters, he went to see Isan. Carrying his bundle of
Buddhist necessities with him, he entered the Law Hall,
marched from East to West and from West to East, and gazed
into Isan's private room. Isan took no notice of him. Tokusan
said, "No, there's nothing to be got here!" and went out.
When he got to the temple gate he said, "There's no need to
be in such a hurry; I will go in and see him again more cere-
moniously." As soon as he had passed the threshold he took
out his cushion and said, "Master!" Isan reached for his *hossu*
(mosquito-whisk, hair-duster). Tokusan immediately shouted
"Kwatz!" dusted his sleeves, and went out. That evening Isan
asked the head monk if there were any newcomers. He replied, "A while ago, someone turned his back on the Hall, put
on his sandals, and went off." "Do you know who he was?"
asked Isan. "No idea who he was," the head monk replied.
Isan said, "That chap will make a hermitage on the top of
the peak and will scorn the Buddhas and speak ill of the
Patriarchs."

> Binnō (Minwang) asked Razan to give the first lecture in
> a temple. Razan ascended the rostrum, took off his robe,
> bade them farewell, and came down. Binnō went up to

him, and taking Razan by the hand said to him, "The meeting at the Holy Mountain was no different from this!" Razan replied, "I thought you were just a common fellow."

The "meeting at the Holy Mountain" refers to Buddha's preaching at Grdhrakuta Mountain, when he silently held up a flower. Binnō was showing off his knowledge of Zen, and Razan seems to be complimenting him on it,—a rather "common" scene. Both Razan and Binnō know all the tricks of the trade.

When Razan first met Sekisō, he asked him, "What shall we do when thoughts never stop rising and disappearing?" Sekisō said, "Be cold ashes and a withered tree! Spotless purity! First impressions for ten thousand years! A box and its lid exactly fitting!" Razan could not grasp the meaning, and went to Gantō with the same question. Gantō shouted "Kwatz!" and asked, "Who rises and disappears?" Razan was profoundly enlightened.

Sekisō adopted what we now think of as Sōtō strategy, but Gantō used Rinzai tactics.

One day Razan went to Senshū, and Tan Chōrō was making tea on the road. Upon the salutation Tan gave a cup of tea to Razan after drinking some himself. Razan was just about to drink the tea when Tan said, "Nice-tasting tea?" Razan spat it out. Tan said nothing, Razan laughed a great laugh.

This anecdote provides us with a definition of Zen. Zen is good manners. "Good manners" means spitting out food or tea or books or people when they are vulgar, affected, sentimental, effusive, or humourless, hypocritical or fanatical,—in a word, when they are what they usually are. Lawrence writes: "Reject people. It is like a poison gas they live in, and one is so few and so fragile in one's own small, subtle air of life."

Zuigan asked Gantō, "What is the Eternal and Fundamental Principle of Things?" Gantō replied, "Movement." Zuigan asked, "What is this 'movement'?" Gantō said, "[When you see things move,] can't you see this Eternal and Fundamental Principle of Things?" Zuigan was lost in thought. Gantō said, "If you agree to this, you are still in the dust of this world; if you disagree, you will be always sunk in life-and-death."

Thinking means deciding one way or another. Zen is deciding both ways. When we see the movement of things, they are not this, but that, and not that, but something else. In this sense, much of Shelley's nature poetry is a good introduction to Zen.

Zuigan (Juiyên) became a priest early in life, and was enlightened by Gantō, and then learned under Kassan. He sat every day like a fool, on a flat stone. He used to call to himself, and answer, saying, "Don't let yourself be laughed at by those who come after you!"

Seppō (Hsüehfêng), 822–908, like Gantō, was a spiritual son of Tokusan; his own disciples were said to be not less than 1500, of whom those who were enlightened numbered 42. The most famous of his disciples was Ummon.

Seppō was cutting trees one day with Chōsei (Chang-shêng) and said to him, "When you cut, cut to the heart, then stop." Chōsei said, "I have cut and finished!" Seppō said, "Former masters transmitted the truth from mind to mind; would you really say that you have cut and finished?" Chōsei said, throwing the axe to the ground, "It is transmitted!" Seppō struck him with his stick.

In general we may say that a (verbal) question should have a physical answer; throwing the axe to the ground was enough, provided it was thrown properly, and saying "It has been transmitted," is legs to the snake. This is not mere addition of unnecessary ornament, but the deformation, the denaturalisation of a living organism. A little too much, or not quite enough,—and what worlds away in the regions of religion and art! Also, we may say, Chōsei was too definite in his assertion. We should be definite about (apparently) indefinite things, and indefinite about (apparently) definite things. Actions, on the other hand, should always be definite. By their finity they attain infinity.

Seppō asked a monk where he had come from. "From Kōzei," said the monk. "Did you meet Daruma anywhere?" asked Seppō. "I just left him," replied the monk.

This anecdote is a refreshing change from the usual reduction of the monk to a half-imbecile silence. The monk has learned to play the Zen game, and airily displays his virtuosity. Though not very profound, it is perhaps superior to ping-pong and such sports.

A monk asked Seppō, "Is the Zen teaching and the Buddhist teaching the same, or different?" "The voice of the thunder is not heard within the room," answered Seppō.

Zen is the religion of nature; Buddhism is the Ten This and Five That, the dividing and subdividing of truth. Amid all this circumlocution and chattering, the simplicity of truth, its materiality, its thusness, is lost to eat and eye and nose.

Seppō said to Gensha, "Monk Shinso asked me where a certain dead monk had gone, and I told him it was like ice becoming water." Gensha said, "That was all right, but I myself would not have answered like that." "What would you have said?" asked Seppō. Gensha replied, "It's like water returning to water."

A monk said to Seppō, "I have shaved my head, put on black clothes, received the vows,—why am I not to be considered a Buddha?" Seppō said, "There is nothing better than an absence of goodness."

The difference between religion and morality, between poetry and emotion, between music and sentimentality, lies here. "Judge not" is usually taken to mean, "Do not condemn others," because you will be yourself condemned. "Judge not" means, "Do not judge your own actions or those of others good or bad, approve or disapprove of them." We must have no principles, no standards, no values. It is true that everything thus becomes wildly subjective, but it can't be helped. You must believe that your real nature is no different from the nature of things, and must somehow try to get at it. This is how, Seppō says, you may become a Buddha.

After Seppō became famous, he opened his own temple, and the monks attending were about fifteen hundred. He used to meet people with his three wooden balls, and when a monk came to be taught he would roll them out. We are reminded here of W. C. Fields, the drunkard-acrobat-humorist. Fields would use his hat. Seppō his three balls. Both were teachers, teachers of Zen. I have learned from both.

A monk asked Gensha, "The Supreme Doctrine,—is there any explanation of it recently?" Gensha said, "We don't hear such a thing often."

This grim understatement nullifies all the books on Zen that ever were or will be written. Zen is how things are said, or heard, but also how they are not said, and "those unheard are sweeter." To talk with Zen is not uncommon, and talking about Zen is more common than it should be, but to talk with Zen about Zen,—it is the rarest thing in the world.

Kuzan entered the gate when Seppō pushed him over and said, "What's this!" and Kuzan was immediately en-lightened. Forgetting himself, he just lifted up his hands and danced around. Seppō said, "Are you behaving rationally?" Kuzan said, "What has this to do with ra-tionality?" Seppō stroked his back, and confirmed his en-lightenment.

Another disciple of Seppō, Chōkei (Ch'angch'ing), had himself many disciples, fifteen hundred, twenty-six being en-lightened under him. He died in 932 aged seventy-nine. When he became enlightened, on rolling up a screen, he composed a famous verse.

What a difference! What a difference!
Raise the blind, and see the world!
If someone asks me to tell him what my religion is
I raise my hossu and strike his mouth.

As noted before, such questions particularly are anathema. "What do you believe?" indeed! Like Walt Whitman, I believe everything and everybody. The learned in his blindness bows down to theology and philosophy.

Hofuku, seeing a monk, struck the (round) outside post of the temple; he then struck the head of the monk, who cried out with pain. Hofuku said, "Why doesn't the post feel pain?" The monk gave no answer.

The answer is; "The question is the same as, 'Have you stopped beating your wife?'" In other words, the answer to the question why the post doesn't feel pain, is, "It does." "Why doesn't it cry out, then?" "It does." "Why don't I hear it?" "You do, but you don't know you do." "Why don't I know?" "Because you are not enlightened." "Why am I not enlightened?" "Because you are too damn lazy!" "Why. . . ."

*

A monk asked, "What is the True Eye of the Law?" Chōkei said, "I have a favour to ask of you: don't throw sand around!"

People ask why and how as an excuse for not doing what they know they should do. In some ways illusion, as Nietzsche said, is life-giving, and we may tell a lie until it becomes the truth, but such truths are not fundamental. We have to learn to look with the eye, and the only way is to keep on looking, looking at a snake until it ceases to be repulsive, looking at a naked woman until she ceases to be attractive, and until snakes and women become supremely interesting.

*

A monk said to Kyōsei, "I am pecking inside the shell; I ask you to peck outside." Kyōsei said, "Are you in a state of active readiness or not?" The monk said, "If I were not, people would despise me." Kyōsei said, "You are still wallowing in the grass!"

The chick pecking inside the shell, and the mother hen pecking outside so that the chick should be born, is an apt symbol of the relation of teacher and pupil, in regard to the enlightenment of the latter. Kyōsei seems to have been famous for his ability in this respect. The monk imagined that his enlightenment was imminent. Kyōsei told him that far from about to reach the summit he was still in the grasses.

*

When Kyōsei's master, Ummon, was asked, "What is this pecking within and without?" he answered with one of his famous laconisms, "Echo."

Hofuku asked a monk, "What is your name?" "Hsientsê, Everywhere-swampy," he replied. Hofuku said, "If you happen to run across a Mr. Dried-up-place, what would you do?" "Who is this Mr. Dried-up-place?" asked the monk. "I'm that man!" said Hofuku. The monk said, "Master, you should not make a fool of people!" Hofuku said, "It's you rather who are making of fool of me!"

The monk, like everyone else, wanted to become rich. Hofuku used the monk's name to point out to him that he, Hofuku, was as poor as a church mouse, spiritually. The monk thought that Hofuku could not be serious. When Bernard Shaw said a rich man was a thief, the rich man thought he was joking.

*

Hōgen (Fayen), the founder of the branch of Zen that bears his name, was born in 885.

A monk, Echō (Huichao), asked Hōgen, "What is the Buddha?" Hōgen said, "You are Echō!" The monk came to a realisation.

Suppose Hōgen had said, "You are the Buddha!" This would be as true as any other statement, according to the meaning. The question is, who and what are "you," and, who and what is the Buddha? Hōgen must adapt himself to the monk's (proleptic) experience of himself, another Buddha, and says, "You are Echō!" "You" meant the Buddha, and "Echō" meant the Buddha, to Echō at that moment.

*

A monk asked Hōgen, "What is a drop of water from Sōgen (Ts'aoyüan)?" Hōgen answered, "It is a drop of water from Sōgen!" Once Shō (Shao), the National Teacher, heard this saying, and was suddenly enlightened.

Sōgen is Sōkei, the place where the Sixth Patriarch taught. The drop of water is the truth revealed to and by him. Hōgen was a master of this repetition of the question so as to be a perfect answer to it. For Hōgen, the question was answered in the asking of it. Doubt and belief were one, not two things, and deep. The danger here lies in the very transcendence, which begins in the use of water as a symbol. The question is the answer, and the answer is the question, that is true, but more important still is that Christ is a door, and a door (if you go through it properly) is Christ.

*

A monk said to Hōgen, "There is a saying, 'One lamp destroys a room's hundred years' darkness; what is this light?" Hōgen exclaimed, "What the devil are you worrying about a hundred years for?"

Each ray of light destroys a whole world of darkness, but there is no need to get sentimental about the time (or even the place).

*

A monk said: "In the *Kongōkyō* it is written, 'If you see all forms as no-forms, you see the Tathagata.' " Hōgen said, "If you see all forms as no-forms, you cannot see the Tathagata."

The Tathagata is the suchness of things, all things as they really are. Hōgen is right, and the sutra is wrong. A thing is a no-thing but it is also a thing. Forms are no-forms, but also forms. Everything is the same, but everything is different. That is the marvel of our life, the supreme problem of philosophy, and the love of this contradiction makes the world go round.

*

One day Hōgen told a monk to fetch some earth to add to that in a lotus-pot. He asked him, "Did you get the earth from the East of the bridge, or the West of the bridge?" "From the East of the bridge," replied the monk. Hōgen asked, "Is this the truth, or is it delusion?"

We are not told the monk's answer. How shall we answer it ourselves. Is the world real, or unreal? The answer is Yes. Is there such a thing as East and West in finite space? You know only if you have been in infinite space, which does not mean in a space-rocket. Earth is very real, especially when you get a little bit in your eye. But Hamlet speaks of "the mind's eye." Does not the mind create the eye and the earth in it? "Nothing is but thinking makes it so." Wordsworth's "imagination" solves the question, for it is the power to create what already exists.

People teach what they can. People teach what they teach. Everybody teaches everybody else. Our teaching is not however what we ostensibly teach. Hitler taught the world that a man may be totally lacking in humanity and yet be remarkable. Many lecturers on poetry teach us that poetry is devoid of value. Kreisler taught us that violin-playing is a mixture of sentimentality and acrobatics. Yakusan taught the monks not to ask to be taught. Buddha had already taught this, but inefficiently. The only way to teach not teaching is really not to teach.

*

Yakusan learned this kind of thing from Sekitō. One day, Yakusan was doing zazen. Sekitō asked him, "What are you doing?" "Not a thing," replied Yakusan. "Aren't you sitting blankly?" said Sekitō. "If I were sitting blankly, I would be doing something," retorted Yakusan. Sekitō said: "Tell me what you are not doing." Yakusan replied: "A thousand sages could not answer that question!"

*

Dōgo was asked by a monk, "What is the deepest?" Dōgo came down from his seat, made obeisance in the manner of women, and said, "You have come from far, and I have no answer for you."

Dōgo's action and words were deepest. To know that there is nothing to know, and to grieve that it is so difficult to communicate this "nothing to know" to others,—this is the life of Zen, this is the deepest thing in the world.

*

Sekisō (Shihshuang) became a monk when young, and studied under Isan, then Dōgo, by whom he was certified. He died in 888.

Nō : Childactor in "Sagi"

Sekisō asked Dōgo (Taowu) 768–835, "After a hundred years, if someone asks about the absolute meaning of the universe, what shall I say to him?" Dōgo called the boy-attendant, who came, and told him fill up the water-bottle. Dōgo waited a while, and then said to Sekisō, "What was it you asked just now?" Sekisō repeated the question. Dōgo thereupon went back to his room. At this, Sekisō became enlightened.

This kind of thing shows a genius above even that of Plato or Michelangelo, or Bach himself. The creation of the world, its evolution, its final destruction, its eternity and infinity is (to be seen in) the filling of a water-bottle, in waiting, in repeating a question, in going back to one's room. No wonder Sekisō was enlightened. But all this was done by Dōgo, consciously; by every Tom, Dick, and Harry also, but unconsciously, by every stick and stone, which "the best of us excel," since they do all that they are capable of; even Dōgo does not do this always.

In the face of death, all competition and ambition is meaningless. Directly facing death is indeed enlightenment itself.

*

A monk asked Sekisō, "Is the meaning of Daruma's coming from the West contained in the Buddhist teachings?" "It is," replied Sekisō. "What is the meaning of Daruma's coming from the West taught there?" "Don't look for it in the sutras!" said Sekisō.

This is very good and clear. The truth is in the Bible, the Holy Bible, but don't look in the Bible for it! As Thoreau said, "When you visit God, don't ask to see one of the servants."

*

Hōgen said to the master Shūzan (Hsiushan), "A hair's breadth of difference, and they are Heaven and Earth apart. What do you think of this?" Shūzan said, "A hair's breadth of difference, and they are Heaven and Earth apart." Hōgen said, "What's the use of talking like that?" Shūzan said, "That's all I can say; how about you?" Hōgen said, "A hair's breadth of difference, and they are Heaven and Earth apart." Shūzan made obeisance to him.

Hōgen's quotation is from the *Hsinhsinming*. It means that the greatest music, played just a little out of tune or out of time is as bad as, or even worse than, cacophony. It means that people are either good or bad, actions are either perfect or imperfect; there is nothing between. You have good taste or bad taste. There are no middle-brows. The slightest touch of egoism, sentimentality, cruelty, snobbery, vulgarity (all the same thing) and everything done is spoiled. The state of Zen does not, of course, cover all these cases, and an "enlightened" man may be spoiled by his native and ineradicable insensitivity or stupidity.

*

Of the Hōgen Sect, besides the founder, the two most famous members were Tendai and Eimyō.

Eimyō was asked by a monk, "What is the Great Round Mirror?" Eimyō answered, "A broken crock."

This comes from the phrase, "Within the bright mirror there is not a hair's breadth of difference," that is, in the Buddhist wisdom there is not the slightest separation between this and that, mine and yours. Thus the monk's question is, "What is the essence of Buddhism?" or, "What is Zen?" The answer is not as destructive and nihilistic as it looks. Oscar Wilde said that art was useless, but he also thought it to be the greatest thing, the only thing, in the world.

A monk said to Eimyō, "I have been with you a long time, but I have yet to grasp your way of looking at things." Eimyō said, "Understand that you don't understand!" The monk said, "If I don't understand, how can I understand anything?" Eimyō replied, "The womb of a cow gives birth to an elephant, and the blue sea produces yellow dust."

Eimyō's intention is clearly to make the unununderstanding monk understand less. When we feel an exhilaration in the non-understanding we are close to Zen.

*

Yakusan (Yüehshan), became a priest at the age of seventeen; he was enlightened under Sekitō. He died in 834 A.D.

Yakusan asked a monk, "Where have you come from?" "From the Southern Lake," replied the monk. "Has the lake overflowed its banks?" asked Yakusan. "Not yet," answered the monk. Then Yakusan said, "So much rain, and the lake not yet full?" But the monk was silent.

This story has a kind of stage irony, two people talking at cross-purposes. Yakusan is not interested in the rain and the lake, but in the monk. The monk is interested in the rain and the lake, but not in Yakusan. In a sense, both are wrong, the monk for his over-simplicity, and Yakusan for over-profundity, and not jolting the monk out of his meteorological complacency.

*

A monk asked Yakusan, "Did the essence of Buddhism exist before Daruma came?" "It did," said Yakusan. "Then why did he come, if it already existed?" "He came," said Yakusan, "just because it was here already."

This *Alice in Wonderland* conversation is a remarkable escape from the scientific world of cause and effect. Five centuries before Daruma came to China, Christ had died to save sinners who were already saved by the eternal love of God.

*

A monk of Kassan's went to Kōtei (Kaot'ing), and had just bowed to him when Kōtei struck him on the back. The monk bowed again, and again Kōtei struck him, and drove him away. The monk told Kassan about this, and Kassan asked, "Do you understand?" "No," replied the monk. "That's a good thing," said Kassan. "For if you did, I would be dumbfounded."

Nyōgen Senzaki has a fine comment on this anecdote. "American Zen is running sideways, writing books, lecturing, referring to theology, psychology, and what not. Someone should stand up and smash the whole thing to pieces. . . ."

*

Kassan was doing zazen when Tōzan came and asked him, "How about it?" Kassan answered, "Just like this."

This kind of conversation is a relief from the sometimes excessive paradox and "mysterification" of the Zen masters, and is nearer to Zen by its thusness.

*

Kassan had a monk who went round all the Zen temples but found nothing to suit him anywhere. The name of Kassan, however, was often mentioned to him from far and near as a great master, so he came back and interviewed Kassan, and said, "You have an especial understanding of Zen. How is it you didn't reveal this to me?" Kassan said, "When you boiled rice, didn't I light the fire? When you passed round the food (*anyaku, gyōeki*) didn't I offer my bowl to you? When did I betray your expectations?" The monk was enlightened.

We teach Zen, if we teach it at all, by the way we write, the way we light the fire, or hold out the bowl to be filled with rice. It is also true, however, that there may be some intellectual obstacle which prevents the (physical) eye or ear or nose from perceiving truth directly. In such a case, the meaning, the intellectual meaning of the words, may cause satori, in the sense of removing that intellectual obstacle.

*

Junfunō (Tsunpuna) said to Shōzan, "About the clear mirror,—I would like you to have a look in it." Shōzan said, "Not a glance." "Why not?" asked Junfunō. Shōzan said, "A broken mirror will not again reflect; fallen flowers will not return to the branch."

This of course refers to the poem-contest between Huineng and Jinshū. Huineng declared that there was no mirror, and Shōzan says that even if there was the illusion of one, that illusion, in his case, had been for ever destroyed; it is as dead as dead leaves. Junfunō was a senior monk to Yakusan.

*

When Tōzan was a child, he became a monk in the temple of a priest who one day was teaching the *Makahannya Shingyō*, and when he came to the passage, "No eye, no ear, no nose, no tongue, no body, no consciousness," Tōzan could not follow the priest. As for the eye, looking at the Vinaya priest, and with his hand feeling his body, he said to him, "The Master has eyes, ears, and so on, and I too; why does the Buddha say we haven't?" The priest was astonished, and said, "I'm not the teacher for you; you will one day be a great Mahayana missionary," and he sent him off to be a monk under Goei (Wuhsieh), a disciple of Baso; he died in 818.

*

Tōzan said to Ungan, "Master, if someone asks me a hundred years afterwards what I thought was your deepest understanding, what should I say?" Ungan answered, "Tell him I said, 'It is simply this.'" Tōzan was silent for a time and Ungan said, "Kai, if you have grasped this, you must carry it out in detail!" Tōzan was still silent. Ungan struck him. Afterwards, when Tōzan was holding a service in memory of Ungan's deepest understanding, a monk said to him, "The dead teacher said, 'It is simply this!' This is the yea-saying spirit?" "It is," replied Tōzan. The monk asked, "What does this mean?" Tōzan said, "At that time, my idea was almost entirely a mistaken one, though I understood what he meant all right." "The dead teacher," said the monk, "did he know It or not?" Tōzan said, "If he didn't, how could he say such a thing; and if he did, how could he avoid saying it?"

"A hundred years afterwards" means "when you are dead"; if taken literally, the speaker would also have gone to the Yellow Springs. "It is simply this" is the very essence of Zen, the point being in "simply." A thing has existence value; infinite meaning in being what it is. Enlightenment is perceiving once for all this poetic factuality, this religious thusness. And if the enlightenment is real, it must be, as Ungan and Blake said, "in minute details" of daily life. Tōzan's answers to the monk's questions are models of modesty, if not of logic, and the former is more convincing than the latter.

*

Tōzan announced: "You must know that there is something beyond the Buddha!" At a certain time a monk asked, "What is this which transcends the Buddha?" Tōzan answered, "Not Buddha!"

"Buddha" means enlightenment, or Zen, or the supreme truth. What is beyond this? The answer clearly is, delusion, non-Zen, all but the supreme truth. God, righteousness, courage, self-lessness,—these are easy to understand. But the Devil, evil, cowardice, selfishness,—who can explain these? As Christ said, "If your righteousness does not exceed that of the Pharisees. . . ." We have to break out of goodness, taste the unique flavour of ugliness, enjoy the lies and hypocrisy of human nature,—as we actually do, whenever we laugh. Real Zen means not to stop laughing.

*

A monk said to Tōzan, "How about when the cart stops, but the ox doesn't?" Tōzan said, "Why not employ a driver?"

The monk says, "The flesh is willing, but the spirit is weak." Tōzan says, "Underneath are the everlasting arms." In (Indian) Buddhism, the ox is the most important of animals. In the *Hokke Sutra*, Buddhism is compared to a cart drawn by a white ox, and in the Yuikyō Sutra, religious practices are illustrated by a pasture cow. In Zen there are many *mondō* connected with cows, and there are the bull-herding pictures, the problem, as with the monk, being to control the bull. Who is the driver? It is Buddha, the Buddha nature, the nature of Nature, Something beyond all these, but closer than breathing.

A monk said to Tōzan, "A snake is swallowing a frog; is it right to save the frog, or not to save it?" Tōzan replied, "If you save it, you do not see with two eyes; if you do not save it, the form does not show its shadow."

If we rescue the frog from the snake, we are looking only on one side, forgetting the snake's point of view. If we let ill alone, we do not express our natural desire to protect the weak from the strong. Anecdotes concerning snakes are not many, but are all interesting. Kyōsei (Chingching), a disciple of Seppō, one day asked a monk what noise it was outside the door. The monk said it was a snake biting a frog. Kyōsei said, "I thought life was suffering; but suffering is life."

According to Christianity the world was made for man, not for itself. The modern view is that things exist for their own sakes, or perhaps just exist, without any "sake" at all. Tōzan says "For your sake," and this is true, though only half the truth, as is every statement. Things exist for their own sake, a hundred percent, and for our sake, a hundred percent.

Tōzan went to see Nansen. At this time they were holding an anniversary meeting for Baso's death. Nansen said to assembled monks, "We are going to celebrate Baso tomorrow. Do you think he will be present, or not?" No one among the monks answered; but Tōzan said, "He will wait for a companion, and will come if he comes." Nansen said, "This man is young, but he can be shaped and polished." Tōzan said, "Your grace should not dislike a good man and regard him as worthless."

"Present, or not present?" Superstition says, "Present"; common sense says, "Not present." Zen is neither. What does it say? It says, with poetry, "Present or not present?" Tōzan says the dead master will wait for a companion. Who is the companion of an enlightened man? The answer clearly is God, but who is God? God is love. If you love Baso he will come and make his abode with you.

The doctrine of the teaching of Buddhism by non-sentient beings originated with Nanyō, born 775, the disciple of the 6th Patriarch. In Buddhism, not in Zen, this would have a pantheistic meaning, but the question arises, what is this Buddhism which rocks and streams teach us? The answer is, they teach us that they teach us. They teach us their existence-value. All teaching is thus non-sentient, not-intellectual, non-emotional. A human being, as Ungan says, teaches before he opens his mouth what in any case he can never say. What is wrong with words is simply that they are late, late arrivals in world history.

*

Tōzan went to see Isan, and said to him, "Recently I heard that Tōzan of Nanyō spoke of insentient beings preaching the Law, but I can't get to the bottom of it." Isan said, "Do you remember what was said?" "I remember it," said Tōzan. "Then try and repeat what was said," said Isan. Tōzan recounted the following. A monk asked (Nanyō) what the mind of the ancient Buddhas was, and he replied, "It is fences, walls, and broken tiles." The monk said, "Fences, walls and broken tiles are insentient, aren't they?" Nanyō said, "That is so." "Do they expound Buddhism?" asked the monk. "Always, and busily," said Nanyō. The monk said, "Why don't I hear it then?" Nanyō answered, "You don't hear it, but you shouldn't prevent others doing so." "Who hears it?" asked the monk. "All the saints," answered Nanyō. "Does your grace hear it?" asked the monk. "Not I!" replied Nanyō. "If you don't hear it, how can you explain the teaching of the Law by inanimate creatures?" asked the monk. Nanyō answered, "It's my good luck I don't hear it. If I did, I would be the same as all the saints, and then you wouldn't have the chance to hear my teaching." The monk said, "If that is so, people would have no part in it." Nanyō said, "I myself expound it for the sake of people, not for the sake of the saints." The monk said, "After the people hear it, what then?" "Then they're not just people any more," replied Nanyō.

There was a monk ill in the infirmary who asked to see Tōzan. When Tōzan went there, the monk said to him, "Why don't you save ordinary people?" Tōzan asked him, "Whose is your family?" The monk replied, "A great (icchantika) family." Tōzan remained silent for some time. Then the monk said, "What shall we do when the Four Mountains come pressing round us?" Tōzan said, "I myself came from under the roof of a family." The monk said, "Is there relativity, or no relativity?" Tōzan answered, "None." The monk asked, "Where will you let me go?" "To a rice field," answered Tōzan. The monk heaved a sigh, and said, "Good-bye," and died sitting there. Tōzan tapped him on the head three times with his staff, and said, "Like this, you knew how to die, but not how to live."

This anecdote has something unusual about it. We feel in it a human warmth that is beyond even Zen. The dying monk is evidently thinking of his old home, and the people in it who have no Buddha nature, no prospect of salvation. Tōzan thinks too of his own. The Four Mountains that hang over us are birth, illness, old age, and death. "Relativity," *ego*, means the under-relation of two things, "No man liveth unto himself." Besides this there is *fu-ego*; each thing is itself, has an absolute independent existence and "owns no other kin." Tōzan answers, "*Fu-ego*," but what he should say is that Zen transcends both. "To a ricefield" is a strange expression.

"Return to the absolute, to nature, to the undifferentiated, where you should have been all your life!" says Tōzan to the dying man. "You died well," Tōzan tells the seated corpse, "but in your life you doubted and dichotomised, you separated yourself from your family in thought, instead of realising that in life, as in death, all is one, and one is all."

*

Sōzan (Ts'aoshan) first studied Confucianism, then became a priest at the age of nineteen. He was taught by Tōzan, whose Zen he received and propagated.

When Sōzan saw Tōzan for the first time, he was asked his name. "Honjaku (Penchi)," he replied. "Why don't you answer me absolutely?" asked Tōzan, "I won't," Sōzan answered. "Why not?" said Tōzan. "Because my name is not Honjaku," Sōzan replied. Tōzan recognised Sōzan's ability and promise.

When Sōzan is asked his name he answers in the relative world. In the absolute world even my cat, let alone God, is nameless. But it is only those who know that all things are nameless, that can truly give names to things.

Sōzan, hearing the voice of the bell, cried out, "Aya! Aya! Aya!" A monk asked, "What's the matter with you?" Sōzan said, "It strikes on my heart!"

Thoreau writes in his *Journal*, 1841:

I hear a man blowing a horn this still evening, and it sounds like the plaint of nature in these times. In this, which I refer to some man, there is something greater than any man.

*

A monk said to Sōzan, "I, Seizei, a poor lonely creature, ask you for your help." Sōzan said, "Master Sei!" Seizei answered, "Yes?" Sōzan said, "A farmer called Haku, though he has drunk three bowls of wine, says he has not moistened his lips."

This episode forms the 10th Case of the *Mumonkan*. Sōzan's answer is usually taken as a reproof of the monk's posing as in a state of spiritual and material poverty. If he were truly in this condition he would be as Christ said the poor are, blessed, and would not need to ask Sōzan for anything. Sōzan's answer may also be taken as an example of the Zen doing-not-doing.

*

A monk said to Sōzan, "Learners are just one mass of illness; won't you cure them?" "Not I!" said Sōzan. "Why not," asked the monk. "Because," answered Sōzan, "if you get me to search for life, I can't find it; death also, I can't find it!"

Animals sleep when they feel unwell and get better or die. We cannot find life, we cannot find death. To look for one or not to look for the other—this is illness.

*

Ungo (Yüngü) was the chief disciple of Tōzan (or Dōzan). He took orders at the age of twenty five. When he first met Tōzan, he was asked, "What is your name?" He answered, "Dōyō" (Taoying). Tōzan said, "Tell me transcendentally!" Ungo replied, "Speaking transcendentally, my name is Dōyō." Tōzan said, "When I saw Ungan, my answer was no different." Ungo remained with Tōzan many years.

An official said to Ungo: "The World-honoured One had a secret message; Mahakasyapa did not keep it a secret; what is this secret word of Buddha?" Ungo called to him, "Your honour!" He answered, "Yes?" Ungo said, "You understand?" "No," he replied. Ungo said, "If you don't understand, that is Buddha's secret word; if you do, that is Mahakasyapa's not keeping it a secret."

A monk asked Ungo, "Who is the teacher of all the Buddhas?" Ungo said "Kwatz!" and added, "You cart-pulling bumpkin!" The monk made his bows. "How do you understand it?" asked Ungo. The monk said "Kwatz!" and added, "You old abbot!" Ungo said, "Fundamentally, I don't understand!" The monk danced around and went off. Ungo exclaimed, "A beggar hanging round the food-table!"

The teacher of all the Buddhas is their own Buddha nature, but we do not really know this fact until our own Buddha nature teaches it to us. It is of course always teaching us. The things around us do nothing else. But being called, and answering, is a remarkably clear, and at the same time profound example of the way in which things are separate and yet conterminous. The monk asked a question. Ungo said, "You are a fool!" The monk said, "So are you!" (so is everybody, so is everything). "What is the meaning of 'fool'?" asked Ungo. The monk danced. (Everything dances; the universe is a dance). Off he went, and Ungo praised him, in his absence, saying, "After all, everybody is out to get something, though of course Zen getting is a no-getting."

One day Ungo had some breeches taken to a monk who lived in a hermitage, but the monk refused them, saying, "The woman who bore me gave me some breeches." Ungo had a message taken to the monk asking, "What did you wear before your mother bore you?" The monk sent back no answer. Afterwards, when the monk died, and was cremated, sharira were found, which were brought to Ungo and shown to him. Ungo declared, "Even if a cartload (of sharira) had been found, it would be nothing compared with the answer to my question?"

Zen requires a certain obstinacy, as well of course as resilience. Both Ungo and the monk persisted in their own activity. Ungo had the last word, it is true, but then the monk was dead and the holy relics found in his ashes could be rightly dismissed as a pious superstition. The monk refused Ungo's charity. He was born with his mother-given fleshly covering on his shanks, and that was enough. He did not wish to be warmed with Ungo's brotherly love. Ungo had his revenge by asking an unanswerable question, and when the monk was dead pooh-poohed his relics and said that the monk should have answered him, forgetting that silence is also an answer, and death the answer to all questions.

UMMON

Ummon is particularly famous for a one-syllable Zen, one (Chinese) word in answer to a question however lengthy. A monk asked Ummon, "What is the Buddha?" Ummon replied, "A dried shit-stick."

This forms the 21st Case of the *Mumonkan*. Pieces of wood were used as toilet paper in China. When the supply of new ones ran out, people would pick up used old dry ones, thus increasing infectious diseases, and by natural selection making the Chinese a disease-resistant race. It would have been more scientific, though less poetic, if Ummon had said that the Buddha, that is, man, is the shit on the stick. But Ummon's intention is a little more complicated. He wants to pour shit on *Das Heilige* for one thing, but he does not wish to say anything pantheistic or panhumanistic. He wishes the questioner to be satisfied with his question. That is the art of living in this world.

Ummon is perhaps the greatest man China produced. He is a mixture of Selden, Swift, Sidney Smith, and Oscar Wilde. He has his superstitions, it is true, Buddhist and Taoist, for example the belief in reincarnation, but it is easy for us, more than a thousand years later, to look back upon him and see how he could not in every way transcend his age and place, but for boldness, succinctness, profundity, universality, transcendentality, only Eckhart and Thoreau come near him. For this reason, he is unknown outside China and Japan. Even in Japan almost no one knows his name, and his *goroku*, the account of his life and sayings, is practically unobtainable.

*

A monk asked Ummon "What is it that surpasses the Buddhas, surpasses the Patriarchs?" Ummon replied, "Buns."

The Buddhas and the Patriarchs are things of the mind, just like generals and prime ministers and policemen, but buns are real, buns are earnest; they have a simplicity, a perfection of being which no man can attain to. Jesus taught us to pray for our daily buns. They are also the spiritual Body of Christ, broken for us. Above all, buns are something which Buddhas and gods and sages are not (except unintentionally); they are humorous.

*

Ummon said to his monks, "The Old Barbarian (Buddha), when he was born, with one hand he pointed his finger at the sky, with the other he pointed his finger to the earth, looked in the four directions, took seven steps and said, 'Above Heaven, and below Heaven, I am the only Honoured One.' If I had seen him at that time, I would have beaten him to death with my staff, and fed him to the dogs, so as to bring peace to the world."

Ummon is not merely praising by blame. Evil arises together with good, delusion with enlightenment. The world of animals, for all the eating and being eaten, is a world of peace, and even the enlightened man can scarcely retain the peace that passeth misunderstanding.

*

A monk said to Ummon, "How about a man whose parents won't let him be a priest?" "Shallow!" said Ummon. "I am not uneducated, but I don't understand." "Deep!" said Ummon.

When we teach, we teach ourselves. If the student also understands something, that's fine, but it is unlikely. "Shallow" means the question is shallow, and the man who will not "Hate father and mother for my sake" is shallow. "Deep" means that to be troubled about a question is deep; not to know is (potentially) deep.

Pointing with his staff, he said, "The patriarchs are all over your heads, dancing about. If you want to know the eyes of the patriarchs, they are all under your feet." Then he went on, "You give the hungry spirits tea and rice, but they are not satiated."

The Bible says, "God is love." This is all right, but it should have said, with Tolstoy, "Love is God." Love of the earth, love of the sky, that is enough. Picking out this, and choosing that for love, it is an eternal task to please these half-gods. Whatever it is, take it, for God offers it, God offers himself in it, God is your taking it.

*

A monk asked Ummon, "What is the meaning of Daruma's coming from the West?" Ummon said, "We see the mountains in the sun."

Ummon asked the head monk, "What sutra are you lecturing on?" "The Nirvana Sutra." "The Nirvana Sutra has the Four Nirvana Virtues, hasn't it?" "It has." Ummon asked, picking up a cup, "How many virtues has this?" "None at all," said the monk. "But ancient people said it had, didn't they?" said Ummon. "What do you think of what they said?" Ummon struck the cup and asked, "You understand?" "No," said the monk. "Then," said Ummon, "You'd better go on with your lectures on the sutra."

The Four Nirvana Virtues are 1. immutability; 2. joy; 3. personal existence; 4. purity. These four virtues belong only to the transcendental realm, from which such things as cups are excluded. We have here the problem of value, or values, which, according to one European school are four, religious, moral, aesthetic, and intellectual. Ummon believes in one only, and practises it, existence-value. The existence value of each thing is infinite, and therefore equal to that of every other thing. Thus a cup or a sutra are "indifferent modes of the Divine Being." Even in Christianity there was the Holy Grail. But, as Wordsworth stated, and proved by examples, value is more accessible in the ordinary, common things of everyday life. So Ummon uses a cup to preach with; his hymn of praise is the note the cup sends out when it is struck.

*

A monk asked Ummon, "How about when the word is uttered that expresses all things?" Ummon said, "Tearing down, breaking up!"

These enigmatic laconisms are not mere encouragements to a state of non-thought. They are exact replies to exact questions. These questions all boil down to, what is the state, what is the activity of Zen? The answer is that morality, beauty, truth, Christ, Buddha, the *Matthew Passion*, the *Commedia*, justice, the soul and its immortality or annihilation,— all disappear.

*

A monk asked Ummon, "What man on earth can understand Buddhism?" Ummon answered, "The outside post of the temple can understand it!" and with a "Kwatz!" added, "You dead toad!"

This calling the monk a toad is praising him too highly, and belittling the toad.

The following is a continuation or corollary of the preceding. Ummon said, "All you monks roam about all over the earth on Zen pilgrimages, but you don't know the meaning of Daruma's coming from the West. The outside post knows it all right. Why don't you somehow find out the post's knowledge of that meaning? Anyway, I'll tell you it myself: nine times nine is eighty one."

When students asked me the meaning of the absolute, asserting that all things are relative, I used to write on the blackboard $2 \times 2 = 4$, which of course might not be true, that is, absolute, in some other world, but what we want is something absolute in this world. Zen is the thusness of things, mathematical no less than material, material no less than mental.

*

A monk asked Ummon, "What is the precise meaning of Sōkei?" Ummon said, "This old monk likes anger, likes joy." "How is this?" asked the monk. "When you meet a swordsman," said Ummon, "meet him with a sword. Don't offer a poem to anyone but a poet."

"Sōkei" means Huineng, the Sixth Patriarch, who lived there. Ummon's first answer has little direct connection with Huineng. Zen means liking what you (really) like, what your (real) nature likes, in Ummon's case, anger, the sinews of the soul, and joy, its wings. He reminds us of Nietzsche, Blake, and of D. H. Lawrence.

*

A monk said to Ummon, "If a man kills his father, kills his mother, he may repent before the Buddha. If he kills the Buddha, kills a patriarch, where can he repent?" Ummon answered, "Quite!"

This is an example of the one-syllable replies for which Ummon is justly famous. Ro! (Lu!) means "expressed," "clear," "nothing hidden," and corresponds very well to the English idiomatic use of "Quite!" What Ummon means is that the question is a very good one, that is, it is rhetorical. Such a man has no place to repent, nowhere to repent; he can't repent. What we can't do, we shouldn't do. As Thoreau says, "Nature never apologises." Dogs fawn, like men, but a cat just licks itself in the corner when slapped.

*

Ummon said to the assembled monks, "Hearing the sound, perceiving the Way; seeing the colour, enlightening the mind. The Bodhisattva Kanzeon brings some cash and buys some rice cakes. Letting them go, they are seen to be dumplings."

"Hearing the sound, perceiving the Way," refers to Kyō-gen (Hsiangyen), who became enlightened on hearing a stone strike a bamboo while he was sweeping. "Seeing the colour, enlightening the mind," regards Reiun (Lingyün), who came to a realisation on seeing the flowers of a plum tree. On the other hand, Kannon does a kind of conjuring trick with cakes. The meaning is that as a result of hearing the sound of a stone hitting a bamboo, or seeing a blossoming tree, we are able to perform the most ordinary tasks in a miraculous way. Hateful things become charming; odious things become indifferent; dust becomes gold, and gold becomes dust,—all at will, and for a few pence, a few *pensées*.

*

A monk asked Ummon, "What is your traditional way of teaching Zen?" Ummon said, "Outside the gate there are learners; tell them to come in!"

This means that Ummon considered himself to be a teacher, no more, no less.

*

A monk asked, "How about when the wind does not pass through the secret room?" "It trembles in the dew, and sounds in the breeze," replied Ummon. "How about the people in that room?" Ummon said, "it's not easy to talk of the same thing twice!"

"The wind not passing through the secret room" means that master and disciple are in complete union and unanimity. It is as natural as the dew on the leaf, and the soughing wind. But if we go on endlessly asking, when the question has been answered once and for all. . . .

*

A monk asked Ummon, "What are the activities of a sramana?" Ummon answered, "I have not the slightest idea." The monk then said, "Why haven't you any idea?" Ummon replied, "I just want to keep my no-idea."

A sramana is an enlightened monk. This monk's question is not so much "What shall I do to be saved?" as "What does a man do when he is saved?" Ummon's answer may be interpreted in many ways. "I know, but I don't want to say." "I really don't know." "I want to teach you not to know." "My state of mind is beyond knowing and not knowing." "You are pestering me!" "Perfect action is unconscious of itself." "Don't ask (foolish) questions!"

*

Ummon was asked by a monk, "What is the dust-samadhi?" Ummon replied, "Rice in the bowl, water in the tub."

The "dust-samadhi" means the supreme state in which each thing is interfused with each other and with ourselves. To put it in a simple way, "It's (universally interpenetrated) love that makes the world (wheel of the Law) go round." Ummon says, "Rice is in the bowl, water is in the tub, God's in his Heaven, all's right with the world."

*

Ummon asked a monk, "Are you the gardener?" "Yes," he said. "Why have turnips no roots?" he asked the monk, who could not reply. "Because," said Ummon, "rain-water is plentiful."

This pseudo-scientific answer by Ummon, who no doubt has his tongue in his cheek, is precisely that of the scientists, who explain how a giraffe got its long neck, but cannot explain why every other animal has not a long neck.

*

Ummon asked a monk, "Where have you come from?" "From Nangaku," he replied. "Usually," said Ummon, "I don't entangle people with words, and bamboozle them with phrases; come a little closer!" The monk went nearer, and Ummon shouted, "Be off with you!"

We are always taken in with apparent kindness, and equally with apparent rudeness. But to be suspicious of everybody and everything is not the solution. To be a dove and a serpent in one,—that's it, but how difficult!

*

A monk said to Ummon, "I ask you, master, to deliver a learner from darkness and illusion quickly!" Ummon said, "What's the price of rice in Jōshū?"

The monk wanted to be delivered from the body of this flesh into a spiritual realm. Ummon wants to put the monk more deeply into the darkness of trade and food and competition. The deepness is all.

*

Ummon said to the assembled monks, "It is said that after we have not seen someone for three days we must look at him anew; what do you all think about that?" Answering himself he said, "A thousand."

Evidently Ummon had not seen the monks for several days, and was looking at them with different eyes, but they gazed at him with their usual blank or ambitious or inferiority-feeling faces, and he was constrained to warn them against such complacency, indifference, or enmity. "A thousand," is used in various ways in Buddhism. Each of the past, present, and future kalpas has a thousand Buddhas. The lotus has a thousand petals. The Tendai Sect has a thousand suchnesses. Kannon has a thousand hands and a thousand eyes. Ummon means by his exclamation that we must look at each thousand-minded man with our own thousand-mind. We are reminded of Christ's "Seventy times seven!"

*

A monk said to Ummon, "What is your age, may I ask?" Ummon replied, "Seven times nine, sixty eight." The monk said, "What do you mean, seven times nine, sixty eight?" Ummon said, "I took off five years for your sake."

An English school-boy was once caught eating an apple in class. Keeping his eye on him, the teacher ordered him to the front. "What are you eating?" "Nothing!" "Open your mouth!" Inserting his finger he pulled out a large bit of apple. "What's this?" "Apple, sir." "How did it get in your mouth?" "Didn't know it was there, sir!" Both Ummon and the boy show their disrespect for the other party by telling an obvious lie.

*

Ummon said, "A monk should know the eye of ancient men. What was this eye?" Himself answering, he said, "It is a toad dancing up to heaven."

The "ancient men" means those who understood Zen. A toad cannot dance, and a man is not immortal, but he can do something impossible, dance out of death into (timeless) life. We learn to do this from the ancients.

*

A monk said to Ummon, "How about the time when there was no Buddha in the Buddha Hall?" Ummon retorted, "Where does Buddha's Brahma-voice come from?"

One way to check a foolish question is to ask another foolish one,—foolish, because we cannot ask why a long thing is long. Matters must remain fundamental. Why do the flowers bloom in spring? But "spring" means "the blooming of flowers." Why does Buddha appear? But Buddha is what appears.

Why has a Buddha a Brahma-voice, strong, pure and melodious? That is the nature of a Buddha. Without his Brahma-voice, Buddha would not be Buddha.

*

Ummon said, "The real Emptiness does not destroy things; the real Emptiness is not different from materiality." A monk thereupon asked, "What is this real Emptiness?" Ummon said, "Do you hear the sound of a bell?" "That's the sound of a bell," said the monk. "Even when you have reached the Year of the Donkey, will you still be a-dream?" said Ummon.

Emptiness is transcendental, and yet it is all-inclusive. Things exist because of the Emptiness; otherwise, they would fall into emptiness, nothingness.

*

One day Ummon ascended the rostrum and said, "Vasubandhu happened to transform himself into a staff of chestnut wood, and, striking the earth once, all the innumerable Buddhas were released from their entangling words." So saying he descended from the pulpit.

Vasubandhu was the twenty-first (Indian) patriarch, who lived perhaps in the 5th century A.D. He was the author of the *Yuishikiron*. Where this anecdote came from, or whether it was Ummon's own invention I don't know, but this Chuangtsean story means that the spirit of worship, the "Idea of the Holy," is the very opposite of true religion, and that the Bibles and sacred writings must be destroyed together with the universe itself before a man can be as free as God was until its creation.

Ummon held up his staff, and said, "We are told in the scriptures that an ordinary man thinks the staff is a real existence; that those of the Hinayana take it as nothing; that those believing in the pratyekabuddha take it as an illusory existence; that bodhisattvas say its reality is emptiness. But I say unto you, take the staff as just a staff; movement is movement; sitting is sitting, but don't wabble under any circumstances! My staff has turned into a dragon and swallowed up the whole world. Where are the poor mountains and rivers and great earth now?"

The above two anecdotes, taken together, show what a staff is and what Zen is, but the second needs some comment. To explain the staff becoming a dragon and gulping down the universe, without falling into mysticism, which is odious, or pantheism, which is intellectual, or literature, which is artificial,—this is difficult. What is needed is first of all energy of mind; second, imagination, a Shakespearian one that

> Doth glance from heaven to earth, from earth to
> heaven.

*

Ummon is going back to the Indian (and the ancient Taoist) view of the world as mutually interpenetrative, each thing containing all things, all-things concentrating itself into each thing. Each thing has every quality; every quality is the same as every other quality, even opposite ones. The question is, how to lift up the whole universe when we lift up a spoon, how to dissolve it together with the sugar in the tea, for if we can do this, there is never a dull moment. It is clear that we approach this state the more we are interested in things. "The lunatic, the lover, and the poet are of imagination all compact"; they have what Kierkegaard calls "purity of heart," for they think of one thing only. What is that One Thing? No one can say what it is, completely, for if we could really say it completely, we should be it, and all the search would be over, and life be at an end.

> Another day he said, "An ancient sage said, "All that touches the eye is the Way," and lifted up the soy-pot and said, "Is this the Way?" The monks had nothing to say. Ummon said, "Good Heavens!" and then in answer to the former question, "Funny cast of mind that is!"

From such an account we feel that Ummon had a mind that in ordinary persons and in ordinary cases would be called frenzied. Here is a man mad to teach, but with nobody wanting to learn. Christ and Socrates seem to have been similar in character, and similarly unlucky in their disciples. The world of today does not listen to any of the three.

*

A monk asked Ummon, "Why does Samantabhadra ride on an elephant? Why does Manjusri ride on a lion?" Ummon said, "I have no elephant to ride on, nor a lion, so I ride on the temple and go out of the temple gate."

Manjusri, the embodiment of wisdom, rides either on a lion or a peacock; he often hold a book. Samantabhadra is the lord of law. Ummon says that we ride on what we please. He himself rides on Buddhism and goes out into the world to save people. Fukuju (Fushou), when asked why Shaka didn't ride on anything, threw up his hands, and said, "He's no good! He's no good!"

*

A monk asked, "How about when the lion growls?" Ummon said, "Never mind about when it growls, try roaring." The monk did so, but Ummon said, "It's an old rat squeaking."

What is important in a question, perhaps the only important thing about it, is the tone of voice, the manner, the intonation, the enunciation. This decides the Zen of the question, that is, if it is a real question or not. If it is a real question, it answers itself. The actual answer is only the wind that blows the crest of the wave over.

*

A monk said to Ummon, "How can we spend the twelve hours of the day without wasting them?" Ummon said, "What are you getting at?" The monk said, "I don't understand; please tell me." Ummon made a verse, and gave it to him:

It is bad not to look at what is pointed out to you;
If you intend just to dichotomise, in what eternity
    will you become enlightened?

Ummon saw that the monk was just a simpleton, and gave him a couplet to think over. What is most difficult of all is just to see what you see, without being for it or against it, without being indifferent to it, believing in it.

*

A monk asked Reiju (Lingshu), "What is the meaning of Daruma's coming to the West?" Reiju was silent. After he died, people wanted to inscribe his doings on his tombstone, and this incident was decided on. At this time Ummon was the chief monk, and one of the monks asked him how to put the incident of the remaining silent on the grave-stone. Ummon said, "Write, 'Teacher'."

We teach silently, and only silently, though we may be silent or talk. Reiju did not teach by his being silent, but by his silence, a Silence which never stopped, even with his death and eternal silence.

Ummon composed a verse:

> A sentence which does not reveal its meaning
> Attains its end before being spoken.
> You press forward, with mouth a-chatter,
> Betraying your not knowing what to do.

The first two lines look like mere perverse contradictoriness, but this is not so. In actual daily experience, or rather, in monthly and yearly, not to say lifely experience, it is always the unspoken intention that is effective, not the words which follow.

THE NANGAKU BRANCH OF CHINESE ZEN

Nangaku (Nanyüeh), born in 677, became a priest when he was fifteen, met Ean, and then studied under the 6th Patriarch for fifteen years. It was he who was responsible for Baso's enlightenment, besides eight others. He died in 744 at the age of sixty-eight. Nangaku is remembered as having been in the Rinzai line of Zen.

When Huineng first saw Nangaku he asked him, "Where are you from?" "I have come from Sūzan (Sungshan)."

"What is it that comes?" asked Huineng. "It is nothing like a thing that comes," answered Nangaku. "Can we attain to it by religious exercises?" queried Huineng. Nangaku answered, "That is not impossible, but it is impossible to spoil it in any way." Huineng said, "Just this unspoilable thing is what all the Buddhas have kept in mind. You have done the same, and so have I. Prajnatara, the 27th Patriarch of India, prophesied concerning you that afterwards you would send forth a horse that would trample to death the people of the world."

The last statement is an apochryphal prophecy of the appearance of Baso, "Horse-founder." "What is it which comes?" The aim of Zen is not to answer the question in words, or even in actions, but to be this "he," or "it," or indeed she or they, in other words the aim of Zen is to come. Never ask a question. Never answer a question. Don't even say anything about asking or answering. "It cannot be spoiled, or soiled." Dirt is said to be only matter in the wrong place, but from the point of view of Zen, dirt is just matter in its place, like a diamond or a cloud.

*

Nangaku practised the Nembutsu, as it was by Hōji, fourth in the line of Gozu Zen, and his own Zen is not quite distinctive enough. The anecdotes are few and not particularly interesting except that of his teaching Baso that doing zazen is not the secret of enlightenment.

When Baso was living in Dembōin, he did zazen every day. Nangaku, realising he was a vessel of the Law, went and asked him, "Sir, what is your idea in doing zazen?" "I intend to become Buddha," said Baso. Nangaku took up a tile and polished it in front of the hermitage. Baso said, "What is it you are doing?" Nangaku said, "Polishing it to make it into a mirror." "How can you make a mirror by polishing a tile?" expostulated Baso. "How can you become a Buddha by doing zazen," retorted Nangaku.

*

We come now to the Nangaku branch of Zen. It produced the Igyō and the Rinzai Sects and the (Rinzai) Sub-sects of

Oryū and Yōgi. The individual masters are all so different from each other that we could not tell on sight whether one belongs to the Nangaku (Rinzai) or Seigen (Sōtō) Branch. The Sōtō Sect does not use, actively, that is to say, the kōan system, as does the Rinzai Sect, in conjunction with zazen.

Nangaku, (Nanyüeh), gave no promise in himself of the vigour of his famous descendents through Baso. (Matsu) 788.

A monk asked Baso, "What is the Buddha?" Baso answered, "Mind is the Buddha." The monk asked, "What is the Way?" "No-mind is the Way," answered Baso. The monk then asked, "Are the Buddha and the Way somewhat different?" Baso replied, "The Buddha is like stretching out the hand, the Way is like clenching the fist."

The Buddha is the Mind of the universe, and this is, must be, our own mind. The Way is not *our* mind; it is free and limitless. The Buddha, the Mind, is active, exfoliating. The way is what we make it. It is motionless, potential.

*

Mugō of Funshu asked Baso, "What is the heart seal of the secret transmission of the meaning of Daruma's coming from the West?" Baso said, "Your honour is in too much of a hurry. Go away for a while, and come back again." Mugō was about to go out when Baso called to him, "Your honour!" Mugō turned round. Baso said to him, "What is it?" Mugō was enlightened, and made him obeisance. Baso said, "What's this fathead making bows for?"

*

Baso said to the assembled monks, "Believe that each and all of you have the mind which is the Buddha! Daruma came from India to the Middle Kingdom to enlighten you with the truth he conveyed, of the Mahayana One Mind." A monk spoke up and said, "Why do you teach this 'the mind is the Buddha'?" Baso said, "To stop the baby crying." The monk said, "And when the baby stops crying?" Baso said, "Mind is not the Buddha." The monk said, "Beside this, is there something more?" Baso replied, "I will tell you, it is not something."

Kyogen actor: Shigayama Senzovo

It is interesting to see that not only Buddhism and Christianity, but even Zen has its progressive revelation, the milk for babes and strong meat for those of full age.

It may be doubted, however, whether this sort of thing is proper on the part of teachers, though it is inevitable in the case of the taught. What is important in teaching is to convey the conviction that there is something which is as yet not understood, but is worth the effort to understand. And this is never-ending.

> Suiryō (Shuilao) asked Baso, "What is the essence of Buddhism?" Baso kicked him in the chest, and knocked him down, and Suiryō had a great enlightenment. He got up laughing like mad, and said, "A hundred thousand Buddhist doctrines, an infinite number of marvellous truths and their Ultimate Origin I apprehend in the tip of one hair!"

This kicking is of course psychological, but it is still nothing if it is not cosmological. The question is, where did Baso hit Suiryō? Below the belt no doubt, but most people wear their spiritual belts around their heads, like haloes; Suiryō had his round his ankles,—that is the great difference. It is like the murderer and the murderee. When they meet, something happens. What did Suiryō laugh at? A bright light makes some people sneeze. Undoubtedly Suiryō was laughing at being rid of the (idea that the) contradictions of life (are of deadly importance).

*

> Baso was one day teaching a monk. He drew a circle on the ground and said: "If you enter it, I will strike you; if you do not enter it, I will strike you!" The monk entered it slightly, and Baso struck him. The monk said, "The master could not strike me!" Baso went off leaning on his staff.

We must do something, or not do it. There is no escape from the alternatives infinite in number though they be. Whatever we do, we are punished, by the Emersonian law of compensation. But oddly enough, at the same time, in our will, though not in physical fact, we may do both, or neither. This is our freedom, and our only freedom, but it is absolute, just as cause and effect are absolute. So the monk entered the circle; it was his fate, and his choice was both free and determined. Baso struck him, keeping his promise; it was Baso's fate to strike him, and the monk's to be struck. But, as the monk pointed out, the striking was free, that is to say, also a non-striking simultaneous with the striking. The monk also was free, free not to be struck, free of being struck. So Baso and the monk played their game, but also aware of a greater Game that involves the little game, and both were satisfied, the struck, unstruck, unstrikable monk, and Baso, who went off leaning on the staff that strikes all men, yet all may be unstruck.

*

Hō (P'ang) said to Baso, "Water has no bones, but it easily holds up a ship of a thousand tons; how is this?" Baso said, "There's no water here, and no ship,—what am I supposed to explain?"

Baso is saying, "Don't cross your bridges before you get to them." If Hō and Baso are on board ship, such a question is proper, because when it is really experienced, with the body as well as the mind, it will be really grasped, but what is done with the mind only is better left undone.

*

Baso was one of the first monks to use a specific Zen technique in teaching, that is, in living, by not being philosophical or paradoxical in speech like Eckhart, not being mystical in manner or apprehension, but by grasping the absolute in the relative, a relative devoid of religiosity, romance, symbolism, beauty, intellectuality, or flower-in-the-crannied-wallness, but with a deep sense of the existence-value of a thing, its animism, its poetry. The respect with which he was regarded may be seen in the following.

One day Baso asked Seidō, "Why don't you read the sutras?" Seidō replied, "What is the difference between the sutras and Zen?" Baso said, "Even so, you should do so for the sake of other people." Seidō said, "I think a man's illness must be cured by the man himself. How can one do things for others?" Baso said, "In after years you will set the Thames on fire."

Seidō is repeating what Buddha says in the *Hokkukyō*, that each man must save himself. This is no doubt true, but not when we say so.

*

Chōshūsai interviewed Seidō, and asked him "Mountains and rivers and the Great Earth,—do they really exist, or do they not really exist? Do all the Buddhas of the Three Worlds exist, or not?" Seidō replied, "They all exist." Chōshūsai told Seidō that Hyakujō always answered "They do not," to such questions. Seidō said, "Let's wait till we come to be like our senior Hyakujō, and then everything will *mu*."

The world exists, it does not exist, it both exists and not exists. That it exists, or that it does not exist can be asserted by science and common sense. Only art can express the third. Seidō's conclusion is admirable, combining loyalty and independence with humour.

*

Mayoku (Maku) was a famous disciple of Baso. A monk said to Mayoku, "I do not doubt the Twelve-fold Canon, but what is the meaning of Daruma's coming from the West?" Mayoku stood up, took his staff, turned round once on it, lifted up his leg, and asked, "Do you understand?" The monk made no reply. Mayoku struck him.

The monk thinks that everything has a meaning. He doesn't know that Everything, that is, every thing, means, or rather, every thing things. The meaning of Daruma's coming from the West, that is to say, the meaning of the universe, the meaning of life, Mayoku's leaning on his staff, twizzling round and lifting up a leg,—these all have the same meaningless meaning, and so has Mayoku's striking the monk, but the monk's being silent has a meaning, and that's the trouble.

*

Hyakujō Isei (Pai-chang Wei-chêng), was co-disciple with *the* Hyakujō, Ekai (Huai-kai), of Baso, but nothing is known of him except that he was nicknamed Hyakujō Nehan.

One day Hyakujō Isei said to his monks, "You make a new field, and I'll tell you the Meaning of Everything." The monks finished the new field and said, "We ask the master to tell us the Meaning of Everything!" Hyakujō Isei opened his arms wide.

The monks "opened" the land; the Master opened his arms. With these two activities the whole work of the world was finished and begun.

*

"Mayoku and Nansen and another monk were on a Nature pilgrimage, intending to interview Kinzan, and met an old woman on the way. "Where do you live?" they asked. "Here," she said. The three went into her tea-shop. The old woman made a pot of tea, and brought three cups and put them on the table and said, "Let the one who has godlike power drink the tea!" The three looked at each other but nobody said anything, and nobody drank the tea. The old woman said, "This silly old woman will show you her full power. Just watch!" and she took the tea, drunk it up, and departed.

The interesting thing is that as Bernard Shaw said, no woman is interesting until she is forty. When some (Chinese) women become quite old, they seem to get some occult power and become witches, or, as here natural Zen adepts.

*

A monk asked Daibai, "What is the meaning of Daruma's coming from the West?" Daibai answered, "His coming has no meaning." The monk brought this up to Enkan, who said, "Two dead men in one coffin." Gensha, hearing of this, said "Enkan is a clever chap."

Daruma's coming is meaningless because it partakes of the nature of the universe, which means, it is true, but does not mean *something*. The two corpses are Daruma and Daibai, both of whom talked too much, and killed themselves and others with their boloney.

Goei (Wu-i), who died in 818, was a disciple of Baso, but was greatly enlightened under Sekitō. Little is known of him, and the anecdotes are few.

Goei went to Sekitō, and said, "If you can say a word, I will remain here, otherwise I will go away." Sekitō simply sat there. Goei went off. From the back Sekitō called him, "Jari! Jari!" Goei turned his head. Sekitō said, "From birth to death, it is just like this. Turning the head, turning the brain, how about it?" Goei was suddenly enlightened, so he broke his staff.

*

One day Impō was pushing a cart, and Baso had his legs stretched out across the path. He said, "Please, Master, pull in your legs!" "What has been stretched out," said Baso, "cannot be retracted!" "What goes forward cannot go backwards!" said Impō and pushed the cart on. Baso's legs were cut and bruised. When they went back, Baso entered the Hall, and said, lifting up an axe, "Come here, the monk who hurt my legs awhile ago!" Impō came out and stood before Baso and bent his neck to receive the strike. Baso put down the axe.

This episode is interestingly similar to the story of *Sir Gawain and the Green Knight*. In both, it is all pretending, it is all a joke, and yet more serious, more meaningful than the most solemn history. Both are a kind of examination. The Green Knight tests Gawain's chastity and faithfulness, Baso tests Impō's. Gawain is a little dishonest and receives a scratch on the neck. Impō is a little rough, and Baso makes a feint of decapitating him. In other words, *Sir Gawain and the Green Knight* has some (humour and some) Zen in it, and so has the other.

The monk asked, "What is the Godhead?" Enkan said, "It is the passing of a bottle with all your soul." The monk was wrong in not listening to Enkan with all his soul. To pass a bottle requires the whole universe, plus our whole soul.

NANSEN AND JŌSHŪ

Nansen said, "Up to today, you and I, brother, have talked over things, and I know how you think, but afterwards, if someone should ask me about your opinion of

the most important thing in the world, what should I say?"
Kisu said, "This piece of land here would be a nice place
to build a hermitage on." Nansen said, "Never mind about
building any hermitages, what is your opinion of the most
important thing in the world?" Kisu gulped down his tea
and stood up. Nansen said, "Brother, you have drunk your
tea, but I haven't finished mine yet!" Kisu said, "If you
talk as you have been, not a drop of water can be finished up." Nansen was silent, and went off.

"The most important thing in the world" is always what
a man is doing at this moment.

When Nansen was living in his hermitage, a monk came,
and Nansen said, "I must go to work on the mountain.
Please make some food, eat yourself, and bring me my
share." The monk made his own meal, ate it, broke up
everything in the hermitage, and lay down and slept. Seeing that the monk did not come, Nansen went back to his
hermitage. Seeing the monk lying there he lay down too.
The monk got up, and went off.
In after years Nansen said, "Before I was living here,
when I was in the hermitage, this clever monk came to
see me. I have never seen him again."

The monk evidently realised that Nansen was enjoying
his ascetic, lonely, Robinson Crusoe life among the mountains. Nansen was becoming attached to his nonattachment.
As Eckhart said the real poverty is absolute and only that
poverty is blessed. That is the meaning of being baptised into
the death of Christ.

A monk once came and stood before Nansen with folded
hands. Nansen said, "A great layman!" The monk clasped
his hands. Nansen said, "A great monk!"

The monk first showed his independence by a lay salutation. Nansen told him ironically, that he was a very fine layman. The monk then reverted to type, and received yet another rebuke. What shall we do when we meet someone? Shall
we say "Good morning," which is foolish, or say nothing,
which is rude? I must confess that I don't know the answer,

and that I don't know anyone (Christ, Buddha, Nansen) who does.

*

A monk asked Chōsa, "What is the meaning of 'Your every-day mind is the Way'?" Chōsa said, "When you want to sleep, you sleep; when you want to sit, you sit." The monk said, "This learner does not understand." Chōsa said, "When you are hot, you cool yourself; when you are cold, you warm yourself."

This half of Zen is both more difficult to grasp intellectually and to put into practice than the paradoxical, A is not A type. This is because it is more poetical, that is to say, it is the thing as it is, simply and deeply perceived by self-consciousness.

Chōsa one day went for an outing in the mountains, and when he came back to the Gate, the chief monk asked him where he had been to. Chōsa said, "I've been walking in the mountains." The chief monk asked how far he had been. Chōsa said, "At first I wandered among the scented grasses, then I followed the falling flowers." The chief monk said, "It sounds spring-like." Chōsa said, "It was better than the dew of autumn falling on the lotus leaves."

The Zen of this is of the highest kind, that can be pointed at only in Chōsa's spontaneous avoidance of anything paradoxical and (in the last sentence) making an (unodious) comparison and choosing the cheerful instead of the sentimental. This anecdote forms Case XXXVI of the *Hekiganroku*.

JŌSHŪ

Jōshū (Chao-chou) became a priest when a child. Later he met Nansen, Obaku, Hōju, Enkan, Kassan, but received the confirmation from Nansen. He later taught at the East Temple in Jōshū, from which he got his name, dying in 897 at the age of a hundred and twenty. He was respected above all the other teachers of his time.

When Jōshū first saw Nansen, Nansen was lying down in his room. Seeing Jōshū come, he asked him, "Where have you just come from?" Jōshū said, "from Zuizō-In, Nansen's temple," "Do you see Zuizō?" asked Nansen. "I do not," said Jōshū, "but I see a Buddha lying down!" Nansen sat up, and asked, "Are you a monk with a master, or master-less?" "I'm a monk with a master," replied Jōshū. "Who is this master of yours?" queried Nansen. Jōshū said, "It is early spring, and still cold, but make obeisance. I see the honorable and blessed master in person!" Nansen called his attendant, and said to him, "Put this monk up somewhere."

*

L'audace, encore de l'audace, toujours de l'audace!

A monk asked Jōshū, "What is the Buddha?" "The one in the Hall." The monk said, "The one in the Hall is a statue, a lump of mud!" Jōshū said, "That is so." "What is the Buddha?" asked the monk, "The one in the Hall."

This becomes easier perhaps, if expressed a little more paradoxically. Even the clay statue of a man who lived a thousand years ago (from that time) is the Buddha. What indeed is not the Buddha? Even the Buddha was a Buddha.

*

Jōshū was one of those lucky people who can say anything that comes into his head, and always make sense, not common sense, but uncommon sense. And after all, when we think it over, it is the mind of (Jōshū) which raises things. If we do not raise rising things, they rise in vain, that is, meaninglessly, that is, they do not really rise, rise livingly, poetically.

A head monk came to Jōshū, and Jōshū asked him, "What business are you learning?" He answered, "I do not allow preaching on the sutras, discipline, or commentaries." Jōshū lifted up his hand, and said, "Can you lecture on this?" The monk looked vacant and did not answer. Jōshū said, "Even if you don't allow lecturing, you are just a lecturer on the sutras just the same, and Buddhism is as yet unborn (in you)." The monk said, "Is not what you said (to me) just now Buddhism?" Jōshū said, "Even if you ask a question and get an answer, the whole thing belongs to the sutras and commentaries on them. Buddhism is still unborn in you." The monk was silent.

We often think, while reading such anecdotes, of the Rich Young Ruler. The monk cannot give up his desire to use his head only, and goes away sorrowful, for he has many prepossessions.

*

Jōshū had a contest of words with the Shami Bunon. The point was to lose, not to win. The person who won (that is, lost) should bring the fruit. Jōshū said, "I am a donkey." Bun-on said, "I am the donkey's crupper." Jōshū said, "I am the donkey's dung." Bun-on said, "I am the worms in it." Jōshū said, "What are you doing there?" Bun-on said, "I am passing the summer there." Jōshū said, "You go and get the fruit."

This is very pleasing. The Zen of it consists in the playing at competition. We should play sports seriously, but otherwise pretend to live and pretend to die.

*

A monk asked Jōshū, "What is the word of the ancients?" Jōshū said, "Listen carefully! Listen carefully!"

It doesn't matter what you listen to, as long as you really listen to it. As Thoreau says: "The squeaking of the pump sounds as necessary as the music of the spheres."

*

A monk said to Jōshū, "I have heard that you said that when the universe is destroyed the (Buddha) nature will not be destroyed; what is this 'nature'?" Jōshū said, "The Four Elements, and the Five Components." The monk said, "These are the very things that will be destroyed; what is this 'nature'?" Jōshū said, "It is the Four Elements and the Five Components."

This is very good. The soul is immortal. The body is mortal. The soul is the body. We can resolve this contradiction only by transcendentalising the terms of it. The soul is unborn, undying, that is to say, timeless, not eternal. The body is the same. Destruction is change of components. The universe is being destroyed at every moment. We, timeless, perceive this timelessness at every moment. This timeless perception of timelessness cannot be destroyed, because destruction is in a different category from time, is eternal, not timeless. All this is as nonsensical as Jōshū's own statements.

Jōshū reached Ungo, who said to him, "You are a good age, why don't you live somewhere?" Jōshū said, "Where is my abiding place?" Ungo said, "In front of this mountain there are the ruins of an old temple." Jōshū said, "Why don't you try it yourself?" Then Jōshū went to Shunyu, who said to him, "You are a good age, why don't you live somewhere?" Jōshū said, "Where is my abiding place?" Shunyu said, "You are a good age, don't you know your abiding place yet?" Jōshū said, "For thirty years I have ridden a horse, but today I was struck by (or, fell off) a donkey."

Between the ages of sixty and eighty, Jōshū wandered all over the country seeking to mature his own enlightenment. Many of his interviews were like those recorded above. Real kindness is helping a man to be blessed, not trying (impossibly) to make him happy. Settling down is not the object of life, but what happens when you are put in a coffin.

*

Jōshū asked a new-comer monk, "Have you just come?" "Yes," replied the monk. "Then have a cup of tea," said Jōshū. He said to another monk, "Have you come recently too?" "No," said the monk. "Then have a cup of tea," said Jōshū. The Chief Monk said, "Why do you offer tea to a monk who has come recently, and to one who hasn't in just the same way." "Injū!" said Jōshū. "Yes?" said the Injū. "Have a cup of tea!" said Jōshū.

This is Zen and humour and kindliness inextricably mingled. It reminds us of the Parable of the Vineyard.

*

One day Jōshū went to see Ōbaku, who, seeing him coming, shut the door of his room. Jōshū yelled out "Fire!

Fire! Help! Help!" from the Hall. Ōbaku opened the door, seized him, and said, "Say something! Say something!" Jōshū said, "It's drawing the bow after the robber has gone."

Playing at Zen is excellent practice for the real thing.

*

A monk asked Jōshū, "What is the way without mistakes?" Jōshū said, "Knowing one's mind, seeing into one's nature is the way without mistakes."

The meaning is that when once we have seen into our mind, which is the Mind of the universe, there is no mistake in the will, though there must be innumerable mistakes of thought and feeling and act.

One day Jōshū was looking at the stone bridge with the head monk, and asked him, "Who made this bridge?" "Rishun," answered the head monk. "When it was made, where did he first begin?" The head monk made no reply, Jōshū said, "Everybody talks this stone bridge, but when they are asked how it was begun, nobody seems to know."

So with everything, so with the creation of the universe. Was it made out of nothing, or out of something. "Let there be light." But how could there be light when there was nothing to shine on? Which came first, the hen or the egg? "It is a mystery," the pious declare. "Yes," say the impious, "so is every thing."

*

A monk said to Jōshū, "I would like you to tell me (what the truth is) without using explanatory words." Jōshū said, "For some time I have been deaf." The monk encircled Jōshū's seat once and said, "I ask you to tell me!" Jōshū also encircled the seat once, and said, "all the Hundred Thousand Buddhas entered from this gate." The monk asked, "What is this Gate of the samadhi of the Hundred Thousand Buddhas?" Jōshū struck him.

To ask a man to talk without using words is nonsense and Jōshū was right to be deaf. The monk then tried a little circumambulation, which Jōshū also performed, and told the monk that in this simple action all the Law and the Prophets was contained. The monk, like a fool, that is, an ordinary human being, went on grinding out his endless questions and Jōshū gave him his quietus.

*

Once Nansen said to the assembled monks, "The Way is not outside things, outside things there is no Way." Jōshū asked, "What is the Way which is outside things?" Nansen immediately struck him. Jōshū caught hold of the stick and said, "From now on don't strike someone by mistake!" Nansen said, "It's easy to speak of a dragon, but difficult to please me!" and throwing down his stick he went back to his room.

Nansen was right, but Jōshū was righter. There is no Way outside things, but there is a Way outside things. The Way that can be called a Way (which is not outside things) is not an eternal way.

*

A monk was saying farewell to Jōshū, who asked him, "Where are you going?" The monk said, "All over the place, to learn Buddhism." Jōshū said, holding up his mosquito-flapper, "Do not stay where the Buddha is! Pass quickly through a place where there is no Buddha! Do not make a mistake and bring up Buddhism to anyone for three thousand leagues!" The monk said, "In that case I won't go!" Jōshū said, "Farewell! Farewell!"

*

The Emperor Chō entered the temple to meet Jōshū, who was doing zazen in his room. The assistant monk announced him. Jōshū said, "Let the Emperor come in and make his bows." The Emperor came in and made obeisance. Right and left they asked him, "The Emperor and many courtiers have come, why don't you stand up?" Jōshū said, "You don't understand me. If it is a visitor of low standing, I go out to the gate to meet him. If he is of middle class, I come down from my seat. If he is of high class, I greet him from my seat. The Great Emperor cannot be treated as a person of low or middle rank; I dread to insult him in such a way." The Emperor was highly delighted and two or three times paid homage to him.

*

A monk asked, "What is the meaning of the First Patriarch's coming from the West? Jōshū answered, "The oak tree in the front garden." The monk said, "Don't express it objectively!" Jōshū replied, "I do not do so." The monk said, "What is the meaning of the First Patriarch's coming from the West?" Jōshū replied, "The oak tree in the front garden."

The mistake of looking for Buddhism, for Zen, for truth, reality, God, apart from this thing at this place at this moment is so ineradicable as to make us think sometimes that perhaps after all God is up there in the sky, and reality is a big block of Something that we must nibble at, and the truth something that must be sought with shoes shod with iron. But as Stevenson said of the touchstone, "What if it was in his pocket all the time?"

*

Seeing a cat, a monk said to Jōshū, "I call this a cat; what do you call it, may I ask?" Jōshū said, "You call it a cat."

What Jōshū means, perhaps, is that Jōshū calls it what the monk calls a cat. He calls it, not a cat but Something which is called by people a cat. But Somebody does not call it a cat; He does not call it even a Cat. He just calls it, and the cat, that is, the Cat, that is, the Something, now exists.

*

Jōshū asked a monk, "Where have you come from?" "From the South," he replied. Jōshū asked, "Who was your companion on the way?" The monk said, "An ox." Jōshū said, "Why should a fine priest like you have an animal as a friend?" "Because," said the monk, "it's no different from me." Jōshū said, "Nice animal!" The monk asked, "How am I to understand the matter?" Jōshū said, "If you don't understand it, give me back my friend!"

The monk evidently liked the ox, and the ox liked him. That is all ye know on earth and all ye need to know. But we must know that we know it and hold fast to that knowledge. Jōshū hearing that ———— reply says: "The ox is big friend, even if he isn't yours."

*

Jōshū asked an old woman with a basket, "Where are you off to?" "I am going to steal your bamboo shoots," she replied. Jōshū said, "Suppose you meet me soon after, what then?" The old woman gave him a slap on the face. Jōshū gave up and went away.

Some of these old Chinese women were more than a match for the greatest Zen masters. By saying she would steal his bamboo sprouts, she meant perhaps his special ways of teaching and so on. Jōshū asks her if she would not be ashamed of doing such a thing, and she immediately strikes him, showing her beyond-good-and-evil mind.

*

HYAKUJŌ AND HIS DISCIPLES

Hyakujō (Pai-chang), 724–814, became a priest when he was twenty years old. He became enlightened when studying under Baso together with Chizō and Fugan (Nansen). Baso said, "Zen is with Ekai (Hyakujō)." His words were simple, but he knew Buddhism thoroughly; he was clever and gentle at the same time; he had nothing ostentatious about him, but was invited to the great temple at Mount Hyakujō, from which he took his name. Many disciples gathered around him, among them such famous ones as Isan and Ōbaku. He died in 814.

*

When Hyakujō was a young boy his mother took him to a temple, and entering, she bowed to the Buddhist statue. Pointing to the statue, Hyakujō asked his mother, "What's that?" "That's a Buddha," she replied. Hyakujō said, "He looks like a man. I want to become a Buddha afterwards."
    Hyakujō said to his monks, "There's a man who eats

sparingly, but is never hungry; there's a man who is always eating, and never full." The monks had nothing to say.

We must be both these men, always overflowing with energy, but never ambitious. By not going we arrive. Fully satisfied at each moment, we never remain with it. Whether Hyakujō meant this is not the question. When a Master of (his own) Zen speaks, I must respond with (my own) Zen, if any.

*

One day it was snowing, and the monk in charge asked Hyakujō to give a sermon. Hyakujō said, "Falling in flakes, the colour scheme and pattern are complete. Why must I go to the Hall and preach?"

*

A non-Buddhist scholar gave Daizui a bowl, and a monk asked, "What did you use before he presented you with the bowl?" Daizui said, "I used the one I shall use on my last day on earth."

This is indeed Zen.

One day, when Daiji was sweeping the ground, Jōshū asked him how to manifest Hannya. Daiji said, "How can we manifest Hannya?" Jōshū gave a great laugh. The next, seeing Jōshū sweeping the ground, Daiji, asked him, "How can we manifest Hannya?" Jōshū put down his broom and laughed aloud, clapping his hands. Daiji went back to his room.

To embody incarnate Wisdom, sweeping, laughing, writing, thinking will do. The great mistake would be, however, to take Wisdom and its manifestation as two things, to suppose that there is a manifestation *of* wisdom, for the Wisdom is the manifestation and the manifestation is the Wisdom. So Daiji repeats Jōshū's question, because the real question and the real answer are always identical like Wisdom and its manifestation. When Jōshū is asked the next day, however, he does not repeat the question, because today's question is never the same as yesterday's question; and the answer is always different from the question. He laughs a different laugh.

*

Isan (Wei-shan) was born in 771, the middle of the Tang Dynasty. He became a priest at the age of fifteen, and a disciple of Hyakujō when he was twenty three.
Most of the anecdotes of Isan concern Kyōzan also but here are some about monks.

At the bottom of Mount I, a monk had built a hermitage, and Kyōzan went there and told him what Isan had said, namely: "Most people have the great potentiality, but not the great function." The monk told Kyōzan to ask him concerning the matter, but when Kyōzan was about to do so, the monk kicked him in the chest and knocked him down. Kyōzan went back to Isan and told him, whereupon Isan gave a great laugh.

*

When Kyōzan was with Isan, he used to look after the cows. The head monk of that time said, "A hundred million lions appear at the tip of a hundred million hairs." Kyōzan made no answer. Afterwards, when he went back, he was attending on Isan when the head monk came and made obeisance to Isan, to speak to him. Kyōzan said, "Wasn't it you, the head monk, who said just before that a hundred million lions appear at the tip of a hundred million hairs?" "Yes, it was I," said the head monk. Kyōzan asked, "Do the hairs appear first, or the lions?" "When they appear there is no first or afterwards," replied the head monk. Kyōzan went out. Isan said, "The lion's back is broken."

This conversation is all a piece of trickery in which Kyōzan is defeated, and has his back broken, but from the point of view of Zen a broken-backed lion is better than an unbroken hair, that is, an undefeated ordinary man.

The whole thing is only sparring, but in Zen also this kind of playing at Zen, spiritual exercises, doing in fun what we must do afterwards in earnest, is necessary, is expedient.

*

Isan said to Kyōzan, "The whole day we argued about Zen; what did we get out of it all?" Kyōzan drew a line in the air. Isan said, "If it were not I, someone would be deceived."

It is always impossible to know what the profit of something is. Time will tell. From a more absolute point of view, the profit is the same, is infinite, like Kyōzan's line. Isan quite rightly will not allow it to end on a serious note but jokes at his brilliant disciple.

This anecdote shows how strongly the Zen masters felt about the creeds and dogmas. The more true and useful the sutras were, the more dangerous, the more devilish. So with societies and groups; the loftier their object the more they are to be shunned. Isan's last remark is not correct. The "minute details" are more important than the general principles. A just eye is of prime importance, but so is a steady hand and so are well-made tools.

*

Kyōzan was washing his clothes, and Tangen asked him, "What should we do at this moment?" Kyōzan answered, "At this moment, where shall we look?"

Perhaps Kyōzan means, "Look at me! I am doing what I should at this moment, so that reality is visible before your eyes. Christ is born again at this instant; suffers again in this tub; is dead and resurrected in my washing these clothes."

*

Kyōzan, seeing a monk come, raised his mosquito-flapper. The monk shouted, "Kwatz!" Kyōzan said, "There is such a thing as saying 'Kwatz,' but tell me, where was my mistake?" The monk said, "In improperly pointing to an external object (and not to the mind)." Kyōzan struck him.

*

One day Isan, seeing the nun Ryūtetsuma coming, said, "So you have come, you old cow?" She said, "Tomorrow there is a big meeting at Mount Tai; will you be there?" Isan relaxed his body and acted as if lying down. Ryūtetsuma went off.

This incident is full of a Zen which is difficult to disentangle from the conversation and activity. Isan is rude, but the universe is not particularly polite. The nun does not beat about the bush; she also does not use any spiritual cosmetics. Isan would rather sleep than attend any meeting. The nun admits his good taste.

*

Ōbaku (Huang-po) became a priest at Mount Ōbaku when a child. He was confirmed by Hyakujō, and was then invited to a big temple newly-built, and named this after the mountain where he had spent his youth. From this time, his fame increased, and more than a thousand priests gathered around him. He died in 850. He wrote a work called Ōbaku Shin-yō, "Ōbaku's Essence of Mind. Twelve of his disciples were enlightened, among them Rinzai, Useki, Chin-Sonshuku, Senkei and Shōkoku.

Hyakujō one day asked Ōbaku where he had come from. Ōbaku said, "From gathering mushrooms on at the foot of Mount Daiyū." "Did you see the tiger there?" asked Hyakujō. Ōbaku roared like a tiger. Hyakujō lifted up his axe and made as if to chop him down. Ōbaku gave Hyakujō a slap. Hyakujō sang out and laughed, and went back to his seat. To the monks he said, "At the foot of Mount Daiyū there is a tiger which you positively must see. Your old Hyakujō has just had a word with him."

This unbuttoned, boisterous Zen is very good, nothing sanctimonious or paradoxical or supercilious, but at the same time not frivolous or exhibitionistic.

*

Once Ōbaku was wandering for pleasure on Mount Tendai when he met another monk. He talked and laughed with him as with an old friend. They looked at each other, and their gaze penetrated to the heart. Together they came to a valley stream full to overflowing, and Ōbaku took off his kasa and stood still on the bank with his staff. The monk pulled Ōbaku to cross together, but Ōbaku said, "If you are going to cross this stream, cross alone!" The monk tucked up his skirts and began to walk over the stream as if on dry ground, and, turning his head, called to Ōbaku, "Come and cross over! Come and cross over!" Ōbaku said, "You self-finishing creature! If I had known before what you were like, I would have cut your legs off!" The monk sighed, and said, "You are a real follower of the Mahayana! I am not equal to you!" and disappeared.

What is striking about this story is the way in which the monk conceded his defeat, the miraculous conquered by the natural. Whether Christ performed miracles or not is not the question. The point is: are you fool enough to be interested in the problem? Christ should not have performed miracles even if he could. Why not? All things are miracles; we need no extra ones. As Whitman says, "A mouse is miracle enough to stagger sextillions of infidels."

*

The T'ang Emperor Daichū, was at one time a sramana and being among those assembled at Enkan's temple, saw Ōbaku making obeisance in the hall, and said to him, "We seek nothing from the Buddha, nothing from the Law, nothing from the monks,—you are making obeisance, however; why is this?" Ōbaku struck him. The sramanera (that is, the Emperor) said, "You rough fellow!" Ōbaku said, "What are you talking about? You judge this as rough and that as smooth?" and he intended to give him another blow, so the sramana ran off.

The point of this story is not the spiritual power of religion as being greater than the spiritual power of irreligion, alias politics, a common phenomenon of Europe and the East and the Far East, but the swindling of Ōbaku. When the Emperor tells him that his bowing antics, superstition if genuine, and weak-minded or opportunistic if not,—are incompatible with his beliefs, the only answer is a blow. When the Emperor calls him rough, Ōbaku immediately flies to the absolute, where there is no rude or polite, and is going to strike him again, though in the absolute there is no striking or non-striking.

The collection of the sayings of Ōbaku, known as "The

Transmission of the Mind," was made by Haikyū, otherwise known as Haishōkoku, a great admirer of Ōbaku. In his Preface, 858, he tells us how in 843 and in 849 especially he questioned Ōbaku intensively and recorded his answers. The following are some extracts and comments on them.

"The material things before you,—that is it. But when the (rational) mind moves, we deny it, we refuse it."

When the universe sees a snake or a hare-lip with our eye, that is the truth. Our "choosey" mind spoils this. Or shall we say, we see something else, which may be also a truth, what we call illusion, but not the truth.

This mind is the Buddha; Buddha is human beings. When it becomes human beings it does not decrease; when it becomes the Buddha nothing is added.

The word "mind" is often written with a capital letter, "Mind." This is a mistake, as we see when we write, as we should, that Buddha is the mind. Ōbaku grasped with especial clarity and strength the fact that illusion is satori, satori illusion.

Buddha said of the sands of the Ganges, "If all the Buddhas and Bodhisattvas, Indra and all the gods walk across them, they feel no pleasure. If oxen and sheep, insects and ants tread on them they feel no anger. They do not desire jewels and perfumes, they do not hate shit and filth."

Ōbaku means that we must be like the sand, but this is neither possible nor desirable. We must be like the sand, that is true, because we are the sand, but we must also be human beings, because we are not the sand, and we must hate the jewels and perfumes and love the sheep and insects.

It is a fact, there is nothing to be attained; this is no falsehood. If you get (enlightenment) in a single act of mind, or as a result of the practice of the Ten Stages, the resulting attainment is the same; one is not shallow, nor the other deep. The only difference is that the latter simply involves ages of pain and labour.

The Mind is not the Mind, and becoming enlightened is not becoming enlightened.

This kind of statement, which Ōbaku repeats again and again, is not an intimation of the inadequacy of words and phrases; after all, the statement itself consists of words and phrases. "The Mind is not the Mind" means that the Mind is both the Mind and not the Mind.

We teach the Law by not teaching it.

Literally, "The Law is not to be taught; this is called teaching the Law." Here again it is not that words are misleading or insufficient. They are so only if the receiving mind is misleadable and inadequate. The Law is not something fixed, to which we approximate in time. The Law itself is changing and growing, in so far as we change and grow. So when we don't catch the butterfly, we reveal its nature. As Jizō said to Hōgen, "Don't-know is the most intimate."

> Haikyū asked, "Does the Buddha save living creatures, or not?" Ōbaku answered, "In actual fact there are no living creatures for the Buddha to save. There is no I, how can there be any not-I. Neither Buddha nor living creatures exist."

Christ as the Saviour disappears. Haikyū's questions are never answered because Ōbaku denies the terms of them, the suppositions behind them, the questioner himself, and the answerer. The mercy and compassion which we extend to all things (including ourselves) is the will for things to be as they are and to become as they will become. What seems, on the relative plane, to be our powerlessness to change the world closer to the heart's desire, is in the absolute realm the will, and this will is a compassionate will. This is the meaning of Jōshū's answer when he was asked by an old woman how she could escape the Five Hindrances of a woman. He answered, "May all human beings be reborn in paradise! May this old woman sink for all eternity in the sea of pain!" Intuitively Jōshū realises that this is "the best of all possible worlds, that the Five Hindrances are at the same time Five Helps, that Lady Macbeth and Medea and Mrs. Gamp and the Wife of Bath and Cleopatra and all the lesser ilk are inevitable, and desirable; the squeaking of the pump sounds as necessary as the music of the spheres. Ōbaku is speaking more intellectually.

If enlightenment is illusion, then illusion is enlightenment. Pity is ruthlessness. But it is not enough to say that Ōbaku is advocating a pitiless pity, or pitiful pitilessness. He is in a realm beyond this paradox, beyond the dichotomy of opposites, one in which, as he says, there is no enlightened Buddha, and no living creatures waiting to be saved by him. This is what he means by the Great Mercy and Compassion. The important word here is "Great," and in *Hannya Shingyō Dokugo* Hakuin explain *Dai* (Great) Hannva Shingyō in the same way.

*

Bokushū (Mu-chou) is the chap who enlightened Ummon by (accidentally) breaking his leg for him.

> A monk said to Bokushū, "We are always putting on and taking off our clothes, and eating our food,—is there any way of avoiding this?" Bokushū said, "By putting on and taking off our clothes, and eating our food." The monk said, "I don't understand." Bokushū said, "Not understanding is wearing clothes, eating food."

Rightly enough, we get tired of doing things mechanically, —when we think of it. Breathing and the beating of the heart we are tired of when we are dead. We must enjoy all we do, consciously or unconsciously. Thus, not to understand is the (happy) wearing of clothes, the (happy) eating of food. And if we have the (Zen) understanding of the matter, the wearing and the eating are a non-wearing and a non-eating, or, as Bokushū says at the beginning, the (Zen) avoiding of wearing and eating,—that is, wearing and eating.

*

> A monk knocked at Bokushū's door, saying, "Clear me up! I ask you to direct me!" Bokushū said, "I have a stick here for you!" The monk had hardly opened the door, and began to ask something when Bokushū immediately struck him.

What the monk can learn from this, what Bokushū wants to teach him, is that when we do something, we are done by something. This doing and being done to is life, and when conscious willingness is added to do and done to, there is Zen.

We therefore revise Christ's words, "Knock, and it shall be opened unto you," to, "Knock, and ye shall be knocked."

*

Bokushū said to the assembled monks, "If you are not yet clear about the Great Matter, it is like the funeral of one's parents; if you are already clear about it, it is like the funeral of one's parents."

This is very good. According to Buddhism, Buddha is always in his abode of bliss. The gods drink and play in their celestial abodes. God created the world and found it good. But Christ was and is a man of sorrows and acquainted with grief.

*

A monk asked Useki, another disciple of Ōbaku, "What is 'the Buddha'?" Useki stuck out his tongue. The monk bowed. "What did you see," asked Useki, "that made you bow?" The monk said, "You stuck out your tongue for me, and I thanked you for doing so." Useki said, "Recently I've got a sore on my tongue."

Teaching is a dreadful occupation. We are always preaching to the heathen, as above, teaching the unteachable; or, preaching to the already converted, which makes us feel even more foolish. What is this sore on the tongue? There are two kinds of sore, corresponding to the two conditions of teaching explained above. When we teach the unteachable we begin to lose our own faith. And when we teach the converted we begin to feel as foolish as they look. The following anecdote is a variation of the one above.

RINZAI AND HIS DISCIPLES

Rinzai was born about the beginning of the 9th century. Precocious as a child, he was however a good son, though he always wanted to escape from others. He became a priest and studied the sutras and then visited Ōbaku. One day Chin Sonshuku, that is, Bokushū, asked him how long he had been there, and was told "Three years." Bokushū asked him if he had interviewed the Master, Ōbaku. "No," said Rinzai, "I don't know what to ask him." Bokushū told him to go and ask, "What is the essence of the Great Meaning of Buddhism?" Three times Rinzai went to Ōbaku and asked the question and three times Ōbaku struck him even before he finished his sentence. Rinzai felt that he was not a man capable of being enlightened, and decided to retire from the monastery and said goodbye to Ōbaku. He was recommended by Ōbaku to go and see Daigu without fail.

Daigu asked him where he had come from. "From Ōbaku," he replied. "What did Ōbaku say to you?" Daigu asked. Rinzai told him he had asked about Buddhism three times and three times he had been beaten. "I don't know whether I was wrong or not," he added. Daigu said, Ōbaku was exceedingly kind to you, forgetting his dignity; why do you come here asking about whether you were this or that?" Rinzai was greatly enlightened, and said, "Ōbaku's Buddhism is not so wonderful after all!" Daigu grasped him and said, "You bed-wetting little devil! Just now you said you didn't know whether you were right or wrong, and now you say it's all a trifle; what did you see? Tell me at once, at once!" Rinzai punched Daigu three times in the ribs. Daigu released him, and said, "Your master is Ōbaku. This is not my concern." Rinzai said goodbye to Daigu, and returned to Ōbaku, who said, "This fellow keeps on going and coming interminably!" Rinzai said, "That's because of your very great kindness to me." Ōbaku asked, "What did Daigu say to you?" Rinzai reported their conversation. Ōbaku said, "When he comes, I'll give that creature a punch on the nose!" Rinzai said, "Why wait? Why not now?" and gave him a blow himself. Ōbaku said, "This crazy chap is pulling the tiger's whiskers." Rinzai shouted, "Kwatz!" Ōbaku said to the attendant, "Take this crazy fellow to the Hall!"

*

As in the case of the Sixth Patriarch, Rinzai's enlightenment is recounted "dramatically," that is to say, minimizing his previous understanding of Zen in order to bring out the great change after enlightenment. Ōbaku's striking Rinzai three times as he was about to ask his (meaningless) question, was the physical manifestation (and there is no other) of the fact that we are not to go cap in hand before the universe and ask it to settle our man-made problems. We are sons of God. Things are our brothers and sisters, as St. Francis knew. We must not ask Brother Fire why he burns. We ask him to cook our rice.

A monk was asked by Rinzai, "Where have you come from?" The monk said, "Kwatz!" Rinzai immediately struck him, and bowing, sat down. A monk was about to speak. Rinzai struck him. Again a monk came. Rinzai raised his mosquito-flapper. The monk bowed. Rinzai struck him. Again a monk was seen to be coming, Rinzai raised his mosquito-flapper. The monk took no notice of it. Rinzai struck him.

There is a certain monotony about the striking which reminds us of that of Nature. But everything is in the will, the will to strike the will to be struck. When these two come together in one person, will is well.

*

Rinzai went to see Hōrin, who said, "May I ask you a question?" Rinzai said, "Why should you gouge the flesh and make a wound?" Hōrin said:

> Into the sea the moonlight falls clear and shadow-
> less,
> But the wanton fishes deceive themselves.

Rinzai said:

> If the moonlight on the sea is without shadows
> How can the fishes be deceived?

Hōrin said:

> Seeing there is wind, waves arise.

> When you speak of Zen
> speak of it poetically;
> Do not criticise poetry
> unless you know some Zen.

*

The attendant O, together with Rinzai, entered the Hall. O asked, "Do these monks read the sutras?" "Not they!"

replied Rinzai. "Then they're learning Zen?" "No." "Then what on earth are they all up to?" asked O. "They're busy becoming Buddhas," said Rinzai, "becoming Patriarchs." O said, "Gold dust is valuable but in the eye it is injurious." Rinzai said, "I thought you were just a mediocre person!"

"Gold dust" means "becoming Buddhas and Patriarchs." "No sutras, no Zen,"—that is all right; the eye is still unharmed, but when we have some ambition to be or become to teach or be taught, then damage is done to our delicate constitution.

*

Rinzai said: "In this mass of red protoplasm there is the True Man, without label or rank, who is forever going in and out of the Six Senses!" A monk asked: What is this True Man without label? Rinzai came down from his seat, caught hold of him, and said, "Speak, Speak!" The monk stood hesitating and wondering what to say. Rinzai pushed him away, saying, "This True Man without label shit-scraper!" and went back to his room.

*

Rinzai said to a select audience, "Sometimes, I take away the person, not the thing; sometimes, the thing, not the person; sometimes, both person and thing; sometimes, neither person nor thing." Kokufu came forward and asked, "What is this taking away the person, not the thing?" Rinzai answered:

> When the sun shines, the earth is covered with
> brocade;
> The baby's hair hangs down, white as silk.

"How about taking away the thing, not the person?" asked Kokufu.

> The Emperor's command is performed through-
> out the country;
> The smoke and dust of war at an end, the gen-
> eral leaves the fortress.

Kokufu asked, "How about when both person and thing are taken away?"

When all relations are broken,
We are really alone.

"And when neither person nor thing is taken away?"
said Kokufu.

The Emperor ascends the jewelled throne,
And the old rustics sing.

All this is not very interesting. One cannot imagine any-body being in any way enlightened by it. It shows how Zen, if confined to itself, goes round like a mouse in a cage. The above is known as Rinzai's Four Kinds of Attitudes. Rinzai, after he became a teacher, used shouts and blows as his teaching materials. Usually when he saw a monk enter the door he would shout, "Kwatz!"

The use of blows has been explained before. They are not a means of enlightenment, not merely a mode of the teacher's sadism and the learner's masochism. The teacher wishes to teach that the universe wishes to teach us. Both teach by striking us. What does the universe wish to teach us? It wishes to teach us that it wishes to teach us. The "Kwatz" is more difficult to explain, and therefore easier not to misunderstand. It is a war-cry, but the fight is a sort of shadow-boxing. The universe shouts at us, we shout back. We shout at the universe, and the echo comes back in the same way. But the shouting and the echoing are continuous, and, spiritually speaking, simultaneous. Thus the "Kwatz!" is not an expression of anything; it has no (separable) meaning. It is *pure* energy, without cause or effect, rhyme or reason.

When Rinzai was still with Ōbaku, he was one day planting pinetrees, and Ōbaku asked him, "Why are you planting such a lot of trees deep in this mountain?" Rinzai replied, "First, to improve the view from the temple gate; second, to be a model and a guide to after-generations." When he had finished speaking, he struck the ground once with his spade, and said, "Phew!" Ōbaku said, "You will make Zen flourish greatly!"

*

This last anecdote is a relief after the ostentation of Zen in most of them. Ōbaku's praise was merited.

Rinzai took leave of Ōbaku, who asked him, "Where are you going?" Rinzai said, "If not South of the River, then North of the River." Ōbaku struck him. Rinzai held the staff, and gave Ōbaku a punch. Ōbaku laughed like mad and, calling the attendant, told him to bring Hyakujō's zenban and mosquito-flapper (to give Rinzai). Rinzai said to the attendant, "Bring some fire!" Ōbaku said, "Just go away, and afterwards you will sit on and silence the tongues of all people under heaven."

When Rinzai says "Either North or South of the River," he reminds us of the school-boy howler, in which we are told that "Wellington was a great general who decided, before the battle of Waterloo, to win or lose it." Rinzai was further like God, unpraisable (how foolish the Psalms are really, for all their poetry!) and unrewardable.

*

Rinzai visited the stupa at Yūji. The Keeper asked Rinzai, "Do you bow to the Buddha first, or to Daruma first?" Rinzai replied, "I don't bow to either of them." The keeper asked, "Why are you and the Buddha and Daruma enemies?" Rinzai shook his sleeves and went away.

When Rinzai says he doesn't bow to either, he does not mean that he does not bow to one more than the other. He means that he does not bow to either. He does not bow to the universe, or to the Truth. He does not bow even to Bach or Bashō. He does not bow at all, any more than the universe bows to him. The keeper of the stupa was suitable to his job in a way; he was stupid.

*

Once Jōshū was on a journey and came to Rinzai's monastery. He was washing his feet in the washhouse when Rinzai asked him, "What is the meaning of Daruma's coming from the West?" Jōshū said, "It's like this washing of my feet." Rinzai went closer, and made as if listening for something. Jōshū said, "If you understand, understand! don't feed me (flattery)!" Rinzai went back to his room. Jōshū said (to himself), "I have been on (religious) journeys for thirty years, and today I made a mistake and gave an explanation."

Jōshū says, "You can't catch old birds with chaff," and then, "That was carrying coals to Newcastle." It should be noted that Rinzai's going back to his room in silence was not a sign of defeat, and Jōshū knew this.

*

Twenty two of Rinzai's disciples were enlightened and there are records of sixteen of them but they are very skimpy, and only a few of these flourished.

*

Sanshō (San-shêng) was perhaps Rinzai's chief disciple. On his death-bed Rinzai passed on his True Law Eye to Sanshō, apparently. Afterwards Sanshō visited Kyōzan, Kyōgen, Tokusan and other masters. Later he lived in Sanshō Temple, from which he took his name, and preached Rinzai's "gospel."

*

Sanshō said, "If someone comes, I go out to meet him, but not for his sake." Kōke said, "If someone comes, I don't go out. If I do go out, I go out for his sake."

Zen has the right attitude here. We must do something for its own sake, *and* for the sake of others, just as each thing exists for itself alone and for all others things.

Kōke's most famous disciple was Nan-yin, who is also called Hōō, because he lived in the temple of that name. He died in 952, and little more is known of him, but the anecdotes are not few.

A monk said to Nan-yin, "What is the Great Meaning of Buddhism?" Nan-yin said, "The origin of a myriad diseases." The monk said, "Please cure me!" Nan-yin said, "The World Doctor folds his arms."

This is unusually poetical, and of a melancholy grandeur. It also happens to be true. Buddhism is both the cause and effect of an unsound mind in an unsound body. Note that greediness, stupidity, maliciousness and so on are not illnesses, for animals have them. Illness means thinking you are ill. And who can cure the illnesses which Doctor Buddha and Doctor Christ have caused?

A monk asked Nan-yin, "What is your special teaching?" Nan-yin said, "In autumn we reap; in winter we store."

Nan-yin ascended the rostrum and said, "Above the mass of red flesh stands one at an immeasurable height." At that time a monk came out and said, "Isn't this 'Above the mass, and so on,' the master's Way?" Nan-yin said, "That's so." The monk then overturned the Zen seat. Nan-yin said, "Look what a rough, wild fellow you are!" The monk didn't know what to say or do. Nan-yin drove him out of the temple.

It seems as if Nan-yin purposely said what he did to draw the monk out and show his mere imitation of such monks as Fuke and Rinzai.

A monk said to Fuketsu, Nan-yin's disciple, "The Western Patriarch came bringing his message; I ask you to tell me it point-blank!" Fuketsu said, "When one dog barks at nothing, a thousand monkeys show their teeth really."

"One dog barking at nothing" is Christ & Buddha and Daruma with their doctrines (or the positive absence of them) and we are the monkeys, afraid of Heaven and Hell or afraid of there being neither, or afraid of not being enlightened before we don't go anywhere.

*

In Buddhism there are eight parjñana, kinds of cognition. These are the five senses, to which is added the intellect. The seventh is discriminated from the sixth as the calculating and constructive mentality. It is the cause of all egoism, of fragmenting into separate things, of all the delusions that assume appearances to be real. The eighth is the basis of all the other "seeds of consciousness." But even this is not the "I," which is thought of as the smouldering end of a rope swung round in the air appearing as a flaming circle because of the slowness of the eye. To mistake these eight for the Real Man is what distinguishes the ordinary man from the Buddha.

It may be thought that when these eight layers have been peeled off nothing remains. This is not so. But if you ask, "What remains?" The answer is, "Peel them off!"

When Rinzai cries: Speak! he means clearly that we must not merely express what impresses us but must express this impression to somebody, somebody real or imagined. Mumon's demand, "Say something so that it is neither speaking nor silence," is not quite accurate. He means "Say something, or say nothing, so that it is neither saying something nor saying nothing." In other words, you must do two opposite things at the same instant. This still is not quite complete. You must do one thing, and at the same time do-it-and-not-do-it, thus combining the relative and the absolute.

One more thing may be said about the "at once," "quickly." This is not, as was explained before, the temporal, or even the psychological speed, but rather the spiritual time-lessness. Nevertheless, we must not despise the timeful speed. Brevity is the soul of wit, and here also we need as few words as possible. The point is to grasp each moment before emotion or intellection has a chance to survey it *independently*. Every act of the soul is to be as full of feeling and thought as possible, but the act is to be whole. A man and his act are to be one.

*

ABOUT THE EDITOR

FREDERICK FRANCK, whose drawings and paintings are part of the permanent collections of a score of museums in America and abroad, including the Museum of Modern Art, the Whitney Museum, and the Tokyo National Museum, holds degrees in medicine, dentistry and fine arts. In memory of Pope John, for whom he had unbounded admiration, he converted the ruins of an eighteenth-century watermill near his house in Warwick, New York, into "Pacem in Terris," a "transreligious oasis of inwardness." Among the artistic and spiritual events at Pacem in Terris are workshops in "seeing/drawing as meditation" and performances of Franck's own contemporary version of the medieval *Play of Everyman*: "EveryOne, the timeless myth of Everyman reborn." He is the author of numerous books, among them *The Zen of Seeing* and *The Book of Angelus Silesius*.